Cliff

Cliff

PATRICK DONCASTER
& TONY JASPER

Written in co-operation with
Cliff Richard

SIDGWICK & JACKSON
in association with New English Library, London

First published in Great Britain in October 1981
by Sidgwick and Jackson Limited

Reprinted December 1981
First paperback edition published
in 1982 by Sidgwick and Jackson Limited

Copyright © 1981 and 1982 by Patrick Doncaster and Tony Jasper

ISBN 0 283 98918 1

Photoset by
Parker Typesetting Service, Leicester
Printed in Great Britain by
William Collins, Glasgow
for Sidgwick and Jackson Limited
1 Tavistock Chambers, Bloomsbury Way
London WC1A 2SG

For two new fans – Sally and Emily

PATRICK DONCASTER

To David, Susan, Andrew, and Megan Cruise

TONY JASPER

Acknowledgements

Special mention must be made of Peter Gormley, David Bryce, Pat and Di of Gormley Management, Hank Marvin, Brian Bennett, Bruce Welch, David Winter, Nigel Goodwin, Cindy Kent, Peter Jones, Keith Skues, John Cabanagh, Brian Munns, Maurice Rowlandson, Eileen Edwards, Janet Johnson, John Friesen, Harry De Louw, The International Cliff Richard Movement, Grapevine, Kevin Wooten – and thanks given to John Foster, George Ganjou, Tito Burns, Jack Good and Ian Samwell for delving into their memories and reliving the eventful days that resulted in Cliff Richard.

Naturally the writers thank Cliff.

Contents

List of Illustrations

Unless otherwise stated, all the photographs are by Dezo Hoffman and come from Rex Features Ltd.

Pictures in section one are as follows:

In the beginning . . . Harry Webb has become Cliff Richard. Shy, a little plump, hair greased Elvis fashion. He is seventeen

The Elvis twitch of the leg. It was all part of the Cliff Richard act

The Richard strut that was to become so familiar, along with black and white stage gear

The agonized Presley mood . . . while the Shadows kick a leg

Always the rock 'n' roller. And Shadow Hank Marvin is all ears

'The Facts of Cliff' – a page from the fan newspaper *Encliff-opaedia*

With his mother

Cliff was an annual 'must' for The Great Pop Prom, staged at the Royal Albert Hall on the Sunday following the last night of the Proms and promoted by the romantic weeklies *Marilyn*, *Roxy* and *Valentine*. Here, during the 1961 Pop Prom, he pauses for the camera during an interview with co-author Patrick Doncaster (*Daily Mirror*)

April 1962 . . . Cliff notches up Gold Disc No. 2 for selling a million records of 'The Young Ones'. 'Living Doll' won the first. In the lower picture recording manager Norrie Paramor hands over a gold disc to the Shadows for 'Apache'

Show time with Jackie Irving

You get to meet the nicest people in showbusiness. The armful is singing star Millicent Martin

How the Germans billed Cliff and company on the street kiosks. Also on the bill, organist Cherry Wainer

Pictures in section two are as follows:

Messing around in boats is always a welcome change . . . especially if you're the skipper

Playback . . . Cliff and the Shadows hear the results of their labours in the recording studio with manager Peter Gormley and the late Norrie Paramor, recording manager

Studio rehearsal. The Shadows pay attention

One-man recording session – in his dressing room

A seat in the stalls during a rehearsal

A solemn Cliff

Up, up and away!

With the vivacious Una Stubbs, who featured in *Summer Holiday* and *Wonderful Life*

With the late Jayne Mansfield during her British tour not long before her tragic death in a car accident

Film time! Cliff turns the camera on to Susan Hampshire, his co-star in *Wonderful Life*

'Cliff! Meet Cliff!' Shaking hands with a puppet of himself created for the *Thunderbirds* T.V. series

With Peter Gormley

David Bryce, protector, aide, lighting expert – 'a tower of strength behind the Cliff success story'

The 1970s Cliff, rockin' on to the forty mark (photo by Harry de Louw)

Rockin' on to the eighties. Still he sings 'Move It', the song that began it all more than twenty years ago (photo by Harry de Louw)

And still he's happy in his work! (photo by Harry de Louw)

Overture and Beginners

On an autumn evening in 1957 a beefy lad named John Foster and some of his pals walked into the Five Horseshoes pub at Hoddesdon, Hertfordshire, for a pint or two.

They were in Teddy Boy rig – long drape coats and drainpipe trousers that might have been moulded to their legs.

John was eighteen, tall and big-chested, and earned his drinking money driving a dumper truck and tractor at a local sewage works. He ordered a pint of black and tan, a mixture of brown ale and light beer.

'It was a kind of long public bar that doubled as a hall,' John recalls, although he can't remember the exact date or whether or not it was a Saturday night.

'I don't think it was,' he says, 'because it wasn't all that busy, but I was a bit of a Teddy Boy in those days and got dressed up at weekends. There was nothing posh about the place and there was this group playing at the end of the bar. Three young lads. They had no lead guitar, just two rhythm guitars and drums and this dark-haired kid doing an Elvis act.

'They didn't have much of a repertoire and were just there to play a few songs. All done in three chords.

'There was something about the youngster who was singing and playing guitar, something that was sort of magic.

'I knew nothing about show business. My one claim was that twice I'd been up to the 2 i's coffee bar in Soho, where the rock 'n' rollers played. It was only twenty-five miles to London from where I lived in the village of Hertford Heath, but it was big-time to go to London in those days.

'Anyway, I said to my mates, "I'm going to manage that kid." They thought I was barmy.

'I went up to him and said, "Hello, my name's John Foster – do you want a manager?"

'His name was Harry Webb and he was about seventeen, a year younger than me. Anyway, Harry agreed. I told him to ring me, because I was on the phone and he wasn't. He lived in a council house at Cheshunt, not very far away . . .'

It was the start of something not only big but sensational.

Within twelve short months Harry Webb would become Cliff Richard; cut a smash hit record for a major label; make his debut on television and tour the land with a variety bill headed by American singing stars the Kalin Twins.

In no time at all he would become a film star, top the bill at the hallowed London Palladium and be a name as well known as soap powder in millions of homes.

John Foster smiles and says: 'I lost my job at the sewage works. They fired me for taking too much time off . . .'

CHAPTER ONE

Birth of an Age Group

Harry Rodger Webb – 'both my father and I spelled Rodger with a d,' he says – was thirteen and a half the day the revolution began; a normal, healthy schoolboy who had failed the dreaded Eleven-plus examination that would have gained him a place in a gram-mar school. Now he was plodding on towards a future that promised little other than a job behind a desk somewhere and a workaday, possibly middle-class life with each new day following much the same monotonous pattern as the previous one.

But . . . came the revolution.

The date was 12 April 1954, and no one knew at that time that it would turn out to be a historic day – least of all one William John Haley, a plumpish twenty-seven-year-old American with family links in Lancashire (his mother's father had been a baker in Ulverston which was, coincidentally, the birthplace of Stan Laurel).

On that April day Bill Haley, who played reasonable guitar, and six colleagues who traded with him as a lively band called the Comets, gathered before the microphones in New York City to record a modest number entitled 'Rock Around the Clock'.

It was like lighting a slow-burning fuse. The song would take its time to travel. In 1956 it would explode with a gigantic roar. Rock 'n' roll would break from its bondage, a lusty offshoot of the black man's music hitherto confined to the ghettos and a few rebellious white youngsters.

In earlier years it had been frowned upon (as was New Orleans jazz in the beginning) and had been generally discarded as 'race music'. More knowledgeable folk called it rhythm and blues.

The usually simple lyrics were strong on two words – rock and roll – although they were rarely linked. The singer was gonna rock his baby. They were also gonna roll. They were words that pictured movement and the movement was definitely sexual, lyrics that would at some stage be labelled by a reprimanding *Variety*, America's show business bible, as *leer-ics* . . .

It was a white disc jockey named Alan Freed who first thought of tying the two words together and giving race music a more acceptable – to whites – description. Rock 'n' roll, he called it. Thus rock 'n' roll it became right across the world. In the end people, being people, would axe it to the one word rock.

Till then rock, at least in Britain, had been a minty pink stick with the name of a seaside town running through it, or something a ship smashed into on a dirty night at sea. Or, as a dictionary defined it – a swaying to and fro.

Freed, then in his late twenties, had entered music accidentally in the early fifties when he was working in Akron, Ohio, as a sportscaster. A disc jockey went sick and Freed took his place, spinning tunes that were middle of the road and intended for all ears, parents and young people alike, sung by balladeers such as Crosby, Nat Cole, Perry Como, Rosemary Clooney and Sinatra. The family then used to listen together. The Teen Age had not yet dawned, when it would become accepted that sons and daughters would have a record-player of their own and play their *own* music in their own dens or bedrooms. They had no music to call their own until Haley and Freed came along – unless you count nursery rhymes.

Freed moved on to Cleveland, where one day a call from Leo Mintz, boss of the big city's largest record store, led him to the three words that would echo around the globe and at the same time bring him a fortune – and catch the ears of Harry Webb.

White kids, said the store chief breathlessly, were now suddenly going for rhythm and blues records by coloured artists. The old cliché was never more true – they were 'selling like hot cakes'.

Alan Freed was not a man to let a trend skip past him. He started to play R&B, as the term had now been abbreviated, and his listening figures were boosted by a new age group – *Teenagers*.

Then R&B was dropped to make way for his new description: Rock 'n' roll. It was the dawn of a new era, both musically and economically. He claimed no copyright on the phrase, but at the outset some disc companies *did* pay a fee to him so that they could use the term.

Freed, who punctuated his shows with excited cries and howls, using such exhortations as 'Go-man-go!' detached himself from the microphone to promote dances and rock 'n' roll concerts, eventually being wooed to New York in 1954 – the year of 'Rock Around the Clock' – to air his adopted music on station W.I.N.S.

Rock was arriving, although thus far the artists were still mainly coloured.

Bill Haley, despite the softness of his looks and the absurd trademark of a kiss curl plastered to his broad forehead, was shrewd enough to notice this youthful rebellion at about the same time as Freed.

In the early fifties, Haley was leading a country and western band – not far from Freed in Ohio – around the adjoining State of Pennsylvania. They called themselves the Saddlemen and, in retrospect, looked and sounded rather square, as the saying then went.

As early as 1951 Haley had begun to record songs with the word rock in the title. One was 'Rock the Joint', which sounded very much like the godfather of 'Rock Around the Clock'. By 1953 he had recorded 'Shake, Rattle and Roll' – still, it is noticeable, not stringing the two all-important words together.

The Saddlemen were renamed the Comets, but his success was for some time purely local. Rock 'n' roll had to wait for 'Rock Around the Clock' for its first white star and acclaimed king.

The song was first heard in the film *The Blackboard Jungle*, which dealt with the new-found movement of youthful protest – this time against the background of school.

It was released early in 1955 but still 'Rock Around the Clock' had a long way to go before it became the battle hymn of the new teenage group and the symbol of rebellion.

A cheap, scrappy movie production made in 1956 did the trick. It was entitled *Rock Around the Clock* and it brought together at last Alan Freed and Bill Haley, the first King of Rock. It was a blockbuster of a hit. The Haley disc was reissued and in Britain alone that year sold a million – a then undreamed of figure.

It was quite a year. The third giant of rock 'n' roll, already waiting in the wings, was unleashed on the world with a song called 'Heartbreak Hotel'. The singer was a truck driver named Elvis Aaron Presley, born one of twins (the other died) and destined soon to oust Haley from his throne.

All three* were to be immense influences on the life and times of Harry Rodger Webb: Alan Freed for giving the world the immortal three words that would describe Harry's eventual trade; Haley for giving them life and soul; and Presley for a new young image with which Harry could identify – a gyrating sexual image with dyed, greasy black hair and sideburns, along with a mean moody scowl.

Here for the youth of the world, like a long awaited messiah, was the real symbol to go along with the music. Presley was twenty-one in that break-out year of rock 'n' roll. He was the rage of the year.

Now the young had built for themselves a solid foundation for the new age group. The word teen began to dominate headlines and crept into song titles. Magazines appeared aimed solely at the teens, along with fashions and movies.

It was a rebellion against parents, against authority, against all forms of rules and regulations, nuclear weapons, fuddy-duddyism, the Church in all its varied branches – against anything, in fact, that wasn't young.

It was a movement that would grow and grow and lead eventually to such anti-heroes as the Rolling Stones and the numerous protesters who wallowed in their wake.

Not that the new, emergent age group found revolution to be a smooth ride in the mid-fifties. Authority started a rebellion of its own, while parents looked on with grave suspicion.

First Alan Freed and Bill Haley took most of the stick, until Elvis the Pelvis, as he was quickly dubbed, became the figurehead of the Big Beat, which some people in the media, endeavouring to ditch the rock label, were now calling the music.

Both Haley and Freed were accused across the States – and

*Not one of the trio survives. Alan Freed died of uremia in January 1965. He was forty-two. Presley died in August 1977, also aged forty-two. Haley died in February 1981, at fifty-five the oldest survivor.

later in Britain – of fomenting rock riots.

Freed, booming with his sellout concerts, was getting pins stuck in him by city fathers and mayors who sagely nodded their heads and decided to ban him from appearing in their cities.

Commented Freed: 'It's a shame that ninety-seven per cent of the country's youngsters must suffer because of the three per cent hoodlum element.'

At the same time in Britain a minority of troublemaking Teddy Boys – a group that adopted rock 'n' roll as their very own – danced in the aisles and ripped up cinema seats in several areas when *Rock Around the Clock* was shown.

Said Haley, 'I don't see why some people get so hot under the collar. Some folks hate to see kids happy. I can tell you honestly – I've never seen a riot . . .'

Which was true, it seems. When he invaded Britain early in 1957 with his Comets, his stage act of around thirty minutes was a harmless run of the mill presentation that was about as sexual as a team of performing seals. The Comets looked like a bunch of oldies desperately trying to hang on to a youthful image by falling around and playing their instruments in unorthodox positions. Rudy Pompilli blew his saxophone standing on his head. Al Rex, lying on his back, plucked away at his bass fiddle held aloft. It was laughable.

But there was no denying the music. It did something to people. It made them get out of their seats and want to dance in the aisles or swarm towards the stage while Haley mouthed the banal lyrics.

Harry Webb, still at school in Cheshunt in Hertfordshire, was swept up in it all. The inoffensive Haley, now at thirty an old man in the eyes of the teens, was unknowingly responsible for getting Harry one of his few black marks in life.

Harry played truant one day – getting up at five – to take himself off to Kilburn, in northwest London, to join the throng scrambling for tickets to see Haley and his Comets in action at the vast 4,000-seater Gaumont State cinema.

Next day the school took Harry's prefect badge away for this evil deed. With a hint of rebellion Harry protested to the headmaster: 'If we'd been to see the Bolshoi Ballet you'd have given us a pat on the back.'

He also promised, tongue in cheek it seems, never to skip school again 'unless Elvis is coming'.

His English teacher, Mrs Jay Norris, was kinder. 'In ten years' time, Harry,' she said, 'I'll bet you won't even remember the name Bill Haley.'

'I'll bet you a box of chocolates I will, miss,' Harry said.

Ten years later he was as good as his word . . .

But Elvis was to be his greater hero and responsible for the enormous eruption in his life that would culminate in Harry Webb becoming Cliff Richard, international rock 'n' roll star.

Harry joined the teen movement along with millions of others. Before Freed, Haley and Presley they had been simply young people, youngsters, youth, in-betweens or kids, and had frequently been dismissed as being at the awkward age.

Not any more.

Now Harry's hero Elvis was finding the knives in his back. Some American critics were crying that he was obscene. One complained that he was just 'a male burlesque dancer'.

In New York for one of his early coast-to-coast TV appearances, Elvis had his guitar taken away for the performance and was seen on screen from the waist up – in case he offended anyone. Elvis without movement was like Hardy without Laurel.

Neither Elvis nor his astute manager Tom Parker, the self-styled Colonel, sought out a dark corner of the studio to weep in. Instead, they pocketed £17,000 (a fortune a quarter of a century ago) for this one innocuous stint on the nationwide box.

Away from television Elvis was also being accused of incitement to riot and causing teenage misbehaviour.

He said innocently and no doubt with a prod from the Colonel, 'If I thought my rock 'n' roll singing was causing juvenile delinquency, I would go back to driving a truck. I don't love money that much . . .'

Nevertheless, a worried pastor in the Deep South held a prayer service that Elvis might 'be granted salvation'. And in St Louis a black disc jockey named James Dillon Burks described rock 'n' roll as 'an ignorant type of music'.

Haley's record company started to show a little concern about the music's image as well, issuing a disc with one side entitled

'Teenager's Mother', whose lyric protested that rock wasn't sinful and 'can't be bad if it makes you glad'. The whole idea went sour. The A-side of the platter was called 'Rip It Up'!

A rather bemused Bill Haley sailed into Britain with the Comets for the first time in the old Cunarder *Queen Elizabeth* on 5 February 1957 for a tour that took in London, Manchester, Birmingham, Leeds, Newcastle, Liverpool, Cardiff and Plymouth.

Earlier, on Wednesday 23 January, the *Daily Mirror* had astonished the rest of Fleet Street and no doubt millions of its readers by devoting the whole front page to announcing its 'big plans' to welcome 'the King of Rock 'n' Roll'. Haley loomed large on the page with his guitar.

The only other story on page one, dwarfed by the bold black type surrounding Haley, disclosed that Prince Charles and Princess Anne had been inoculated against polio, which had been claiming many young victims up and down the country.

Despite the wave of criticism rock 'n' roll was now attracting, the *Mirror* was not only sponsoring the Haley tour but also extending a big hand. It gave away seats at the concerts and Haley discs in simple competitions and also hired a train – a Rock 'n' Roll Special – to greet him at Southampton and escort him in triumph to London.

Mirror columnist Noel Whitcomb was despatched to the United States to join Haley at his home in Chester, Pennsylvania, to ghost a daily column by Haley as he journeyed to New York to embark aboard the *Queen Elizabeth* and as the liner sailed the Atlantic.

All the Comets were married men and, like Haley, brought along their wives – the whole party travelling tourist class.

At Waterloo Station in London, 3,000 fans besieged the baffled Haley as he tried to enter his limousine. Hundreds of girls lost their shoes in the great scuffle and some were injured. The New Battle of Waterloo, screamed the headlines.

Haley didn't know what hit him. 'Fantabulous!' he kept mouthing, a new word to go with the new music.

'My feet didn't touch the ground for fifty yards,' he said. 'I lost my gloves, the buttons off my overcoat and a case with my overnight gear in it.'

Thus rock 'n' roll, to which Harry Webb had now sworn his devotion, had arrived and now seemed about to achieve its first acknowledgement of respectability in Britain.

The *Mirror* had done its homework. Some months before deciding to sponsor Haley it hosted a small rock 'n' roll party in a suite at the Waldorf Hotel in London's Aldwych to find out what the music did or could do to people.

Disc columnist Patrick Doncaster and writer Tony Miles (later to become chairman of Mirror Group Newspapers) took along several attractive secretaries from the office, the Rev. John Hornby, an East End vicar, and a tame psychologist.

Keith Waterhouse, creator of Billy Liar and then a *Mirror* feature writer, scoured parts of London in a cab and plucked a handful of likely lads off the streets to be guinea pigs – with some difficulty, it must be said, because they were all a little suspicious of a character who suddenly halted a taxi at the kerb to invite them to a rock party!

Records of Haley and Presley were played for more than two hours to the assembled participants in what was seen at the time as a bold experiment.

But there was no mini riot, no horseplay, no rave-up. Just some honest to goodness unsexy dancing which consisted mainly of the girls being twirled until their skirts ballooned. The Rev. Hornby managed a twirl or two himself.

He summed up rock 'n' roll thus: 'It's exciting rhythm, enormous fun. It's a red herring to blame it for the bad behaviour of Teddy boys.'

The psychologist had this to say, 'This is music stripped bare – a persistent, insistent beat. A perfectly good outlet for the exuberance of youth. But,' he added as a possible warning, 'the impact depends on the person . . .'

This, then, was the way it was in Britain as Harry Webb steered his course towards the world of rock, taking in one of the *Mirror*'s Haley concerts at Kilburn late in February 1957 (the one that cost him his prefecture).

There were still the fors and againsts, but the movement was swelling. Already Britain had someone who had been heralded as the nation's answer to Presley – a tousle-headed blond merchant seaman with a wide toothy grin, a Cockney from Bermondsey born Tommy Hicks but now renamed Tommy Steele.

He had been launched into Discland in September 1956, the first of many, after discovery in the 2 i's coffee bar in Soho – a location that would become a Mecca for the pilgrims and hopefuls of rock 'n' roll.

But Presley? 'I hate him!' Tommy had said, all of nineteen years and ready to set the world alight.

Honestly?

'Well, I don't really hate him. I just don't like his style.'

His own style, however, was little removed from Presley's. When told by one critic that he sounded something like Elvis he retorted: 'I was singing like this *before* Presley . . . Bill Haley's my man . . .'

That September week of Tommy's launch in 1956 with a British-made song, 'Rock with the Caveman' on the Decca label, founding father Haley had *five* records in the Top Twenty chart (early charts were limited to twenty placings but grew with the industry until the weekly lists took in fifty and then seventy-five).

One of the writers of 'Rock with the Caveman' was to be found at the 2 i's coffee bar, an unassuming East-Ender with a lot of ambition but at that time a silk-screen printer and a dab hand at décor.

In fact he decorated the tiny cellar beneath the little café – barely roomy enough to swing a guitar – and incorporated two large eyes. The cellar was where the music blasted forth and when this Cockney wasn't splashing paint around he sat in with the various hopefuls and groups, strumming his fingers up and down a washboard in rhythm.

His name: Lionel Bart. Even then he was dreaming of writing a musical based on Dickens' *Oliver Twist* and had roughed out a first act in a Woolworth's sixpenny lined notepad.

When someone pointed out loftily that no producer would ever look at a first act with something like fourteen scene changes, Bart was undaunted and forged on.

He was to figure large in the life of Harry Webb, write a song that would be a turning point in his life and his career when he became Cliff Richard, and help mould him into someone above the average rock 'n' roller who swivelled his hips and curled a lip, exuding rebellion. Someone a little nicer . . .

The 2 i's would also be forever a landmark in the life of Harry Webb. Like a magnet, it would draw him as it did thousands of others, including one Terry Nelhams, from Acton way, who would become Adam Faith.

Literally thousands would fall by the wayside and go back to their jobs or the dole. Only Steele and Cliff Richard would emerge as giants, go forward into manhood and still be names that could fill a theatre when they had passed the forty mark a quarter of a century later.

CHAPTER TWO

Indian Sunset

The long trek to the 2 i's in Soho and fame as a rock 'n' roller extra-ordinary began for Harry Rodger Webb halfway across the world in India, where he was born on 14 October 1940 at Lucknow.

Britain was at war with Germany and Italy, standing alone, fighting for survival and her freedom. The Battle of Britain had been won – just, but enough for Hitler to call off Operation Sealion, his much-trumpeted and feared invasion of England set for 15 September – a month before baby Harry weighed in at Lucknow.

The Battle of Britain was the first German defeat of the Second World War and America had yet to play its hand.

For Harry's parents, Rodger and Dorothy Webb, England was still the homeland, although neither of them had ever seen it. Both had relatives braving it out in bomb-battered Britain.

He had been born of English parents in Burma and was now an area manager employed by the well-known catering firm of Kellner. His wife Dorothy had been born of English parents in India, her father a British regular soldier. They married within six months of meeting.

India was then British India and for exiles the bonds were close. They were, however, peaceful days in the Indian empire while Britain still felt the lash of nightly air raids and Mr Churchill stalked the ruins in a steel helmet next morning.

Japan would be the obvious threat to India and invasion was always a possibility, although it wasn't until late 1941, when Harry was fourteen months, that Japan attacked neighbouring Burma.

Ironically, it would be the Indians who ran the Webb family out of their home and livelihood in the end, after partition in 1947 . . .

When Harry was born Lucknow was a garrison town of some half million souls and the home base of a celebrated Indian division which was fighting for Britain in the western desert.

Father Rodger was thirty-five when his first-born arrived. His wife was some fifteen years his junior, small, with the dark eyes that Harry would inherit.

They found Lucknow a pleasant town, situated on the Gumti River, a tributary of the Ganges, 303 miles southwest of Delhi and a little over 600 miles northwest of Calcutta, where the Webbs would later settle.

Lucknow boasted spacious parks and traditional industry, being noted for its *Chikan* work of fine hand embroidery. It also produced gold and silver thread work, cotton fabrics and perfumes.

From Lucknow, where Harry had his first lessons in paddling in the Gumti, the family moved on to Cawnpore and Jaipur before taking up their final residence in a company flat in Calcutta. The Webbs were now five, with the addition of Donella, more fondly known as Donna, and Jacqueline – two sisters to annoy Harry, who at least on one occasion demonstrated that he was the eldest and therefore the boss.

His mother has said, 'Of course they squabbled, like all children do. But my husband always drummed it into Harry that a gentleman never hits a lady.

'Donella, who is two years younger, sometimes took advantage of this and teased him terribly. One day he got really mad at her and chased her with a rolled-up newspaper. But he said it was all right – it was the newspaper that did the hitting!'

Dad ordered him to count up to ten before ever thinking of doing it again.

Young Harry accompanied his father on fishing trips and found kite flying, Indian style, great fun as well as something of a challenge. Kite-fliers indulged in air battles, trying desperately to sever each other's slender controlling threads and put the kite out of order. It was a deadly serious sport, with some fliers coating their threads with particles of glass to slice through an 'enemy' kite and thus bring it down or send it soaring into the heavens on the breeze.

In India it was the good life for the Webbs, with four servants and a style of living far beyond the dreams of the majority of the population.

Thus, after India gained independence, British families were targets of retaliation for the have-nots of the British Raj days. There were riots, Britons were pelted with stones and other missiles, and to stay on in such conditions seemed decidedly dangerous. 'Why don't you go home to your own country?' an angry demonstrator yelled at Mrs Webb.

The Webbs uprooted and, after debating whether to pick up the pieces in England or Australia, sailed for Britain in the autumn of 1948 in the S.S. *Ranghi*.

Harry, his eighth birthday not very far away, was unable to cope with the rock 'n' roll of the ocean during the three-week voyage to Tilbury and spent a lot of the time in his quarters with the sea's most dreaded malady.

England, still punch-drunk from the war that had ended only three years earlier, was as yet no land fit for heroes and certainly no attraction for a family of five bent on making a new life. Mr Webb set foot on British soil for the first time with only £5 in his pocket. The prospects were anything but hopeful.

Britain was in a shabby state. Food was still rationed and the transition from war to peace was still painfully slow. Men returned from the forces were still gloomily waiting for somewhere to live, with homes being allocated on a points system. Clement Attlee was Labour Prime Minister and with President Truman of the United States was finding that peace was not an easy road.

Life for the Webbs, after the comparative luxury of India, was indeed spartan when they settled in one room in Carshalton, Surrey, alongside one of Harry's grandmothers. They ate, slept and lived in that one room, all five of them.

For Harry there was his first British school, Stanley Park Road Primary, where he was to discover how merciless childish tongues could be.

His skin had been burned dark by the Indian sun and he spoke

English with a trace of the accent much parodied by Peter Sellers. 'Nigger!' the kids taunted Harry. And 'Inde-bum!' when they found out that he had been born in India. He had to learn how to defend himself in frequent playground battles.

One misguided teacher goaded him on one day by saying: 'Come on Webb, you can't run off to your wigwam any more!'

England was definitely hostile and he didn't like it one little bit in those early days.

There was little improvement in the Webbs' living standards when later an aunt took them into her home at Waltham Cross, Hertfordshire. Again it was one room with everyone getting in each other's way and life threatened to become increasingly difficult when Mrs Webb was expecting a fourth child.

Their plight resulted in the allocation of a council house in Hargreaves Close at nearby Cheshunt. Joan, a third sister for Harry, was born just prior to the move.

By now father was working as a clerk at Atlas Lamps, part of the Ferguson complex at Enfield in Middlesex, on the A10 route into Hertfordshire and Cambridge. But the going was still hard and conditions still in sharp contrast to those they had enjoyed in India.

There was no money to lavish on furniture and Mr Webb even had to make some of it, fashioning sturdy chairs from packing cases which he bought for a few pence. They lasted for years.

Mrs Webb, her hands already full coping with four children, went out to work part time in the evenings at a paint-brush factory at Broxbourne, cycling to and fro to save pennies.

She recalls that Harry 'was marvellous. He always gave his sisters their tea and put them to bed for me.'

He remembers seeing his mother in tears at times when the pressures became just too heavy for her.

For Harry there was another primary school at Waltham Cross, where he swotted for the eleven-plus examination that he felt sure he would pass but didn't. It was a sad blow.

By this time he was completely anglicized and the harsh British winters had worn away any traces of the Indian tan.

He moved on to Cheshunt's secondary modern school for the formative years and, without being brilliant, proved himself an adept pupil, becoming a prefect and something of a sportsman. At soccer he was a reliable right back and was good enough to be chosen for a place in the county's under-fourteen side.

He swam, played badminton and basketball and was a fair hand with the javelin, setting a school record that wasn't broken for many a year.

To raise a few shillings he occasionally caddied at a local golf course. One day, as his mother's birthday came around, he went there with swimming gear beneath his jeans, stripped off and plunged into the stream that ran through the course to retrieve lost golf balls, which he sold. For mother there were two pound notes to help make it a happy birthday.

He played in school theatrical productions, putting his all into the title role of *Toad of Toad Hall* and Bob Cratchit in Dickens' *A Christmas Carol*.

At fifteen he could have left school to go to work but, encouraged by his parents, he stayed on for another eighteen months to take O-levels, achieving a pass in English.

In the world of pop music the revolution that would engulf Harry Webb was beginning to take hold with skiffle and rock 'n' roll.

Skiffle worked itself up into a national craze. All across the nation youngsters were banding themselves together with hastily-learned guitars and a do-it-yourself bass which conjured a deep twang from a tea chest by means of string and broom handle.

Harry was still only fifteen when along came Elvis, who would be his idol and responsible for a giant upheaval in his life.

Thus far, however, Harry had given only a slight indication of where his future path might lie by being part of a boy and girl vocal group, calling themselves the Quintones, which made its first public appearance at a Youth Fellowship dance in Cheshunt.

The transition to rock 'n' roll was to be as slow as Presley's take-off in Britain. Elvis was certainly no overnight sensation when he was launched here on record in the first week of March 1956, with his first major disc on the powerful American R.C.A. label – 'Heartbreak Hotel' and 'I Was the One' (issued here under the H.M.V. banner).

Strangely, it seems in retrospect, the publicity material that came with the record said nothing about his being a foremost exponent of rock 'n' roll and revealed instead that American teenagers were hailing him as the King of Western Bop, an odd linking of two musical styles – country and western and bebop, a jazz phase of the early forties.

The *Daily Mirror* critic, introducing Elvis to Britain's discophiles, posed the question, 'Will British girls fall for him?' And supplied his own answer, 'I think it's likely – in time.'

He was partly right. The record moved incredibly slowly, but was a smashing great hit by summer.

Young Harry Webb, along with sister Donna, was an early devotee.

Around this time his father had spent a fiver on a guitar that both of them played. Dad used to strum a banjo in India with a traditional jazz outfit and could also play guitar. He gave Harry his first lesson, teaching him the simple three-chord trick that was sufficient for struggling skifflers and early rockers.

As Presley zoomed to fame with 'Heartbreak Hotel', Harry's worship of him grew. He tried to look like Elvis, growing sideburns, greasing his hair, imitating his scowl in front of a mirror at home, the same curl of the lip that was taken to be some demonstration of protest or defiance. And he began to try to sing like him, giving an Elvis impression when he appeared with the Quintones.

'He was my idol,' he has said frequently over the years.

Yet it was skiffle rather than rock that put Harry Webb on the glory trail.

He had left school when it happened and had become a £4.15s a week credit control clerk at Atlas Lamps, working in the same large office as his father, the pair of them cycling the dreary miles from Cheshunt to Enfield daily.

Word came via a schoolfriend that a local outfit called the Dick Teague Skiffle Group was in need of a singer. Harry went into his act at an audition for Teague, passed and was at last on his way.

On drums in the Teague group was one Terry Smart whose leanings, like those of Harry, were towards the more vital rock 'n' roll. Within a short time both broke away from Teague and

28

set up their own rock group, the Drifters, along with a third member – Norman Mitham, a schoolmate of Harry's.

They met nightly to practise this new art in the Webb council house. The incessant racket brought down the wrath of the neighbours and the housing authority, after investigating complaints, decreed that the music would have to cease by ten o'clock. But the Drifters were now an entity and treading the path to fame as Harry Webb and the Drifters, belting out rock at local dances and youth venues.

The road would lead one evening to the Five Horseshoes at Hoddesdon, where their pay was measured in pieces of silver, and to the encounter with John Foster, the sturdy Teddy Boy from the sewage works.

To this day John – now back with his mother some two miles from the scene, living in the same house in which he then lived – doesn't know exactly what prompted him to ask Harry Webb if he could be his manager.

'It was just this magic,' John says now, shaking his head slightly in bewilderment, 'and he certainly aroused a lot of excitement with the girls.

'I was just doing a funny little ordinary job at the sewage works and knew absolutely nothing about show business, but I had this feeling that this boy could be a star.

'I went over to Cheshunt to the Webbs' council house home and met his mum and dad. His father wasn't interested and just didn't want to know, but then we were all pretty young and naive and, after all, I was only a year older than Harry.

'Anyway, I believed in this lad and my mother and father put together the money to make a private recording of the Drifters. How much was it, Mum?' he asked her as we talked in the little house where Harry and the Drifters used to practise as well as sleep occasionally in those primitive days.

'Ten pounds,' she said as if it were only yesterday.

'That's right,' John said. 'They recorded two songs, "Lawdy Miss Clawdy" and "Breathless".

'I slapped around with our tape trying to get people interested in Harry Webb and the Drifters, but no one was terribly impressed,' John remembered.

'One of the people I went to was Ian Bevan, Tommy Steele's agent. Tommy was making it big by this time. Anyway, Mr Bevan did listen to the tape. Afterwards he said, "I like rock 'n' roll – it's a great thing, but if I was you I'd tell this fellow not to give up his day job!"

'A long time later when I met Bevan he recalled the occasion and asked me, "How'd that boy do?"

' "He's Cliff Richard now!" I told him . . .'

Nothing could sway John Foster in his early enthusiasm for Harry Webb and his great belief that he had discovered a star. He thought there might be more interest in his charges down at the 2 i's in Soho. That was the Mecca of rock 'n' roll, people were always telling him, which had produced not only Tommy Steele but some other names that would have their moments of triumph in the ever-changing world of pop.

So Foster sallied forth to London once more by Green Line bus.

Surely there was someone who would give a break to Harry Webb, star in waiting.

CHAPTER THREE

In Darkest Soho

It was a different Soho in the fifties, abounding in coffee bars and characters, a cosmopolitan, colourful quarter where you could smell the cheeses and salami on the evening air.

There were no porn shops, no marital aid stores or erotic cinemas proclaiming 'Hard Core Porno Films Now Showing' or warning 'that persons under eighteen are not admitted to these premises'. Striptease was in its infancy and mostly inoffensive.

Soho, however, was still a honeyed invitation from a doorway. It was still an ugly white scar down a mobster's cheek, for the habitués included a fair proportion of tarts and gangsters and their protection heavies. Yet somehow the atmosphere was more *Guys and Dolls* vintage than sleazy and sinister.

Thousands of ordinary citizens – at that time the majority of them teenagers – were able to trek there to drink coffee and listen to music, in coffee bars or jazz clubs, without being coaxed to sample the pleasures of sex.

The 2 i's was at the Wardour Street end of Old Compton Street, sandwiched between a delicatessen and another neon-signed coffee lounge called Heaven and Hell.

Heaven and Hell was as harmless as a fairground ghost train ride, offering nothing more exciting than coffee and music from a jukebox. Heaven was simply the ground floor. Hell was the basement. It was hot all right, because of lack of ventilation, and lit only by red-eyed devil masks on the walls and the jukebox.

'Everybody wants to go to hell,' the then proprietor said. 'We had a parson in the other night. He started up in Heaven on the ground floor, but after a while said "I must see what it's like down there." He found Hell quite pleasant . . .'

The 2 i's didn't try to be clever at all. It was a rather plain little establishment, no larger than an ordinary high street café, which it closely resembled. There was a bar with stools, a jukebox and a gleaming espresso machine – then the newest thing. Along with your coffee you could munch a hot dog.

The big attraction was the basement, where young people could belt out their new revolutionary music and hope for instant fame.

Two brothers with the surname Irani had been the first proprietors. Thus the 2 i's. The original hand-painted sign spelt it with a small i – although a neon sign proclaimed 2 I's with a capital. The hand-painted sign described the establishment as a coffee bar. A small neon sign called it a café.

It kept its name when it was taken over by two young all-in wrestlers. The one most in evidence at night was Paul Lincoln, a stocky Australian then in his early twenties – a man who nursed a dark secret. He was, in fact, the celebrated mystery figure known as Doctor Death, who fought countless bouts in the ring wearing a black mask.

Nobody – certainly not the newspapers or the hopefuls who descended on the coffee bar from many parts of Britain – had any idea that this cheerful chap who encouraged rock 'n' rollers to come play for him was the much-feared Doctor Death. He kept his secret until he retired from the wrestling ring several years later.

Said Mr Lincoln, as most of us knew him, 'There are bags of kids these days who have talent but don't get the opportunity of showing what they can do. We try to give them a chance.'

Not everybody who appeared at the 2 i's received payment. It was principally a showcase, but there were those willing to toil away nightly for something like ten shillings (50 pence now). They included Harry Webb and the Drifters . . .

But there was the excitement of it all: being on display at the 2 i's where the elusive talent scout might be the man leaning against the wall in the shadows, waiting to dispense a fat recording contract and put your name up in lights.

It had happened to Tommy Steele. It had happened to the skiffling Vipers group and briefly to a lad named Terry Dene.

Terry had been eighteen, came from London's Elephant and

Castle district and worked as a packer by day – packing records in H.M.V.'s Oxford Street store, where Harry Webb made his demonstration recording!

One night Terry, determined to be heard and seen, jumped on to the stage at the 2 i's while a perspiring group took a break, and sang to his own guitar accompaniment. Paul Lincoln listened, became his manager and Dene's enterprise won him an immediate week in cabaret and a contract with a major recording label, Decca – sworn rivals of his H.M.V. employers.

The up and coming boss of the Parlophone company was the man to watch for, a slim ex-Fleet Air Arm flier named George Martin. 'I make a regular visit to Soho,' he said at the time. 'It has become a breeding ground for talent. Six months ago I wouldn't have dreamed of going there.'

It was George who signed the successful Vipers – but passed up Tommy Steele, who was singing with them! He never made another mistake like that. Within a few years he would be the only recording manager to open his door to a struggling foursome calling themselves the Beatles when everyone else was slamming them shut in their faces . . .

Thus there was much excitement in the Drifters' camp when John Foster managed to book them into the 2 i's for a week's engagement. This, at last, could be it! But that week proved a great disappointment for Harry Webb and his colleagues Terry Smart and Norman Mitham.

There were no show business moguls in Teddy Bear overcoats, smoking long cigars, waiting to make them famous.

There was no George Martin waiting for the right singer to come along to compensate for having missed out on Tommy Steele.

There was no Lionel Bart, whom Harry had dreamed of meeting; of having Bart force a song on him and spin him headlong into stardom. 'I was really disgruntled with the 2 i's,' Cliff says today. 'Nothing seemed to happen and it was a great letdown at the time.' (Lionel Bart has said that he *does* remember seeing Cliff perform at the 2 i's, but Cliff is sure that they never met there.)

Even Paul Lincoln wasn't much impressed with the Drifters – although years later he did count the cost and estimate that he had kissed more than a million pounds goodbye through not having involved himself in the golden-lined futures of Tommy Steele, Adam Faith and Harry Webb.

At that time Lincoln was attracting the attention of 5,000 teenagers a year, he estimated, all seeking discovery either in person or by writing to him.

'Most of these kids wanted to throw up their jobs, come to town and work for almost nothing. I told them how tough it was, to stick to their jobs and try to make a go of it part time.'

For Harry Webb the nightly journey to the bright lights held little fascination. As John Foster remembers: 'We used to get the Green Line into London – number 715a, Hertford to Oxford Street – and Cliff was always sick on the bus.

'But it used to take us past the old Finsbury Park Empire, a famous variety theatre at that time, and one night I pointed it out to Cliff as we went past and said "Some day your name will be up there in lights . . ." '

Cliff still recalls John Foster's words fondly. 'We used to have a giggle and laugh as well on the old 715a bus,' he says.

Despite the overall disappointment, the 2 i's would turn up some trumps for him. It was there that he met a young red-haired R.A.F. man named Ian Samwell, nearing the completion of his two-year national service and popularly known as Sammy.

Samwell, a Londoner, was a regular pilgrim to Soho on off-duty nights, with a hankering to be up there as one of the boys making music. He had learned piano when younger and had recently taken up the guitar when Harry Webb and the two Drifters came into his life.

Sammy, like John Foster, sensed the magic in this dark-eyed, chubby lad; a magic that cried out to be set free on a far wider public. He also noticed that there was something not quite all there about the Drifters: they had no lead guitar.

He saw his chance. When the music stopped he sought out Harry, pointed out the deficiency and asked him if he needed a lead guitar. 'I just went up to the stage and asked – it was as easy as that,' he recalls today at the age of forty-three.

There was no hesitation on Harry's part and so Samwell became the third Drifter whenever the Royal Air Force let him out for a night. Within a short space of time Ian Samwell would have a leading part to play in the transformation of Harry Webb into Cliff Richard . . .

Says John Foster, 'While we were at the 2 i's a promoter – I believe his name was Bob Greatorex – came in one night and took an interest in what the Drifters were offering. In fact he was so keen he couldn't wait to book us for a one-night stand at a dance hall in Ripley, Derbyshire.

'We all adjourned to The Swiss pub, a few doors down from the 2 i's in Old Compton Street, to talk the deal over.

'Bob asked us what we called the lead singer? "Harry Webb," we said. Bob didn't like it; it didn't sound exciting enough, he said, and he asked us to think of another name. And he wanted it quickly because he had to get the bills printed for the dance hall show and there wasn't much time left.

'It wasn't easy. We threw around a lot of names and agreed eventually that Cliff sounded pretty good as a first name. We got as far as Cliff Bussard – why Bussard I don't know – but it didn't sound quite right. Then I came up with Cliff Richards. "That sounds all right," this Bob fellow said.

'Then Sammy Samwell had a bright idea. "Why don't we leave the s off the end? A lot of people would get it wrong and call him Richards, but having to correct them would get the name known and talked about." '

So it was Harry Webb is dead! Long live Cliff Richard!

The dropping of the s gave great publicity value in those fledgling days. Even now some people who ought to know better still refer to him as Cliff Richards . . .

As far as John Foster can remember the fee for the Ripley gig was about ten pounds.

'I know there was nothing left after we had paid all our expenses. Even so we couldn't afford the cheapest of digs. After the show that night we slept in the dance hall! But it was all experience.'

It was on a night at the 2 i's that John Foster was alerted by a poster advertising a talent contest to take place on a Saturday morning at the Gaumont Cinema on the Green at Shepherd's Bush. Conducting this free for all was a Canadian radio personality named Carroll Levis who, like Hughie Green, roamed the country searching for new names with his discovery shows.

Cliff's mother had already written for an audition with the Hughie Green setup, but thus far the negotiations had only reached the form-filling stage. Earlier, Cliff had entered a talent contest at the Trocadero Cinema at the Elephant and Castle – only to have his amplification gear fail, forcing him to retire from the competition extremely hurt and near to tears.

Now there was another talent contest . . . Foster, still not out of his teens and the man to whom Cliff and the Drifters were looking for miracles, dreamed up one of his inspired super-moves.

Why should they enter some crummy talent show and run the risk of coming nowhere? They were a going concern, starring, albeit practically for nothing, at the famous 2 i's.

Why shouldn't they go along to the Gaumont and offer their services free – provided the management would let them top the bill as an attraction? Not just as miserable contestants.

Full of enthusiasm, John Foster put it to them. 'They fell for it,' he smiles now. 'They thought they were getting something for nothing, I suppose, even though the Drifters were still a little bit raw and sounded thin without a bass guitar.'

It was felt at this time, too, that perhaps the Drifters and their star turn, now officially Cliff Richard, might make more progress if they had an agent.

'It shows you just how much I knew about show business,' John Foster says. 'I went along to see an agent named George Ganjou and asked him if he'd come along to Shepherd's Bush to take a look at Cliff and the boys.'

Ian Samwell told us that he had picked out Ganjou's name and address in *The Stage*, the theatrical weekly, and had made the same plea to him earlier.

The world of agent Ganjou was as far removed from the new world of rock as an Eskimo from a palm-fringed beach, but there were few agents devoting themselves to rock 'n' roll at this period.

He was then coming up towards sixty and had been a member of a celebrated variety and cabaret act called the Ganjou Brothers and Juanita. They were billed as an adagio dance presentation, with the three brothers bewigged and magnificently attired like

French courtiers in silk breeches. They tossed Juanita gracefully around the stage, sweeping high and sweeping low in poetic motion, a beautiful act that needed no words and which they performed with immense success right across the world.

George, now turned eighty – 'I was born on the first day of the century' – says Juanita must have flown more than a thousand miles through the air via his brothers Serge and Bob and himself.

He had been born in Warsaw of a Russian father and Polish mother and in his teens played second flute in a Warsaw symphony orchestra. He also played piccolo. 'I was no James Galway,' he smiles, 'but I leaned towards classical music from those days.'

The brothers left a Europe in turmoil after the end of the First World War and settled and worked in America, arriving in Britain with their adagio act in 1933 to 'join the Crazy Gang at the London Palladium', George remembers.

'We finished our career appearing on television in *Sunday Night at the London Palladium* in 1957 – a year before I discovered Cliff Richard.'

George, still sprightly and dapper, still playing golf, had started his variety agency business three years before in 1954 and now began to devote all his time to it.

'Speciality acts were my forte,' he says, and he covered the world in search of them. When Cliff and the Drifters intruded into his life he had also become the sole agent for entertainment at the Butlin holiday camps.

He appears to have complete recall of the advent of Cliff Richard and even remembers that it was a Friday afternoon in July 1958 when an insistent caller came knocking at his door.

'It was John Foster,' he says, 'and John told me that he had this young man appearing in the morning at the Gaumont at Shepherd's Bush and how great he was and that I should see him.

'I tossed a coin to see whether I should play golf on that Saturday morning or try to do some business. The coin came down business, so I went along.

'I was not a rock 'n' roll expert. I didn't care for it, to be truthful, but I sat back in the stalls as I usually did. Then came the band with Cliff Richard. They started to do their gyrations and music and everybody went absolutely mad about Cliff. The audience screamed and yelled and Cliff gave what I thought was a very clever performance.

'He was something new. I liked his looks, his behaviour, his personality. I could see that he had great potential. It was music that lots of other people would like even if it wasn't my type of music.

'He was not a Caruso, but as far as crooning was concerned he had something which appealed to girls and women. Vocal and visual – that's what he was. I knew then that he would become a star, although he was dressed a bit peculiarly.'

John Foster says he had decked Cliff out in something like a Teddy Boy rig. The drape jacket was pink, with pink day-glow socks to match, burning brightly like neon signs. The pants were black along with the shirt. The obligatory suede shoes were grey.

'Cliff was a very beautiful young man,' George mused as we talked in his flat on the Chelsea Embankment, 'and he looked too nice to be a Teddy Boy.'

George wasted no time after witnessing the explosion caused by Cliff and the Drifters at the Gaumont. 'Next day – Sunday – I took the tape of Cliff and his band to Norrie Paramor, a friend of mine.'

Norrie was a soft-spoken, sparse-haired ex-pianist who had led his first band at the remarkable age of fifteen. He had been with an R.A.F. orchestra during the war and later with a lively outfit called Harry Gold and his Pieces of Eight, frequently heard on radio.

In the summer of 1958 he was artistes and repertoire manager of the Columbia label, part of the E.M.I. recording complex. He had been having considerable success with an Irish thrush from Belfast named Ruby Murray who sang four hits at a time into the then Top Twenty; with golden trumpeter Eddie Calvert, a million-seller with 'Oh Mein Papa', and Michael Holliday, a big-band singer who sounded like Bing Crosby.

Mr Paramor had yet to catch up with rock 'n' roll.

Says George Ganjou, 'Norrie was neither here nor there about Cliff's tape, but he did say he would like to meet him and have another go with him and his boys in the E.M.I. studios. Then Norrie went off on holiday for two weeks.'

Those two weeks bothered Mr Ganjou who, despite the fact that he was no rock 'n' roll fan, was increasingly convinced that he had a winner, although so far no contract had been signed. 'During those two weeks, if they had known,' says George, 'anybody could have had Cliff Richard!'

Nobody did.

Along with the Cliff Richard tape George left another for Norrie's consideration – made by an opera singer named Tino Valdi. 'He was Ukrainian,' George says, 'and a wonderful singer of opera.'

When George rang Norrie on his return from holiday it was to enquire first about Tino Valdi – not the good-looking kid who belted out rock 'n' roll in the style of the now unstoppable Elvis.

'But Valdi was not Norrie's type,' George says, 'though he *was* interested in Cliff. We went to the studios at Abbey Road to audition and that was the start of it all. Norrie said afterwards: "I think we've got something here!"'

'I signed Cliff to a sole agency agreement, guaranteeing him that he would be earning a thousand pounds a week within six months. I was really sticking my neck out! I started by booking him into Butlin's at Clacton for three weeks for thirty pounds a week and my first wife, Adela, who had been a dancer, began to advise him on his appearance. He would not look up enough with those dark eyes, for one thing.'

It was an all-happening July for Cliff Richard and the Drifters, as they were labelled on their debut disc. It was recorded at Abbey Road during that month with the added help of two seasoned session musicians – professionals who backed various artists and remained anonymous.

Ian Samwell recalls today that Columbia really didn't want the Drifters on the disc at all–'only Cliff. I got a seven pound fee for playing guitar on it in the end!'

The two titles were 'Schoolboy Crush' and 'Move It' and the release date was set for 29 August 1958.

With little subtlety, the recording industry was intent on snaring the early teens or the Nellies, as the diskeries fondly called the hordes of screaming girls who were now worshipping idols of their own age.

39

Already a fourteen-year-old coloured American rocker named Frankie Lymon had topped the bill for a fortnight at the London Palladium with his group the Teenagers (what else?) – a visit simply inspired by the fact that his record 'Why Do Fools Fall in Love?' had been a smash hit in Britain (he died of a drug overdose by the time he was twenty-five).

Therefore the trend showed that a title with *teen* or some young-oriented word such as *schoolboy* in it might well hit the bell in a big way. So 'Schoolboy Crush' was made the A-side, or main side, of Cliff's first record.

This song had been brought to Norrie Paramor by singer/music publisher Franklyn Boyd . . . another name that would have some bearing on the early career of Cliff Richard.

'Move It', the B-side, was a home-grown effort, conjured up by Ian Samwell and given its title by John Foster. 'He wrote it on top of a bus,' says John, 'and it was on top of a bus that I said why not call it "Move It"? Lots of things seemed to happen to us on buses,' John smiles.

Samwell recalls: 'It was a London Colney-Cheshunt bus. I was stationed in the R.A.F. at this time at Hendon but lived at home in St Albans on compassionate grounds because my mother was ill.'

The lyric, he says, was based on recurring reports that rock 'n' roll was beginning to fade and included a line that said 'they say it's going to die'.

True, there had been something of a lull after the earlier explosions of Haley and Presley in 1956. Cliff was, in fact, two years late coming to the scene, but rock 'n' roll continued to produce an endless belt of new names and new songs, many of which made only a fleeting impression on the recording scene – songs, for instance, such as 'The Teen Commandments', which qualified for a bad-taste award at the end of 1958. Alongside this 'Schoolboy Crush' sounded almost distinguished.

But again, like the initial stint at the 2 i's, Cliff's first record did not make any immediate waves. There was no star-overnight sensation, no rags-to-riches-all-in-a-week story. Cliff Richard was as yet just another new boy on the treadmill and it would be up to the Nellies, with their spending power, to either make him or break him.

Norrie Paramor felt confident in his new find and refused to join in the pessimism about the future of rock 'n' roll. 'I just can't see the kids giving up these personalities with a beat,' he said, interviewed for Patrick Doncaster's column in the *Daily Mirror* on 31 July 1958.

Paramor had given him a sneak preview of Cliff's record a month before it was due for release and the *Mirror* devoted the whole top of page ten to the dawn of Cliff Richard. NEW RECRUIT FOR THE DISC WAR was the bold black heading alongside a two-column picture of the lad, looking mean, moody – and chubby, it must be said – in an open-necked shirt, a gold cross on a chain around his neck.

He was seen as an ace up the sleeve of Columbia when the record companies would do battle for the annual autumn sales boom that followed the end of the summer holidays.

The story told how Norrie had done his homework via his daughter Carolyn, who was then nearly fourteen. He had taken home a test pressing – a metal disc thinly coated with shellac and not meant to last more than a few spins, perhaps as little as thirty.

Carolyn's copy was worn out in a few days.

The *Mirror* column summed up that Cliff Richard's personality shone through the grooves and decided that he could succeed in Discland. It also disclosed that his favourite artist was Elvis and that his ambitions were to win a gold record for a million sales and to meet Elvis.

This was the first-ever mention of Cliff Richard in a national newspaper. Within a year the cutting libraries in every Fleet Street office would have a considerable section devoted to him . . .

Around the end of July our new recruit for the disc war gave up his job as a credit control clerk with Atlas Lamps where, he was told on parting, it had been realized that he had never been cut out for it.

So he joined the Discland militants, became officially a professional artist on 9 August and began to look and present himself even more like his idol Presley.

Off went the Drifters to Butlin's at Clacton where Cliff, the Discland rookie, soldiered on resolutely, wondering when or if his first record would ever achieve one of those elusive little lines of types in the hit chart – one line that could really bring sudden fame and put up your money along with your name in lights.

The group had travelled one light – minus original Drifter Norman Mitham. 'He dropped out when we became professional,' Cliff explains. 'It was all amicable. Norman didn't want to continue with us. He didn't feel he was up to the standard now required.'

Oddly, Mitham, the guitarist who hadn't considered himself good enough in those days, has in recent years been giving guitar lessons, so Cliff has heard.

For Clacton, too, Ian Samwell transferred to bass guitar and a professional lead guitarist working at the camp was brought in for the Drifters' appearances.

When they reached Butlin's John Foster was once again delivered of a shaft of promotional inspiration.

'They wanted us to wear the usual red coats that entertainment staff had become famous for. But we weren't Redcoats, I told them. We were Cliff Richard and the Drifters – something different, even though Roy Hudd, the comedian, was there as a Redcoat!'

Foster won. They were given white shirts – on which was emblazoned a red V which no one seems able to explain.

The camp management, however, couldn't quite make up their minds where to place this ambitious but pernickety bunch of youngsters.

'They put us in the ballroom,' says John, 'but we didn't quite fit. "We're a rock 'n' roll band," I told them. We played one night and they took us out. So they tried us in a sort of Hawaiian room and again I protested that we were a rock band. Same thing, one night and they took us out.

'Next they put us in the rock 'n' roll room – where we should have been from the start. Anyway, we played there lunchtimes and evenings. All the time Cliff was getting better and better and the reaction was fantastic when he tried our "Move It", which was the side we liked better and always played.

'Norrie rang while we were there to tell us that the record was to be played that night on Radio Luxembourg. There was great excitement and we all crowded into a chalet to hear it. Funny thing, but Luxembourg turned the record over as well and played "Move It" instead of the A-side, "Schoolboy Crush". We were delighted.

' "Move It" started to show some signs of really moving. Other disc jockeys began to play this side now and "Schoolboy Crush" was forgotten.'

Someone else had turned Cliff's record over – a young television whiz kid named Jack Good, who could scarcely believe that anyone British could sing rock 'n' roll as good as this. 'Get him!' the order went out . . .

When Cliff and the lads returned home after Clacton there was a message waiting from George Ganjou. 'It was sensational,' John Foster says, still with much enthusiasm.

Cliff Richard and the Drifters had been signed for their first tour in the coming October on a bill headed by a bright new duo from the United States, the Kalin Twins.

It was all happening and seemingly at once.

It was goodbye 2 i's, farewell Soho. No more cramped cellars, no more Five Horseshoes. Big time here we come – at £200 a week for a start . . .

Sadly the 2 i's is no more. Where a sign once proclaimed 'Home of the Stars' there stands a pleasant French restaurant. In the cellar where rock 'n' roll gave birth to Steele, Faith and Richard, diners ease escargots from their shells and quaff cool wine instead of coffee.

Even Heaven and Hell next door has gone the way of all flesh. The delicatessen still stands and so does The Swiss pub.

Squeezed between them is a cinema showing nothing but dirt . . .

CHAPTER FOUR

Oh Boy! It's Cliff!

One record hit was enough to bring the Kalin Twins, Hal and Herbie, hurtling across the Atlantic to tour Britain. That was the power of a shiny, spinning disc in 1958, a year in which the industry really didn't know where it was going; wondering if rock 'n' roll was here to stay; wondering if ballads – still popular with such stalwarts as Dean Martin hitting big with 'Volare', that year's winning song at the San Remo Festival in Italy – would take over once more; wondering if there would be something completely new from Latin America.

Elvis had been drafted into the American Army and was now a number – 53310761 – serving in Germany, leaving behind a stockpile of records to keep his fans happy. But, it was asked, would his absence for two years tend to make people forget him?

America's merchandizing merchants did their best to keep him very much alive. During the eventful July of the advent of Cliff Richard in Britain, a million and a half youngsters in the United States bought bracelets, anklets and key chains featuring an auto-graphed picture of Presley, his army number and his blood group.

The new disc names launched to fill any gaps included the smoothie Johnny Mathis and the vivacious Connie Francis. A sixteen-year-old Canadian named Paul Anka sold a million copies in Britain of his teenage love song 'Diana'. Sinatra sang 'Witch-craft', Max Bygraves came up with 'You Need Hands', which he's still singing. Jim Dale, now a Broadway star, was hosting the B.B.C.'s pop show *6.5 Special*, Buddy Holly was big with 'Oh, Boy' and 'Peggy Sue'. And to prove that Discland really was scratching its buzzing head in the great search for something different the Parlophone label burst forth with their discovery

Sparkie Williams, who recited nursery rhymes and gave a reasonable impression of an American TV cop-show. He was a budgie living in a cage at Forest Hall, near Newcastle-upon-Tyne . . .

Thus this headlong pursuit for something fresh off the disc presses resulted in the pairing of newcomers the Kalin Twins and Cliff Richard and the Drifters on a variety tour of Britain.

At twenty-four, the Kalins were almost old men in this world that was getting younger and faster every day (on 12 August a Comet IV jetliner set up a new record for a transatlantic flight from New York to Britain with a non-stop crossing in 6 hours 28 minutes; six days earlier Australian runner Herb Elliot cut the mile record to 3 minutes 54.5 seconds in Dublin).

But in the Kalins' favour was the fact that they were new and in the charts – and that was what mattered most.

Their lone hit song was 'When', a runaway smash. Yet a year earlier Herbie had been a salesman in a clothing store in Washington and brother Hal had been a singing telegram boy for the famous Western Union cable company, standing on Washington doorsteps warbling 'Happy Birthday to You'.

'We made a private record and took it to New York,' Herbie said, 'but nobody wanted to know. Three minor disc companies turned us down, so we took our record home again.

'Then we met songwriter Clint Ballard, who had more faith in us. He took the record back to New York and managed a hearing with a big company.'

The result was a first record that missed hopelessly – followed by 'When' and blast-off!

What they didn't know was that Cliff Richard, who had been clerking at his desk only months earlier, would prove to be an even greater sensation, but when they arrived to top the bill for their first British tour he was just a kid with a first record on the market and as yet looking nothing like a threat . . .

To vary the possible monotony of the show, top heavy with singers, the promoters had put in golden-disc-winning trumpeter Eddie Calvert, blowing his middle of the road tunes. Also on the bill were the Most Brothers, a twosome who weren't even related, comprising Mickie Most and a fellow named Alex Murray. Their star would not endure and before long they would part. Mickie would later become one of the world's best-known record producers in his own right, watching over the disc destinies of top-line British and American artists. As yet, however, the Mosts were as raw as the Kalins and Cliff and the Drifters.

While they waited for the tour wagon to roll the all-important call came for Cliff to make his bow on television for the first time. The programme was Jack Good's *Oh Boy!* The date was 13 September.

This programme was Independent Television's answer to *6.5 Special.* The brain behind both shows had been Mr Good, an unlikely, studious-looking genius in his mid-twenties, bespectacled and with an Oxford degree in philosophy and English language.

6.5 Special had been born in February 1957 and was initially meant as a magazine programme for young viewers. There was a sports section introduced by one-time British boxing champ Freddie Mills, for instance, but the main presenters were D.J. Pete Murray and hostess Josephine Douglas. Gradually the show became a pop showcase, especially for the stream of rock 'n' rollers who inc ded such rising stars as Marty Wilde.

Cliff and his Drifters had been invited to audition for *6.5* as 'Move It' came out. Astonishingly they failed – perhaps because Mr Good had already fled the coop across channels to I.T.V. with the A.B.C. company. He readily welcomed Cliff Richard into this rival camp instead and immediately became a tremendous influence on him and his career.

The one thing Jack Good didn't want was a carbon copy Elvis. What he did to Cliff could well have been reported to any Society for the Prevention of Cruelty to Rock 'n' Rollers.

First he took his guitar away, leaving him feeling almost naked. Then he ordered 'off with his sideburns!' He left the curl of the lip and the shocking pink jacket and glowing, matching socks.

This was the advent of Smoulder Eyes, as Cliff was dubbed in the *Daily Mirror.* And it worked . . .

Jack, who today lives in Santa Fe, New Mexico, between show business commitments in both Britain and the United States, told us, 'You have to remember that Cliff was one of the few people I discovered for television who, in fact, I heard on record first rather than saw first.

'I saw Adam Faith singing with the Worried Men first and saw Jim Dale at an audition. P. J. Proby and Cliff, I think, were the only two I heard first on record.

'I was thrilled with both of them, but I was even more thrilled by Cliff because in those days it was unheard of that a rock 'n' roll record coming out of Britain should sound as genuine as "Move It" and be performed with such confidence and assurance. He *sounded* like a rock 'n' roll singer. Better than anything we had.'

Jack spun the disc for the already established Marty Wilde, who had also crossed channels. Marty too couldn't believe that this was a British-made effort. From that moment on Cliff Richard was a must for the *Oh Boy!* show, but not without a stack of fears on Jack Good's part.

'I was very worried about the audition,' he says, 'because I thought he would probably have a terrible squint, or an uncontrollable twitch or two heads or three fingers or something, but anyway he was all there and he was quite normal and, in fact, quite a good-looking young man.

'So I was delighted, but he wasn't a strong personality in his performance. He was terribly shy and inexperienced, as most of them were.'

Jack knocked some of the rough edges off his new find with a week of gruelling rehearsals – not only for Cliff but all the cast. These were held at the Four Provinces of Ireland Club in Canonbury Lane, near Highbury in North London. A tattered runthrough schedule still in John Foster's possession gives the details.

Rehearsals began on Sunday 7 September 1958, and the schedule points out coldly that each time shown 'is the time that the artist is expected to be in the rehearsal room, set up and ready to go'. Cliff and the Drifters had to be in full throttle on the dot at nine-thirty on that Sunday morning.

This meant an early start from Hertfordshire to reach the venue, cart the gear in, put it into position and full electronic working order with instruments tuned, and somehow manage to look daisy fresh when Jack Good raised his finger to let the rock 'n' roll rip.

From nine-thirty there was an hour and a half of rehearsing 'Move It' and another song called 'Don't Bug Me Baby' before the Vernon Girls and Dallas Boys were called upon to do their bit at eleven.

There was an hour's lunch break and a four o'clock a tea break of twenty minutes (on another day they managed a half hour break).

Monday was a free day, then off the artists went to Canonbury Lane again on the mornings of Tuesday, Thursday and Friday for more rehearsals.

Live transmission of the programme was scheduled for six p.m. on Saturday 13 September, going out to millions of viewers from the variety stage of the Hackney Empire in East London. It was another never-got-a-minute day for the artists, who had to be present and correct by eight-thirty in the morning for 'preliminary sound balance'.

From ten till one o'clock there was a 'vision only' rehearsal. At two o'clock there was a 'sound and vision' rehearsal. By the time six p.m. came around and the expectant viewing public were drawing up their chairs to make themselves comfortable for the rockin'est show on the box, there were those taking part who had had a real bellyful of singing or playing the same songs they had been rehearsing through the week. But that's the way the programme worked and there was a certain excitement about it which gathered in a steadily growing viewership, eventually estimated at five million.

Suffering on that debut programme along with Cliff and his band were Marty Wilde, balladeer Ronnie Carroll and the John Barry Seven. John would later become one of the big screen's foremost composers, making his mark with music for the James Bond films. These were early days for a lot of people . . .

For Jack Good, a meticulous man who has left his imprint on pop television, the show was all-important. He told us, 'The show came first and the artists definitely came second in *Oh Boy!*

'What you must remember is that compared with Tommy Steele and Marty Wilde, who had already been going round the theatres topping the bill, Cliff was raw and though he threw himself into his songs with conviction he did not project a personality. In fact, he was probably more in a transitional stage than a lot of the other young men.

'Not only was he very young [seventeen], he hadn't finished growing. People say he hasn't changed over the years, well, he may not have changed since about 1961 or 62, but in 1958 he was about four inches shorter than he is. He was a good two inches shorter than me and I'm about five foot ten. So he was about five foot eight. I think he must be a good six foot now [he is around five foot eleven].

'One noticed how dark he was. He looked as if he had come from a romantic place with a strange-sounding name. His black hair was almost blue-black and I suppose this was accentuated by the grease and the Elvis Presley haircut and the famous sideburns that I ordered off.

'He was a different Cliff Richard and a very shy one and very immature in a way, so one really could pick a personality out of a hat and try to stick it on him. He was *tabula rasa* [a mind not yet influenced by outside impressions and experiences: *Chambers 20th Century Dictionary*].

'Not like Wee Willie Harris, for instance,' Mr Good goes on. 'You had to turn him into a comic. I mean, you had to do something and give him a red jacket and grow his hair long and make it orange, because if you didn't get away with the comedy angle you weren't going to get away with Wee Willie Harris at all.

'What we did with Cliff was give him a *persona* that he could use in front of a television camera and on stage until such time as he developed his own personality, which he subsequently and so successfully did.

'We had to develop a character and a look that would come across in a couple of minutes. He had to register that he was different from (a) Elvis Presley and (b) all the other seven people who were featured on the show, and memorable in his own right. So, of course, we built the personality that was usable on *Oh Boy!*

'It was no good creating the Boy Next Door when you had numbers like "Blue Suede Shoes" and "Move It" to do. We had to create a personality that would come across singing these tough songs.

'Now we had a slightly-built, romantic-looking young man with

49

fine features,' Jack Good recalls. 'There was nothing coarse about the face – the eyes big and dark, the nose small but well-shaped. He looked younger than his almost eighteen years. So compared with Elvis – who looked at least twenty-three and as if he had knocked around a bit and was a good deal more extrovert and vulgar in his performance – what we had here was a teenager.

'We could make him mysterious – the Quiet Smoulderer – the boy possessed of smouldering fires of sensuality of which he was as yet barely aware. That sort of stuff.

'This is what we could make work on our show – that's all that mattered to us. We obviously didn't discuss that sort of thing with him; it would have driven him crazy!

'We gave specific advice. The angle of the head . . . tilt the head down. The eyes . . . look up towards the lens because it'll give a better effect. Shoulder forward, not square on to the mircophone . . . grab the arm on *this* line because it will give more impact . . .'

When a rock 'n' roller was performing without a guitar a good dramatic stance could be achieved by grabbing one arm around the elbow with the other!

Jack Good made it all work superbly. Perhaps too well – within a short time Cliff would be taking the same sort of stick that had come the way of Freed, Haley and Presley . . .

Meantime, however, while Jack Good had managed to solve his initial problem of what to do with the lad, the Drifters had problems of their own as the tour with the Kalin Twins drew uncomfortably nearer. They were still without a regular lead guitarist now that Ian Samwell was playing bass.

There was only one way out of the difficulty, John Foster decided, boarding the 715a bus once more to visit the place that seemed to have all the answers – the good old 2 i's in darkest Soho.

'I dearly wanted a fellow named Tony Sheridan,' he says. 'He used to knock about in the 2 i's – everything seemed to happen there.

'When I went up to meet him there they told me he'd be in soon, so I waited about and waited – growing very annoyed when he didn't show up. I'm a busy man, I kept saying. What'm I doing hanging about here? While I waited a guy wearing glasses walked in carrying a guitar case. I watched him unpack it and I heard him play. He could fit the bill all right, I thought.

'So later I went up to him and asked him if he had ever heard of Cliff Richard?'

He had. He had heard 'Move It' on the radio and liked it, he reported.

'Well,' John went on, playing the big time, 'I'm his manager. Would you like to go on tour with Cliff? My name's John Foster.'

'I'm Hank B. Marvin,' the bespectacled fellow said in a Geordie accent that didn't exactly tie up with such a distinctly American-flavoured name.

After John had outlined the rough details of the tour, Hank B. Marvin nodded his head. Yes, he would like to go on tour with Cliff Richard on one condition – 'that's if my mate can come along. He's Bruce Welch . . .'

Hank and Bruce, like so many others, had trekked from Newcastle to Soho in search of stardom and in July – only some weeks earlier – had taken a tilt at Discland as members of a group calling themselves the Five Chesternuts.

A private backer had heard this teenage quintet performing in an espresso parlour in Hampstead and splashed out £40 to make a production record of them which was good enough to lease to E.M.I.

Leader of the group was a sixteen-year-old schoolboy named Peter Chester, who penned both the songs on the disc – 'Teenage Love' and 'Jean Dorothy', inspired by a thirteen-year-old girlfriend.

What the backer and E.M.I. didn't know until the release date was set early in July 1958 was that Peter was the son of the celebrated comedian Charlie Chester.

They went on TV with their disc in *6.5 Special* and, what's more, proud Dad introduced it. The two sides were no better and no worse than some of the American teenage offerings that had hit the top of the best sellers. But the Chesternuts failed to set the world ablaze and here were Hank Marvin and Bruce Welch ready and waiting to become Drifters instead.

'Up till then they had been living on baked beans in a flat at Finsbury Park,' John Foster smiled.

Within months of their joining Cliff Richard after John's on-the-spot invitation at the 2 i's they would become two dominant members of the Drifters, later to emerge as the Shadows and as international stars, standing on their own without Cliff singing in front of them. It would be an association that would last through the years . . .

What of Tony Sheridan, the guitarist Foster had gone in search of? He went off to Hamburg, where in 1961 he recorded a rock arrangement of the traditional song 'My Bonnie' with a British group labelled the Beat Boys. It was the record that would lead to the discovery of the Beat Boys under their rightful name – the Beatles. Tony Sheridan never did share their fame . . .

Cliff reached his eighteenth birthday during the tour with the Kalin Twins – and also reached high in the charts with 'Move It'. It zoomed to second place, overtaking the Kalins' number 'When', which had been a topper but which now slipped as Cliff became Britain's newest rock 'n' roll sensation. All of which made it an embarrassing tour for both Cliff and the Kalins.

The contract had said that Cliff and the Drifters would open the second half of the show, immediately preceding Hal and Herbie, who would close it with a big finale.

But as 'Move It' got its big move on the twins were shouted down each night with cries of 'We want Cliff!' from the audience.

Says John Foster, 'There's no doubt that Cliff was *the* star of the show. He was mobbed every night. At one stage the Kalin Twins asked us if Cliff would close the show, as they had no chance now that our record was higher than theirs. No one could follow him, they said. But we stuck to the contract.

'We were now seeing what fan worship meant. Cliff couldn't move without girls clamouring and chasing after him. One night, at Hanley, we had to pull a real nasty trick. Cliff said he was starving and wanted to go across to the café near the stage door to get a bite.

'The stage door was besieged by girls, about fifty or more. So we put on an act. Cliff pretended to be ill and I told the girls he was pretty grim and coughing something awful and I had to get him to a doctor. They parted like the Red Sea.'

He made a remarkable recovery when he had eaten, even though it was only baked beans. 'The fans were a forgiving bunch,' John recalls.

Cliff spent the evening of his eighteenth birthday rocking 'n' rolling on stage at the De Montfort Hall in Leicester. It was a touching, unforgettable scene. Fans littered the stage with flowers in his honour and lifted their seats to stand like a massed choir to sing 'Happy Birthday' to him.

For Cliff these were not only crucial, formative days, but long wearing days that would soon threaten to take their toll. Things were beginning to happen swiftly to him and around him in that all-important autumn of 1958.

Around the start of the tour with the Kalins he found that he had acquired a new manager.

He was the singer and music publisher Franklyn Boyd, the man who had first interested Norrie Paramor in 'Schoolboy Crush' – only to see it crushed by Ian Samwell's bus-top hit 'Move It'. Not that this could have worried Mr Boyd unduly. The publishers of the songs on both sides of a disc shared an equal royalty on sales of the record.

Agent George Ganjou told us: 'I appointed Franklyn Boyd.'

The deposed John Foster, who took the new appointment philosophically, says that he thought Boyd had been brought in by Paramor. There is no doubt that it would have been a move approved by Norrie.

John Foster reflects today, 'I was beginning to learn the business, but I had begun to realize my limitations as well. I was naive and so was Cliff. We never had a contract between us and we took each other totally on trust. It was a big mistake, I suppose.

'However, I'd gone as far as I could as Cliff's manager. He was in great demand and now in the big league. So when I stepped down I became his personal road manager at £18 a week.

'To be nearer things Cliff and I had taken a flat together over Sainsbury's in Marylebone High Street in town, sharing the expenses fifty-fifty.

'Of course we entertained girls there! We were normal, healthy young men, so why not? We took a drink at times as well.

'There was one night when we both felt a bit down. I can't remember why, but we were going on tour the next day. We had several bottles of stuff in the flat and we poured the lot in together and made a punch. It packed a punch all right. We drank ourselves paralytic and didn't feel very well in the morning!'

Some weekends John's mother Carol would pay a visit to the flat – 'to give it a bit of a tidy up' she says.

Today she treasures a Yardley pink heather compact which Cliff gave her. 'Thanks for everything. Love . . .' the inscription reads.

'He was like another son,' she recalls, looking around the lounge at her home in Hertford Heath. 'Many a time he slept here in this room.'

She treasures as well a signed photograph of the young rock 'n' roller on which he wrote 'lots of love and beans'.

'He loved baked beans in those days,' she explains . . .

CHAPTER FIVE

The Wild One

For Cliff Richard 1958 was undoubtedly the most astonishing year of his life. From being an obscure clerk at the beginning of August he was within weeks a rapidly rising celebrity rushing headlong towards a sensational December.

All in quick time he had become a recording star, a television personality with five million or more pairs of eyes on him during his now regular *Oh Boy!* appearances and a film actor in the making, George Ganjou having booked him into an unpretentious movie called *Serious Charge*.

In the midst of it all, following the tour with the Kalin Twins, the Drifters were having more teething troubles. Ian Samwell was replaced on bass in favour of Jet Harris, an impressive guitar man with blond hair who would emerge as a personality in his own right.

He had come to notice during the tour, where he appeared in support of the Most Brothers.

At the time it was said – and has been repeated since – that Samwell, having been a guitarist for only a short spell, had decided to stand down because he had not yet reached the professional standard required. What's more, having penned a walloping great hit in 'Move It', he would like to devote more of his time to songwriting.

He had been approached by a publishing company to work for them, he says today, but he really didn't want to leave the group.

'It was a mixed-up situation,' he recalls, 'and I wasn't all that happy about it. I would have liked to have continued with the Drifters and, given a little time, I think I could have been good enough to carry on as bass guitar. I felt sad, but there was nothing

I could do about it. It was a *fait accompli* – they wanted Jet Harris in and me out.'

Not that he was left completely in the cold – after 'Move It' he wrote Cliff's follow-up hit, 'High Class Baby', which reached seventh place in 1958. Another success was 'Dynamite', a 1959 chart entry.

Later he penned 'Feeling Fine', the first solo record by the Drifters when they became the Shadows. He also acted as their temporary manager for a period.

'I have tremendous admiration for Cliff,' he says, 'and we are still friends today.'

Following Samwell's dropping came the resignation of the only remaining founder member of the Drifters – drummer Terry Smart.

Says Cliff, 'It was his own decision. Terry felt that he was not able to keep up the standard and that the way we were developing was beyond his capacity. "I think you should get someone else," he said. It's always been like that – all very friendly. Nothing like the story of the fifth Beatle.*

'Terry went into the merchant navy for some nine years,' Cliff continues. 'I still see him now and again, maybe every two or three years. I'm not quite sure what he does now, but he's not in show business.'

Drummer Tony Meehan replaced Terry Smart, but this upheaval amongst the Drifters was, in comparison, only a minor event.

As the season of goodwill to all men approached not everyone was entering into the spirit just yet. There were rumblings that parents were now showing some considerable concern about Cliff's act on *Oh Boy!* His movements on screen were being viewed with alarm and deemed by some people to be exceedingly sexual.

A crushing criticism came from the most unexpected quarter. Around two weeks before Christmas, the trade weekly *New Musical Express* astonished its mainly young readership with a sensational

*The fifth Beatle is a reference to Pete Best, who was the Liverpool group's drummer for two years before being suddenly sacked in 1962 shortly before they made their first British record, 'Love Me Do'. In an interview in 1980 he told Patrick Doncaster that he still didn't know why the other Beatles dropped him to make way for Ringo Starr. 'It will always be in the back of my mind,' he said. 'When they became famous I just couldn't ignore the fact that I should have been part of it. I don't try to forget that I was ever a Beatle.'

attack on Cliff Richard, describing his performance on the small screen as 'the most crude exhibitionism ever seen on British T.V.'.

His violent hip-swinging, it went on to say, was 'revolting' and 'hardly the kind of performance any parent could wish his children to witness . . .'

The *Daily Sketch* headline on Monday 15 December asked, IS THIS BOY TV STAR TOO SEXY? The story repeated the *N.M.E.* blast and ended, 'This is Show Business 1958 . . . Do you want it?'

N.M.E. tried to temper its outburst against Cliff by apportioning some blame to producer Jack Good.

Jack, then aged twenty-six, took it like a man. 'If there's anything too sexy or offensive about the show, it's my fault,' he said. But he pointed out, 'I can't see anything wrong with the act. I don't intend to do anything about it.'

However, in the *Oh Boy!* programme following the trade paper tirade, the *Daily Sketch* noted that 'the cameras showed little more of Cliff than his head and shoulders . . . In the finale, the cameras revealed a display of knocking knees.

'But all the way through, the teenaged audience squealed with ecstasy over the half-closed eyes, the pouting lips, and the agonized Presley look . . .'

Cliff's reply to all this mud-slinging was careful and considered for a lad not long past his eighteenth birthday. 'I don't set out to be sexy,' he said. 'If people want to find me sexy they will. If they want to laugh then they'll laugh.

'We are a lively, jumping-bean generation who don't have time to sit down and listen to Beethoven. Rock expresses our feelings and gives us a chance to let off steam.

'I am not violent – nobody I know is violent. Rock won't inspire violence in anyone who is not inclined that way already.'

Jack Good, thinking back today to those controversial appearances by Cliff in his *Oh Boy!* show, had this to say to us, 'We were accused of wild bumps and grinds and all that sort of thing – but it was not so.

'What helped to make such an impact were the close-ups and the carefully considered cutting [from camera to camera] on the beat to the line of the music that gave the impression that there was something really wild going on.

'I worked very close to the artist, physically close, to show how close the image would be to the viewer at home. Even the mere flicker of an eyelid counted.'

Jack confessed that he sometimes discussed the feeling to be got across in a song, 'but obliquely', he says, giving as an instance, 'You know, "Here you're waking up in a hospital in a daze. You've just had some sort of injection that makes your head fuzzy", that sort of stuff. Anything to give him something to think about, something to direct his performance towards – without saying "you're a teenage idol" . . .'

Appearing to be sexy, it would seem, was hard work in those days, even if it were largely an act. But nevertheless, here was Cliff Richard, the nice Boy Next Door from Cheshunt, picking up a new label as the Wild One.

More viewers – people who wouldn't normally watch a television show beamed at kids – switched on to see what all the fuss was about; but there were no protest marches to the A.B.C. studios by furious parents or a storming of Number Ten Downing Street, where Prime Minister Harold Macmillan was in residence; and there was no instant change in Cliff Richard or his act.

There was, as Christmas neared, something of a silver lining. There he was starring at the Finsbury Park Empire, just as John Foster had said he would one day.

'They were really tough days,' John remembers. 'Cliff was getting up at five in the morning to start filming in *Serious Charge* and doing two shows a night at Finsbury Park. It was all too much for him and his voice went on the Saturday night, last night of the engagement.

'He was obviously being worked too hard. When Franklyn Boyd arrived in the dressing room we were melting butter on a hot spoon to try to ease Cliff's throat. I told Franklyn to find an all-night chemist and get something for the boy.'

Nothing could have worked the miracle that night. Cliff *did* go on stage for the final performance and mimed – not to his own records but to the voice of unseen rocker Wee Willie Harris, who gave a Cliff Richard impression from the wings. No one in the audience knew the difference, not amidst the squeals and screams that tended to drown Cliff's act anyway.

It spelled the end for Franklyn Boyd. After three months as Cliff's manager he was out. Some days before Christmas a letter from Rodger Webb told him that his services were no longer required.

On 20 Decmber 1958 the *Melody Maker* carried the headline CLIFF RICHARD'S FATHER SACKS HIS MANAGER. In the text Franklyn Boyd explained that he had no contract with Cliff other than a verbal agreement and a letter empowering him to sign contracts.

Mr Boyd lamented, 'I got him the *Oh Boy!* series and his film work.'

Cliff's mother said that the firing of Boyd 'was a family decision'.

She told how Cliff had been up at dawn to film *Serious Charge* while singing twice nightly at Finsbury Park and that on the Sunday following the loss of his voice he had been due to rehearse for another *Oh Boy!* appearance.

Instead he was in bed. He had collapsed into it as soon as he reached home after the final curtain and in the morning croaked, 'Mum, I can't stand this life in show business any longer. If it's all going to be like this past week I'd rather go back to my old job at Atlas Lamps.'

His mother later said, 'After that my husband wrote to Mr Boyd saying we didn't need him any more.'

Cliff's father explained, 'We hadn't realized that Boyd was a very busy entertainer and music publisher. This meant he just didn't have time to be with Cliff as much as we would have wished.'

Clearly both parents were worried about their son, who had now become the hottest property in British show business. Cliff, of course, soon conquered his bout of depression, regained his voice and bounced back into the pell-mell life of a rock 'n' roller. But still the Webbs had fears about the kind of life he might be living, fears that resulted in the exit of John Foster within a few weeks.

'There was a letter from Cliff's dad waiting for me in the flat at

Marylebone High Street when I returned one day in mid-January 1959,' he says. 'It was to give me two weeks' notice.

'When I saw his father he complained that Cliff wasn't being looked after or eating properly. "Look," I said, "I love your son. I'll cook for him!" We had a big blazing row and Cliff walked out. He was sickened, but there was nothing he could do about it.

' "I'm leaving you," I told Cliff afterwards and packed my bags and went home. We'd come through a lot together, but we were both too young to make decisions in the big business that was happening around us. Meantime, I'd got the sack from the sewage works for taking time off!'

Foster was still only nineteen and legally unable to sign anything. The *Daily Sketch*, announcing his departure, described him as Cliff's personal bodyguard. There was a quote from Cliff saying, 'He's pulled me out of a few jams, especially with fans in the north, but now he is to try to do better for himself. I'll miss him.'

John went on to become Walt Disney's London publicity chief before setting himself up in his own public relations business.

'I have no regrets about those days with Cliff,' he says. 'We are still pals . . .'

Appointed to succeed Franklyn Boyd as personal manager was Tito Burns, a former popular band leader.

Strangely it wasn't until September 1960 – nearly two years later – that the Sunday newspaper *The People* worked itself up about the saga of John Foster and Franklyn Boyd. The story was headed, 'To the girls he's a heart-throb. To his two ex-managers CLIFF IS A HEART-BREAKER!' (the words in capitals were in type an inch and a half deep).

Excerpts from the story are worthy of repetition because here was one more rare occasion of our number one rock idol being knocked not only so long after the events, but for two happenings which, as a minor, were beyond his control.

The article, signed by Peter Bishop, began, 'He is short, plump and curly-haired and has a remarkable knack of appearing to rotate his knees in opposite directions as he bellows out the latest pop tunes.

'Cliff Richard is the name, and he's the current dreamboat of rock-'n'-roll-mad teenage girls.

'But last week two men who helped this bouncing small-town clerk to climb to stardom confessed to me that sometimes Cliff features in their dreams too. And they wake up screaming.

'Why? Because both of them were his managers . . . once.

'Since he dropped them they have seen him soar to the stage where his weekly pay is about £1,200.

'And to think they might have had five or ten per cent of it. It's enough to break any man's heart.

'Take tall, quiet-spoken John Foster, for example . . .'

The article then tells how John discovered Cliff at the Five Horseshoes in Hoddesdon and of his efforts to launch Cliff.

The piece continues, 'For months John took days off from his labouring job to hawk his "find" around the West End agents.

'But no one was interested. Everywhere he met shrugged shoulders when he played the boy's tape-recorded voice and was told "rock and roll is on the way out".

'Then one day he walked into Mr George Ganjou's office. And they clicked.

'Ganjou, an agent, signed Cliff Richard on a five-year contract – his cut being ten per cent on all earnings.

'John was naturally delighted. His parents urged him to get a contract from Cliff's parents. But in the glow of success he didn't think it necessary.

'Cliff was my pal and I was confident he would look after me,' said John.

'But it turned out that Cliff, being under twenty-one, had very little say in the matter. A new manager with a greater knowledge of show business was called in, singer and music publisher Franklyn Boyd.

'John Foster – discoverer of the Cliff Richard talent – was relegated to road manager . . . His duties: book hotels and play strong-arm-man if the fans got out of hand.

'But he wasn't worried. He thought his turn in the Cliff Richard organization would come when he had learned more about show business.

'He got his first sharp lesson in January 1959. It was a letter from

Cliff's dad, Mr Robert [sic] Webb, giving him the boot . . .

'But by that time Franklyn Boyd had got his cards too . . .

'Said Mr Boyd at his tasteful Byfleet, Surrey, home, with a sleek grey Jaguar car in the garage: "I've never been so stunned or hurt in all my life as the day I opened that letter [from Mr Webb].

' "At the time my wife and I were living in town and for six weeks Cliff stayed with us because his home was too far out for convenience.

' "I spent days with him during those early recording sessions, guiding him, trying to inject some professionalism into his act."

'Mr Boyd's pretty wife broke in: "We took him out on his first big social engagements. Franklyn spent a lot of his own money on Cliff. We even borrowed an evening suit for the boy to wear at the Tin Pan Alley Ball at the Dorchester."

'Why did Mr Webb sack him?

' "He thought we were working his son too hard," said Mr Boyd. "But we had to work the boy pretty hard to get some polish on his act fast. Anyway, we're still pals."

'After Mr Boyd came manager No. 3, Mr Tito Burns . . .'

The People writer then went on to ask Mr Webb why so many changes had been necessary?

'Mr Webb shook his head as he sipped a glass of beer.

' "I was green in this game to begin with and I wanted good advice for my boy," he said.

' "Foster? He didn't know enough about show business.

' "Boyd? He didn't quite suit. He seemed to work my boy a bit hard.

' "But Mr Burns now – we get along fine. He seems just right for my boy.

' "But managers," he reflected again, "you got to keep your eye on 'em." '

In the midst of all the managerial hoo-ha of December 1958 Cliff could at least take some heart. The *Daily Mirror* disc page bestowed on him the title of New Boy of the Year . . .

CHAPTER SIX

The Great Transition

The pace wouldn't slacken during 1959. It would be another
helter-skelter year for Cliff Richard, watched over now by the
experienced Tito Burns, a forthright man who said what he
thought and usually got what he wanted. There would be some
brickbats to take – some of them physical – along with the
bouquets and they wouldn't be long in coming.

There would be the achievement of one of his great ambitions –
a number one record selling a million – a performance before
royalty despite the wrath rock 'n' roll was still bringing down on its
head in some quarters, and another film to make.

The Cliff Richard story was beginning to shape up like one of
those old Hollywood movies in which the underdog becomes the
toast of the world all in twenty-four hours. Things began to
happen almost at machine-gun pace although, strangely, this year
of the Great Transition from rocker to Mums' Delight would not
be all that obvious at first and the protests about his being too sexy
would be slow to diminish.

For Tito Burns the going wouldn't be easy at the outset. 'In
those days there were a lot of knockers in the business,' he says,
'and I was battling my arse off trying to batter them down. When
they knew I was looking after Cliff Richard they'd say "that little
bit of rubbish, that rock 'n' roller", dismissing him. They couldn't
see the talent that was there, that he wasn't just a rock 'n' roller.

'I didn't know in those days that Franklyn Boyd had been
involved with him. Anyway, it didn't seem to be a full-time job for
him and he was mainly a music publisher.

'Cliff's father had now become very strong behind the scenes
when he approached me. I had a message asking me if I would be

interested in managing this new boy. So I had a look at him and was quite enthralled with his image. He looked good and was so great – *is* great, not only *was*,' Tito, now sixty, corrects himself.

'He had made *Serious Charge*, was on television and making records and it looked like he was really going to take off.

'I had two or three meetings with his parents – it had to be that way because Cliff was under age as far as contractual matters were concerned. I explained to them what I would do and what I was looking for in the end, but I felt that the old man [Mr Webb] was a bit suspicious.

'I wanted Cliff to stand on his own two feet. I didn't want him to die with rock 'n' roll, if ever it was going to die, that is. Who could know?' Tito shrugs his broad shoulders.

'Cliff took direction beautifully and understood what I was trying to do. "I see what you mean," he said. And he would do it.

'I began negotiating things for him on his own, away from the Drifters as they still were when Cliff came to me. They were marvellous now in their own right, but I had to bring him to the stage where he wasn't depending on anyone else.'

The transition began slowly, with minor adjustments. 'When he went on *Sunday Night at the London Palladium* – then the top I.T.V. slot –he was preparing to go on without a tie. So I pulled mine off and he went on in that. Ties were important at that time. But he did begin to come away from the Elvis thing and he did agree with this. Never once did he say "don't try to change me, I'm a rock 'n' roller". He always understood what I was trying to do. He is the easiest man in the world to work with. What you see – that is Cliff. No façade, no bullshit.'

While 1959 was still an infant, Cliff found himself standing on his own two feet for a different reason. On the evening of Monday 2 February, when he opened his act on his first night at the Lyceum Ballroom off London's Strand, he found himself on the receiving end of an uncooked omelette of eggs and tomatoes hurled his way by a bunch of Teds. There were also some bottles in the barrage of missiles, along with rolled-up balls of newsprint.

Cliff stood firm and tried to continue singing. A gang of louts then stormed the stage and he found himself ready to sling punches with at least one of them until the ballroom manager held him back.

Some time earlier, when the bills first went up announcing him as a forthcoming attraction, this hooligan element had been boasting around that they were preparing a welcome for him. They kept their word.

After the third number the management brought the act to a close.

Cliff came through it all not particularly dismayed. He knew exactly why he had been on the receiving end and said, 'Boys out for the evening with their girls get jealous. It's nothing personal – just jealousy . . .'

Anyone watching a Cliff Richard performance at that time would have to agree. He had only to twitch a knee and a thousand girls would begin to scream. He had only to mouth the word 'you' in a song and young hearts accelerated. He had only to be in range for a hundred girls to try to tear him to pieces.

It was something that irritated boyfriends – everywhere.

He would have to endure more eggs and tomatoes or a shower of copper coins at Chiswick, at the Trocadero, Elephant and Castle (already a sad landmark where his amplification gear had failed at an early talent contest), and in Manchester and Nottingham. But nothing would stop the onward march of Cliff Richard – certainly not a handful of Teds.

One song from the film *Serious Charge* proved to be the great turning point in his career – 'Living Doll', which had been sung on to a tape by the much-gifted songwriting Lionel Bart, the washboard player from the 2 i's. (Lionel couldn't put music down on manuscript paper or play the piano – someone else had to do this chore for him.)

In case there is still doubt, let us emphasize that the title of the song was 'Living Doll' and not 'Livin' Doll', as it is referred to so frequently. The word Living with a g is on the original record label and on the sheet music copies. The confusion possibly arises from the fact that, prior to its release, Cliff recorded an entirely different song entitled 'Livin' Lovin' Doll' earlier in 1959. It reached twentieth place in the main chart of the day in the *New Musical Express* – and it upset Mr Bart considerably.

He saw this overlapping of titles as an attempt by the powers that be at Columbia to move in first and therefore take some of the shine off his effort – which by contract Cliff *had* to record to tie in with the film's release.

Bart need not have had any fears. 'Living Doll' was the runaway victor, romping to number one and doing extraordinary things for Mr Richard.

Serious Charge was the story of a clergyman (Anthony Quayle) working amongst a bunch of yobs. Cliff, as Curly Thompson, more or less played himself as an embryo pop singer, although Curly was something of a delinquent himself. There was also a background of homosexuality. But all that mattered really, in retrospect, was that one song.

In his book *Pop from the Beginning*, published in 1969, author Nik Cohn is emphatic about it.

' "Living Doll",' he writes, 'was by far the most influential single of the whole decade. It was cute and sweet and bouncy. It was tuneful and ingenuous. It was the British equivalent to high-school – and it was desperate. In months it took over completely. No rage, no farce, no ugliness left . . .'

It was certainly sugary and catchy with a lilt far removed from the rip-it-up type of rock 'n' roll. And it certainly knocked some of the fire and smoulder out of Cliff Richard, who despised the song from the beginning, thought it was 'chronic' and says that he sang and recorded it 'under duress'!

Certainly, as well, it chipped away at what was left of his Elvis image. You couldn't sing 'Living Doll' with a snarl or a curl of the lip or be mean and moody about it. It was too nice.

' "Living Doll" changed the whole course of my career,' he has said over the years. 'I parted company with the greasy-haired rock 'n' roll scene and began attracting the mums. And that's how it stayed.'

It was also, he said, one of the key factors in his life, ranking with his becoming a Christian.

On subsequent tours he was astonished to find grandmothers in the front stalls. 'Aged sixty-five at least, some of them!'

Before 'Living Doll', he felt that he had been acceptable only to the teens. Now in came the family, dads as well.

'They came along to see what the apparition was all about,' he thought. But they stayed and were converted. He was still a rocker at heart, but there would be no going back. 'Living Doll' paved the way for more up-market ballads – hits such as the standard 'It's All in the Game', works with a more sophisticated lyric.

This was a number that simply oozed 'establishment'. The tune had been written in 1912 by an ex-vice president of the United States who had also been ambassador to Britain – General Charles G. Dawes.

He penned it as a waltz. It was simply called 'Melody' and was played mostly by military bands, although Kreisler did have a go at it.

Some years later lyricist Carl Sigman gave it some words and changed the title to 'It's All in the Game', which resulted in waxings by jazz king Louis Armstrong and Nat King Cole. In 1958 American singer Tommy Edwards had another go at it and this version carved a niche in the British charts at the same time as Cliff's 'Move It'.

General Dawes, an eminent banker as well, died in 1951 – never knowing that eventually he would have his melody warbled by a rocker who had been called the Wild One!

Thus, because of 'Living Doll', Cliff would move out of the rock-for-the-kids class into the adult class . . .

Despite his initial loathing for Lionel Bart's song, he took it very seriously when he went into the studio to record it and demonstrated at the same time how much a professional he already was at the age of eighteen.

Says Tito Burns, 'He hated the up-tempo treatment of the song in the film and when he made the record he slowed it down. It was his own idea. Nobody told him to do it.'

Bart, then aged twenty-eight, was on holiday in Spain in early August when 'Living Doll' reached the number one position in the charts on its way to the million sales and a coveted gold disc. Patrick Doncaster rang him up from the *Daily Mirror* office in London to tell him the good news. It caused him little excitement.

'I was on the beach working on *Oliver!* when you rang,' Bart said flatly, as if he really didn't want to be disturbed.

At that time he, too, had moved away from the simple early

rock that had helped to put Tommy Steele on the show business trail and had scored some of the music for Tommy's latest film, *Tommy the Toreador*, which featured the Bart hit 'Little White Bull'. He had also written the lyrics for the Bernard Miles hit show *Lock up your Daughters*, for which Broadway was hankering.

Now his mind was fully occupied with *Oliver!* which would be a resounding hit and all his own work. He went back to the Spanish beach to slave away at it, not dwelling overlong on the fortunes of 'Living Doll'.

Lionel Bart has said in recent years that when he was asked to write the songs for *Serious Charge* he suggested Cliff for the roll of singer after having seen him at the 2 i's.

Cliff agrees that this could very well have been the case but has no recollection of having ever seen or met Lionel at the coffee bar.

'I remember how disappointed I was when we played the 2 i's that Lionel wasn't there. I'd hoped that he would be one of the people we might meet.

'My memory of first meeting him was at his flat. I remember that Larry Parnes [then a pop impresario] was present and that when you went to the loo and shut the door it switched on Handel's "Water Music" somewhere!

'I think we talked about the music scene, but there was no discussion about a film part that I can recall.'

What has to be considered is that all these events took place well over twenty years ago when the principals concerned were young men living and working in a breathless, thriving and thrusting new world where more could happen in a day than in a year for most people. What was indisputable at that time was that Cliff's stock was now rising with each day that passed.

Tito Burns recalls that he was receiving fifteen telephone calls an hour from people who wanted Cliff Richard – impresarios, agents, bookers, promoters, television – people who were now seeing the great potential.

'The demand was fantastic,' he says, 'and it really wasn't necessary to have an agent, although George Ganjou was still acting in this capacity and getting his ten per cent every week for doing practically nothing! It became easier and easier to look after Cliff.'

Serious Charge, which has been described as a moderate success smoothed the way for a more ambitious film for Cliff,
Expresso Bongo. Laurence Harvey was signed to star and Cliff
was again a rock 'n' roller, playing Bongo Herbert to Harvey's
manager Johnny Jackson.

With the shooting of *Expresso Bongo* there came a slight hint of
scandal. Or was it merely a groping for publicity?

On 30 September 1959, some weeks before the film was premiered, the headline over Peter Evans's Inside Show Business
column in the *Daily Express* said, 'This love scene makes an hotel
angry'.

The story read, 'The Dorchester Hotel, the London resting
place of many international stars, has taken legal advice over a
scene in the new film *Expresso Bongo*, in which Yolande Donlan,
playing a famous star, seduces a young rock 'n' roll singer, Cliff
Richard – in the hotel's famous penthouse suite.

'Last night rock star Richard said, "It's not a sordid scene. I
play a youngster infatuated with an older actress. And she likes
me.

' "Then one night I go back to her suite at the Dorchester Hotel
and I've had a bit too much to drink, and you know, I'm feeling a
bit tired.

' "Then she begins to sort of, well, take my tie off and that.
And, it's very delicate really, the camera moves down and you see
her take her shoes off. And that's it.

' "I wouldn't say it was sordid or torrid." '

One more event that year did much to dispel any adult doubts
that might still have lingered on about Cliff Richard and rock 'n'
roll: he was invited to appear before the Queen Mother at what
was seen as a mini Royal Command Show at the Palace in Manchester.

Show business writers were stunned by his inclusion and wrote
about 'the biggest surprise in years'.

Cliff was in august company, with such pillars of variety as
Tommy Trinder and Arthur Askey, and there to bring a touch of
culture to the proceedings was the celebrated Hallé Orchestra
under Sir John Barbirolli.

So rock took another step forward and Cliff enthused about the graciousness of the Queen Mother, whom he saw as an example to every woman in the land.

Performances before members of the royal family would become commonplace for him before long and one day reach the ultimate with an invitation to a matey lunch with the Queen and Prince Philip at Buckingham Palace with only a handful of guests all at one table.

As the fifties gave way to the sixties there seemed to be few ambitions left to be realized. Once he had merely dreamed of making a disc that would reach the hit parade. Now everything he recorded seemed to head there automatically. Even his number one ambition to win a gold disc had come true in quick time – when he was nineteen.

The odds against having a number one record were at that time assessed in the *Daily Mirror* disc column as being 125 to 1. The reasoning was that of the 2,000 or so discs issued during a year an average of only sixteen occupied the number one position during the twelve months. As the majority of the top perch residents were established stars the odds must have been considerably lengthened for a new boy – possibly to something like 250 to 1, it was argued. This shows what Cliff's 'Living Doll' was up against . . .

There was still an important ambition to fulfil – to tour America. It wasn't long in coming.

In January 1960 he flew off to take part in a rock 'n' roll package playing venues in the United States and Canada. With him went his father and Tito Burns and as the plane winged high above the Atlantic Cliff, scarcely able to believe it, said to Tito, 'We're *actually* going to America!' Understandably. So much had happened since he quit his desk at the Atlas bulb factory less than eighteen months earlier that life sometimes seemed to lose reality.

The tour, a barnstorming series of one-nighters spread across five weeks, was a strange and largely disappointing introduction to the nation that had given the world the rock 'n' roll music that had produced Cliff Richard.

Because of the gruelling itinerary, most of the time was spent in the tour bus, where the artists ate and slept. The packed schedule of a different town every night meant journeys of eight to fifteen hours between dates. Few of the venues were theatres and many were in vast stadiums with sometimes only a makeshift stage.

Cliff was billed as an added 'attraction from Britain' and introduced on stage as Britain's top singer in a cast that was headed by Frankie Avalon and included such hit-makers as Freddy Cannon, Bobby Rydell and Clyde McPhatter. Any of these could have topped a bill in Britain but Cliff was given third billing.

He left his guitar at home – nothing negligent – and explained the reason at the time, 'My act is so short I didn't want to play the guitar on it. I just sing here and leave the instrumentals to my group the Shadows.'

These, of course, were the former Drifters with Hank Marvin and Bruce Welch and company, who had been obliged to change their name to avoid possible confusion with an American outfit recording as the Drifters. Watching over the Shadows on this trip as acting manager was Ian Samwell.

Cliff, who had by this time been appearing on stage at home in a white jacket, black trousers and white leather shoes, wore all-white for his American debut. 'I thought I'd go all the way,' he said.

Strangely, he gave the Americans back their own songs, singing 'Forty Days', 'My Babe' and 'Whole Lotta Shakin' Goin' On' – the Jerry Lee Lewis classic and 'a real wild one to wind the act up with' said Cliff – wedging 'Voice in the Wilderness' from *Expresso Bongo* and 'Living Doll' between them.

The tour played to thousands of American youngsters, but Cliff didn't reach the pinnacle of fame that was his at home in this competitive company.

'He did sensational,' Tito Burns says today. 'My one regret is that we didn't conquer America when I first took him there, but there were so many artists doing the same thing and Cliff was singing other people's material.'

It was all experience, of course. For the 'Whole Lotta Shakin' Goin' On' finale he would go down on one knee – but first pull a white handkerchief from a pocket to kneel on.

'The stages are so dirty,' he explained, 'that my trouser leg would be black if I didn't. And that mustn't happen because it's the only white suit I've brought – and it has to last till 21 February.'

That was when he left the tour to fly home to Britain for a day to

71

receive an award as the country's favourite rock 'n' roller. Then he winged back across the Atlantic to rejoin the whistle-stop bus tour – taking his mother with him because, he said, he was homesick.

'I'll be glad to be back in Britain. I've had four weeks in America and I'm a little bit sick of it.'

For Mrs Webb it was her first flight and she confessed to having 'butterflies'.

Three stage suits had been ordered for the visit to North America, but only one was ready in time, mainly because the tour had been so hastily put together. 'Living Doll' had begun to attract some chart attention in America and reached the 30 placing there, which resulted in his inclusion in the tour.

It was the number that really 'sent' the American kids, staff correspondent Stan Mays cabled to the London *Daily Mirror* from New York.

Cliff's big regret was that rarely could he meet these young Americans who had taken him to their hearts. This was because the police, nightly fearing fan hysteria or rioting, hustled the artists out of the stadium via an escape route straight into the waiting bus, engine purring, which then hurtled off into the night.

Even so, American fans he did manage to meet did not impress him all that much and he found them and Americans in general lacking in manners. 'Fans would ask for an autograph as if they were doing me a great favour.'

On the credit side there was some television exposure here and there, principally in New York when Cliff guested on the Pat Boone Show. The clean-cut, all-American Boone talked allegedly like an Englishman in a banal exchange of scripted words.

Example: Boone tells the viewers that Cliff was 'born in India but left when he was a year old. How was that?'

Cliff: 'Frankly, Pat, when you have shot one elephant you have shot them all!'

There was some compensation on that show: Cliff did sing 'Living Doll', which no doubt helped to lift American sales of the record.

During the tour he also had a meeting with Elvis Presley's colourful manager, Colonel Tom Parker, and wondered when he might meet up with his idol.

Parker said that he would like the two to meet sometime but couldn't arrange anything because when Elvis (still in Germany) was due to leave the American army Cliff would be back in Britain.

They would never meet. It would be the one great unfulfilled ambition.

Said Cliff, 'I almost made it when I was in Germany during his army service. The first time I went to see him he was away on manoeuvres. The second time he was in hospital having his tonsils out.'

The nearest he would come to meeting Elvis was in 1962 during a promotional tour of the United States to boost the showing of his film *The Young Ones* (retitled there *Wonderful to be Young*).

'Elvis was filming on the west coast when we hit the south, but there was a phone call from his father inviting us over. We saw Elvis's home and we were treated with that old southern hospitality.'

He found the Presley home 'a bit frightening' he admitted, with its white leather chairs, the bed with gold panels at the head, and Elvis portraits everywhere, including one woven into a carpet.

In those days Cliff carried his worship of Presley to extremes, even to trying to copy his eating habits. At a swish dinner he ordered sauerkraut because Elvis liked it. He called it ghastly stuff and said that his hero was welcome to it. But he did like the peanut butter and banana sandwiches that were a favourite of Presley's and said that this was one recipe he intended to keep.

The adoration would not last for ever. After Elvis died in 1977 and the stories began to creep out of his sexual exploits and drug addiction, Cliff had this to say in a *Daily Mirror* interview, 'It makes me squirm to think this is the guy I idolized for so long.

'He may have been the most successful artist, but as a man he never made it. I don't mean sexually, but just as a human being.

'When I think of what my sister [Donella] and I went through all those years ago with Elvis as our pinnacle, it's sad.

'I didn't want to read that he picked up a girl out of the audience and within a week she was an absolute wreck on drugs. Or about the pills he was taking. Pills to make him thin, pills to make him fat . . .'

But back in 1960, during that first American tour, Cliff's admiration of the man who had been his inspiration continued unswervingly.

Back home, on his return from the States, a year of triumph awaited Cliff: his first 'full' royal show, a long summer season at the London Palladium, his first own television series, plus negotiations for further, more ambitious movies. And, of course, more records.

The pattern would be set, in fact, for his show business future during the relatively short term that Tito Burns would be his manager. The forthcoming years would be much the same except for changes of venue or location. Cliff Richard had truly arrived and was here to stay.

Only now was the big disc money beginning to roll in – royalties can take an age to come through – and only now, after his return from the largely disappointing American tour, did the Webb family uproot once more and leave their council house at Cheshunt to move into their first home of their own.

It was a modest little place even so and bore no comparison with the big luxury homes that would be a feature of the pop star life style for years to come.

The new abode was a semi-detached in Percy Road at Winchmore Hill – not so very far away in North London – which cost around £7,000. Cliff had a bedroom decorated in primrose yellow where his mother would bring him a cup of tea in the mornings and he would sometimes ask her to pinch him to see if life was real.

To save space he had the attic converted into a room to house his stage clothes. In his bedroom there was one wardrobe set aside for shirts. And, according to one report, he was becoming rather blasé about his footwear, wearing a pair of suede boots only two or three times before giving them away when they needed cleaning.

Now he drove a red Thunderbird with white hard-top that at £4,000 cost nearly as much as a lesser home in those days.

Cliff described it as one of his proudest possessions and piloted himself to the Palladium and back during the long five-month season.

When this same-every-day life tended to become monotonous

he would sometimes drive aimlessly around quiet streets in the early hours, soul searching, occasionally feeling low in trying to cope with the penalties of fame and wondering if he might be far happier as just plain ol' Harry Webb instead of Cliff Richard. When he did arrive home mother would always be waiting.

Says Tito Burns, 'Material things never seemed to bother him outside of his big love for cars. I went with him to Lex in Brewer Street in Soho to buy that Thunderbird. He loved that car.'

What did begin to bother Cliff at this stage of his career was the weekly siege of Percy Road.

At weekends upwards of a hundred fans would descend on this hitherto quiet suburban haven for a glimpse of their idol and perhaps an autograph. Some just gawped, peeping through cracks in the seven-feet-high fence that had been put up to provide some privacy. Others lolled around on the wall of nearby gardens, which didn't exactly please Cliff's new neighbours.

A woman living opposite the Webbs thought this fan activity lowered the tone of the area. 'When I went out to water the hydrangeas,' she said, 'I asked the girls to move away, but they were very rude and one of them said, "Why should I? This isn't bloody Russia!" '

The woman decided that she would have to set up home somewhere else if this kind of behaviour continued, she said.

Cliff's mother had some sympathy for the neighbours. 'I know this must be annoying for them,' she said, 'but some of these youngsters come all the way from Scotland and places as far off as Leeds. Cliff can't just turn them away.'

Whenever he did appear he would sign autographs and tell the fans as pleasantly as he could to move off from the house.

If the good neighbours of Winchmore Hill had yet to take this rock 'n' roll star to their hearts they were lagging a long way behind the Establishment. A few weeks after moving into his new home Cliff was chosen to sing in his first full Royal Variety Performance at the Victoria Palace on 16 May before a smiling Queen in white satin.

The Crazy Gang were in attendance and, with their usual impudence, walked on stage wearing bridesmaids' dresses that were exact copies of the one Princess Anne had worn ten days earlier at the marriage of Princess Margaret to Mr Antony Armstrong-Jones.

It was a mammoth evening featuring more than 200 artists, numbering Nat King Cole, Sammy Davis Jr, and Liberace, who closed the show. The cast was thick with comics apart from the Crazy Gang and included Max Bygraves, Benny Hill, Bruce Forsyth, Jimmy Edwards, Harry Worth, Frankie Howerd, Norman Wisdom and Charlie Drake.

Rock 'n' roll, along with pop, was squeezed in early as Item 5 in the first half of the show. Still, it was a start.

In the programme the item was described as 'Focus on Youth', which was one smart way of not having to mention either pop or rock. It consisted of Cliff, Adam Faith and Lonnie Donegan coming on to perform their hit songs. Also in attendance were the Vernon Girls. But the big sensation of the evening was the sparrow-like little one-eyed Sammy Davis Jr . . .

Cliff was still packing 'em in at the London Palladium to the accompaniment of thousands of girlish squeals twice a night when he said goodbye to his astonishing teen years on 14 October 1960.

'Just think – I'm twenty!' he said incredulously. 'When I was fourteen I used to think how marvellous it would be to be twenty and shave every day. Now I shave every day and I wish I didn't. That's life. Always want what you can't have.'

Asked what he thought he might be doing in a further twenty years' time in 1980 he said, 'Well, I see myself doing a bit of singing, a bit of acting. A sort of Bing Crosby type.'

He wasn't far out.

They had been truly magical teens for Cliff Richard. He was up there with the greats of show business, playing his part, standing on his own two feet the way Tito Burns had planned it.

He was earning more than the entire British Cabinet put together and the Great Transition from Wild One to The Boy Next Door was almost complete.

Leslie Grade would see the job through . . .

CHAPTER SEVEN

The Image and the Makers

Leslie Grade was a sandy-haired pleasant man with large blue eyes who didn't look a lot like his two brothers, Lew and Bernie. They were the fabled, all-powerful brothers Winogradsky, whose family had come from Russia to settle in London's working class East End.

Lew and Leslie anglicized the name to Grade; Bernie called himself Delfont. Between them, in 1960, they controlled or watched over a lot of ground in show business: theatres up and down the country, including the historic London Palladium and television via A.T.V., where brother Lew was the big wheel with the big cigar.

Now the new thing from the Grade Organization was going to be nice, clean musical films for all the family, masterminded by agent Leslie.

With all this going for them the Grades were super people to have on your side. Those who weren't with them or were untalented and unwanted or both made envious jokes about Lew and Leslie Greed or Low and Lousy Grade. It didn't matter. In the end there would be Lord (Lew) Grade and Lord Delfont and the jokers would be nowhere.

The perceptive Leslie Grade saw the potential in Cliff Richard early on and knew that here was a very hot potato indeed. It was inevitable that he would eventually become his agent, but first there would be some hard bargaining between Grade and manager Tito Burns and a deal with agent George Ganjou.

'Leslie was never Cliff's agent in those days when I was operating as manager,' says Tito, 'but he'd been after me for Cliff and he wanted to "buy" him for a period of weeks, as it were, as a promoter, putting him into theatres in various places, good spots such as Coventry.

'I wanted something as well in return – I wanted the Palladium for Cliff and a series on television. So I asked for twenty-five per cent over the going rate if I were going to let him have Cliff – plus the guarantee of an A.T.V. series and the Palladium.

'Leslie eventually agreed and "bought" him for thirteen weeks, six days a week. I leased him, you might say.

'Then I got him into Leslie's films with a deal for three movies. There was a lot of argument and to-ing and fro-ing. "Look what I've done for the boy!" Leslie said when I asked for a certain figure plus a percentage of the film profits. "I can't give the boy away because you did something for us," I told him. I got the deal as I asked in the end . . .'

To clear the way for the Grade films Cliff had first to buy himself out of a contract negotiated two years earlier with another British company. The price for his freedom was reported to be in excess of £10,000. Said Tito at the time, 'It was hefty, but we feel that it was worth it. The contract was signed when Cliff was only just becoming known. Now he is free to take up one of the bigger offers that has come his way.'

In retrospect the sum was peanuts. For the first film would be *The Young Ones* – one of the most successful British-made movies ever – which began to evolve on the drawing board in November 1960.

At this stage freelance producer Kenneth Harper, who had joined Leslie to set up the Grade Organization's film section, had been observing a new phenomenon – that when Cliff Richard and the Shadows appeared at a cinema in place of the movies they did more business at the box office than any film did.

'We must make a musical film with those boys in it,' Harper told Grade.

It sounded a good idea and the people concerned started remembering the smash-hit films Hollywood had made years back with young ones such as Mickey Rooney and Judy Garland, all-time musical winners like *Babes in Arms* and *Babes on Broadway*. They were nice clean homely films that really entertained, caused nobody any heat under the collar, had good songs, good dancing and some laughter and maybe a tear or two.

Writers Peter Myers and Ronnie Cass were called in to produce a script for the Grade musical; a young Canadian named Sidney Furie was invited to direct and choreographer Herb Ross was whisked across the Atlantic from America to put some zest into the dancing. For too long the dancing in British films had always managed to look as if it belonged in a parish hall production.

The story was simplicity itself. A bunch of kids put on their own show (à la Rooney and Garland) to stop their youth club being taken over by some spoiling bigwig. That was it. First rehearsals were called for May 1961, at the Elstree Studios in Hertfordshire. But Cliff didn't arrive . . .

The year had started troublesome and by May the Webb family would experience a crisis.

But first, on 4 February 1961, a headline in the long-gone *Daily Herald* read, 'Cliff and his boss part – so amicably'.

The story beneath began, 'Pop idol Cliff Richard has broken away from his manager, Tito Burns – the man who put him at the top.

'He announced it yesterday in a joint back-slapping statement with Mr Burns that emphasized the parting is amicable, by mutual consent – and not caused by any row.

'The end of the two-year partnership was announced by Richard's publicity agents, the Leslie Perrin organization. Richard had agreed on the wording of the statement with Burns's lawyers.

'The statement added Richard's thanks for his work. Burns said he had "enjoyed" their association. Then each wished each other "the best of luck" for the future . . .'

The headline on the *Daily Sketch* story the same morning was nearer the mark: 'Now dad handles disc star'. The text was terse: Cliff Richard, £1,000-a-week rock 'n' roller, has broken with his manager, Tito Burns. The hinted reason: a difference over his contract.

'Commented ex-band-leader Tito, who "owns" ten per cent of the singer: "Cliff and I have separated as from today, but that's all I can say."

'Last night a spokesman for both the singer and his ex-manager said, "Cliff's father, Mr Roger [sic] Webb, is now looking after him."

'Twenty-one-year-old Cliff signed with Burns after a wrangle with his first manager Franklyn Boyd.'

Cliff, of course, still had a great chunk of the year to go to reach twenty-one which, in the circumstances, was important. Legally he was still under age and considered a minor. But what was more important at this crucial time in his development was that his father was far from well. He had been seriously ill for several weeks at home in Winchmore Hill during Cliff's previous summer season at the London Palladium. To be with him as much as possible at this time Cliff cancelled a number of other personal appearances and engagements.

Tito Burns doesn't mind recalling those days, 'We agreed to separate because of Cliff's father, who fancied himself to be the power behind the throne. It's funny,' he smiles, 'but all kinds of people in England seem to have two businesses – their own and show business! Anyway, Cliff had to be pushed to the front and stand on his own two feet and I just couldn't work with his father. He, like a lot of others, thought he knew it all, but maybe that was because he was a very sick man.'

Sadly, Mr Rodger Webb was dead a little over three months after the announcement that Cliff and Tito had ended their partnership.

He died from heart trouble in a North London hospital on 15 May 1961. He was aged fifty-six and had been in and out of hospital since the previous October. Said Cliff, 'I never did anything without consulting him first. He helped me in everything.'

Because of his father's death he had to call off the first rehearsal at Elstree of *The Young Ones*.

Now Leslie Grade would loom larger than ever in Cliff's career. He got what he wanted. 'In 1961 I sold Cliff to Leslie Grade for £12,500,' George Ganjou revealed to us in 1981.

'So Leslie, who was a great friend of mine, became his agent. I was sorry to part with him because Cliff was just wonderful to me and very grateful for what I did for him.'

Brought in to succeed Tito Burns as personal manager was a shy, reticent but forceful man from Australia named Peter Gormley – a man who today still tries to shrink from the limelight (even pictures of him don't come easy).

His predecessor, Tito Burns, has this to say about the events of those early days of 1961, 'At the time Peter was managing the Shadows and had proved a very knowledgeable person. So when Cliff's father and I could no longer get on together Peter became the automatic choice to take over from me as Cliff's manager.'

Like most other people, Tito has nothing but admiration for Gormley. 'I had a great friendship with him and we're still friends,' he says.

Gormley was to be the last in the line and endure right through to today, steering the fame and fortune of Cliff Richard through two decades and somehow managing to keep him at the zenith of his profession of pop star even in his forties. It says much for the dedication of the man who, with little outward show, has said yes or no in the right places and at the right time year in and year out.

He has none of the flamboyance of Presley's mentor, Tom Parker, who had Elvis's name emblazoned on the back of his jacket; none of the gimmickry that goes hand in hand with the pop business; no pushing and shoving into the headlines. He is immensely brilliant at his job, shrewd without giving any impression of how thorough he is, a man of great integrity, and much respected.

He made his London headquarters and diaries available to the authors during the preparation of this book – but kept discreetly out of the way . . .

Peter Gormley, born in a Sydney suburb, was drawn towards journalism in his teens and joined the staff of a country paper as a cub. At eighteen he left to go into the film game with a company that also turned out a weekly newsreel. Then the Second World War came along to take a slice out of his life and he saw service in the Solomon Islands.

When the peace came Gormley went first into film journalism and then into cinema management, being responsible for a group of picture houses that sometimes put on live entertainment, all of which was to lead to a meeting one day with a country and western singer named Frank Ifield.

Their liking for each other was mutual and Gormley now

81

devoted his energies to managing this good-looking green-eyed lad who yodelled and didn't give a cuss for this thing called rock 'n' roll.

The Ifield-Gormley partnership boomed, but an artist can go only so far in Australia. Then he has to spread his wings and take off for Britain or America to find new and more rewarding fame. The ties with Britain, naturally, are strong and were particularly strong for Frank Ifield. He had been born in Coventry in 1938 when his father – who had hailed from Australia – was working in the motor trade. The family returned Down Under when Ifield was eight.

So Britain was the choice for Frank's future – and Gormley's. But the methodical Gormley didn't arrive here in 1959 with his charge and start pounding the streets and knocking on doors looking for the big, elusive break for his boy.

Instead he arrived three months ahead of Ifield with tapes, Australian records and press-cutting albums to sell him first, and had a start neatly packaged for him with radio and TV appearances when he did touch 'own.

By January 1960 Ifield was making his bow on the Columbia label with a song called 'Lucky Devil' – all very pleasant, but not ear-catching enough to start a stampede to the record stores. That would come some eighteen months later with the Ifield yodelling smash hit 'I Remember You'.

The year 1960 would be a turning point year for Peter Gormley rather than for Frank Ifield.

While the Shadows were appearing with Cliff in the Palladium summer show they cut a solo record, a home-grown composition penned by singer-songwriter Jerry Lordan, an ex-London bus conductor. Title: 'Apache'.

Norrie Paramor, who was guiding the disc destinies of Cliff, the Shadows *and* Frank Ifield, thought its potential so high that now was the time for the Shadows to employ a full-time manager. Gormley was the right man, he decided, and approached him. After seeing the group in action and hearing 'Apache' Gormley agreed.

'Apache' (Cliff played a Chinese drum on it) became a blockbusting international hit after its release early in July. At this time in 1960, of course, Cliff was still in the capable managerial hands of Tito Burns. When Tito departed early in 1961 the lifeline was thrown Gormley's way.

He was now on the threshold of becoming one of the most successful managers in the history of pop – but it wasn't a lifeline that he hastily grabbed. He weighed the situation carefully and particularly didn't want to tread on the toes of any predecessor.

'Do you know,' Cliff confides to us in a great tribute to Gormley, 'Peter didn't take a percentage of my earnings for a year after becoming my manager, saying that they came from arrangements made by Tito. Where can you find people like that in a business that is notorious for its rip-offs?'

In 1961 the final image of Cliff Richard was perfected under the guidance of Peter Gormley and Leslie Grade. It was an image that Cliff was naturally assuming as the days of wild rock receded. The real Cliff.

There would be no more managerial upheavals to complicate his professional life; there *would* be two more Grade movies much in the same nice-guy groove as *The Young Ones*, and records that would continue to hit. No more would anyone see even an itsy-bitsy suggestion of offensiveness in anything that Cliff Richard would do.

The path into the future had been determined. Not even the fantastic explosion that was the Beatles in 1962–3 would ruffle a hair on his head . . .

The Young Ones not only packed the cinemas of Britain when it was screened but caused a sensation in the movie world when the money was counted. Cliff, it was announced, was the nation's most popular film star of 1962 – head and shoulders above anyone Hollywood could offer. This was the finding of the *Motion Picture Herald* in its annual survey and poll of the film business in the United Kingdom.

The movie itself came second in the money-spinning league, which was topped by *The Guns of Navarone*, which cost around £2 million to make. *The Young Ones*, with an original budget of £100,000, had eventually cost £230,000.

Headed by Cliff, the list of the ten most popular stars showed an astonishing array of talent that just couldn't keep up with the boy from the council house at Cheshunt.

His idol Elvis was second, Peter Sellers third. After this the runners-up were: 4, Kenneth More; 5, Hayley Mills; 6, Doris Day; 7, Sophia Loren; 8, John Wayne; 9, Frank Sinatra; 10, Sean Connery.

With his usual modesty Cliff told interviewers that it was 'ridiculous'. It wasn't, of course, and there were the box-office totals to prove it.

He went on, 'For my own ego it's great to be named the top star, but my next film may be a flopperoo. Of course I'm not as big a draw as Elvis. He's made a lot of pictures. It's not just a oncer for him. After I've made more films I'll be in a better position to judge my own worth.

'I dare not compare myself with established stars like Sellers. That would be stupid. Let's face it, I didn't do anything at the box office with my other two pictures, *Serious Charge* and *Expresso Bongo*.

'*The Young Ones* was just meant as a happy little film, or so we thought. It was Sidney Furie who injected the magic.'

He summed up, 'It really is fantastic. I'm terribly proud, but if I was making the choice I wouldn't choose me!

'I know I was being used as a guinea pig to see if a British musical could be a success and I think it happened because it was a simple film with a kind of amateur charm. But the public like something simple.'

Ironically, a vaudeville segment in the film was shot in the old Finsbury Park Empire, which Cliff used to pass in the Green Line bus before he was a star and where he lost his voice. It was, when used as a location for *The Young Ones*, a doomed theatre, killed along with variety by television . . .

The *Motion Picture Herald* poll and survey results came just a week before the second of the three Grade films was due to be premiered in London's West End – *Summer Holiday*, which was screened at the Warner Theatre in Leicester Square on 10 January 1963. It was a premiere that Cliff missed.

More than 3,000 fans were swarming around when his car arrived in the square. Hundreds pressed in close and twice when he tried to leave the car the sheer weight forced him back.

Worried police advised his chauffeur to try to make his way out of the square through the throng. He managed to edge the car out and drive Cliff to Peter Gormley's flat in St John's Wood, where he watched boxing on television while the premiere went on without him. 'I am bitterly disappointed,' he said. 'I put off a South African tour so that I could be there.'

One girl fan went to hospital with a leg injury. Others were treated at the cinema's first-aid centre . . .

Cliff was in the Canary Islands a year later shooting the third Grade film, *Wonderful Life*, when he received a cable which read, YOU'VE DONE IT AGAIN BOY.

It was to tell him that for the second year in succession he had topped the poll in the *Motion Picture Herald* survey and was the most popular film star in Britain still.

This time Peter Sellers was second and Elvis third. The other placings were: 4, Sean Connery; 5, Hayley Mills; 6, Elizabeth Taylor; 7, Marlon Brando; 8, Albert Finney; 9, Dirk Bogarde; 10, Norman Wisdom.

Summer Holiday had done the trick . . .

The now completed image of Cliff Richard, top pop star and top film star, was far different from his original stage image. Gone was the chubbiness of the early rock 'n' roller, along with the dreadful drape jacket and pink, light-up socks. He was neat, well groomed and now ranked amongst the nation's ten best-dressed men.

A few years earlier he had been shocked one evening as he sat watching television to hear Minnie Caldwell – a character in *Coronation Street* – saying, 'I love that *chubby* Cliff Richard'.

He decided to do something about it. As Tito Burns says, 'Cliff's a great believer in not abusing his body. Not that he's a health food nut, but he will eat the right kind of food – except for curry!

'He was tending to be a little plump when he was with me, but no one gave him a diet sheet. He sorted it out himself. He also had the usual teenage problem of acne. He found out what to do about it himself and got some treatment.'

Some of this early skin trouble was caused by using the wrong stage make-up and not taking it off afterwards in the approved fashion with cold cream.

During the mid-sixties he could be observed arriving at the

Palladium, where he was once more resident in *Aladdin*, carrying a string bag holding a mysterious package. What dark secret lurked there? Just a whack of cheese, it transpired, mostly Cheddar.

Cheese, he revealed, was his staple diet. By nibbling at it instead of wolfing curry he had reduced his weight to ten stone from his former twelve stone seven pounds.

'I have one real meal a week,' he confessed to Patrick Doncaster's column in the *Mirror*, 'and I had it last night. A tin of stewed steak.'

He also admitted to indulging in his mother's home cooking on his one day off on Sundays. 'I'll eat anything then, but I know exactly what the result will be. I'll put on four pounds.'

The spartan cheese diet shed it again, almost as quickly, he reckoned.

This then was the prototype of the Cliff Richard, superstar, we know today – the Cliff who has endured in a business as hard as steel and strewn with pitfalls.

The final image was not the work of one influence. No one could point a finger at any one person and say that's the man who made him what he is today. Cliff Richard evolved because of a bunch of people who were close to him or simply crossed his path.

In chronological order they were his father Rodger; John Foster; Ian Samwell; George Ganjou; Norrie Paramor; Franklyn Boyd; Jack Good; Lionel Bart; Tito Burns; Leslie Grade and Peter Gormley.

Cliff admired his father very much, but has always said that they were really never close until his father's last illness. He had been strict and something of a disciplinarian.

'There's no doubt he was a great influence,' Cliff told us. 'He was also very much a balancing factor. He liked to know exactly what was going on and whether or not it was good for me. Whatever he did was for me and when he felt that I had too much to do he put his foot down.

'Yes, he taught me guitar – he'd played a banjo in a jazz band when we were in India, but not professionally. The original guitar he bought me on the never-never when I started out professionally was stolen on that first tour when we played the Colston Hall in Bristol – before he'd even finished paying for it!

'He was a great Jerry Lee Lewis fan and loved "Whole Lotta Shakin' Goin' On".'

This was the rock classic with which Cliff closed his act on that first American tour in 1960. Cliff said at the time, 'My father is really enjoying himself. Like me he too has never been to America. He fusses over me.

'During the show he sits in the stalls and listens to how the mike is reacting to the other singers' voices. Then he tells me how far away from it I should sing.'

The record of his son's which he most liked, Cliff told us, was 'A Girl Like You', which reached fourth place in the charts the year that he died.

'It would have been lovely if Dad had stayed alive to see all that has happened,' Cliff says today a little sadly . . .

He will always be thankful that John Foster strolled into the Five Horseshoes at Hoddesdon that memorable evening in 1957.

'He was the first to have any faith in me,' Cliff says now. 'He gave me confidence – as well as a giggle and laugh on the old 715a bus to London!'

And he will always be grateful that his first agent, George Ganjou, took the private recording to Norrie Paramor and wonders – almost with a shudder – what might have happened if he hadn't. 'Because no one else was taking much notice of us. George knew nothing about rock 'n' roll, but he saw the potential that was there,' Cliff says.

He remembers ex-Drifter Ian Samwell not only for writing 'Move It', the song that began it all, but for a master stroke in having suggested that the letter s be dropped from Richards when Harry Webb was looking for a new name. 'Brilliant!'

Samwell, who now has his own music publishing company and also produces records, says he still collects royalties from 'Move It'. He works in Britain and the United States and commutes across the Atlantic.

'I'm in the middle of a new song for Cliff,' he said when we talked to him. 'He's recorded about fourteen songs of mine over the years.'

87

Norrie Paramor died in September 1979. Five years earlier he had ended the long association with Cliff when he went to work for the B.B.C. in Birmingham. He felt that he should make way for a younger man to preside over Cliff's recording career, he said.

Remembering him today, Cliff says, 'What can I say? He was a kind of father figure. He gave me fifteen years of consecutive hit records. I never had a miss – until the first record I made without him. It was called 'Brand New Song'. A sort of epitaph in a way. It's nice to think – with no disrespect to his successor – that the first record without Norrie didn't make it. It was the end of an era.'

Norrie once paid this tribute to Cliff, 'He's always so unassuming. Above all he has humility – the humility to listen and take advice even though he has firmness of opinion. In his position he could easily throw his weight about and make demands – but he never does.'

Cliff has long forgiven Jack Good for taking away his guitar and curtailing his Elvis sideburns and he never forgets that Jack turned over that first record in favour of 'Move It', the B-side. Jack's *Oh Boy*! programme pushed him to fame – and some notoriety – in those all-important early days.

'I used to look glum, sad, brooding – whatever word you like,' Cliff said. 'That was the way I was told to play it in close-up on telly. But,' he added, 'that wasn't me. After a few years I tried to set a happier mood.'

Jack Good agrees, of course, that the personality he developed was only a temporary one for television and that Cliff would grow out of it.

Answering our question, Jack says, 'What were my thoughts about his future prospects at that time? I didn't think about that at all. We lived from day to day and it all seemed rather a joke. I wasn't prepared or cut out for this sort of career and in a sense neither was he, because rock 'n' roll had only just happened.

'Cliff and I just grabbed on to it. I said publicly that I thought he was going to be a huge star, but I certainly never conceived that in 1981 I would still be alive – I thought I was going to die at about thirty – and telling anybody about these events. Even as I say this it sounds absurd. And I suppose it is absurd . . .'

Tito Burns left his mark on Cliff Richard as well. 'I have him to thank for my early film entry,' Cliff says. 'Again, when our association came to an end, it was an amicable parting. I can't pay tribute enough to all these guys. You know what a rip-off business this is. I have been fortunate, but of course there have been little bits of sadness – and some smiles.'

Tito himself, today an impresario who represents in certain countries such names as Victor Borge, Sacha Distel and Tony Bennett, says, 'I look back on my association with Cliff with great satisfaction and the big thrill for me these days whenever I'm in California is turning on the radio and hearing a Cliff Richard record. He has an incredible love of music. That's his whole world and his whole life.

'Only once did we ever come near to possibly breaking up while he was with me.'

It happened towards the end of 1959 when they were preparing for Cliff's first American tour early in the coming year. Cliff was recording twelve songs that could be released during his absence when Tito noticed that something was lacking.

'He had only two more songs to do and there was not a song yet from his new movie, *Expresso Bongo*,' he tells us. 'So I suggested one.

' "I don't like it," Cliff said.

' "You have to learn politics," I told him. "You have to back up your own movie." But he still didn't like it. "It's obvious," I said, "that you've reached the stage where you don't need me any more. Okay, you can carry on on your own." I walked out – but he ran after me.

' "You have to take my advice," I told him. "Oh, all right!" he said and everything was well again.

'The song was "Voice in the Wilderness". The record reached number two in the charts.'

This was one of a batch of songs from *Expresso Bongo* written by Norrie Paramor and Bunny Lewis, a former Decca executive who had guided the early career of the powerful-voiced hit singer David Whitfield.

Cliff's EP from the film also hit the singles chart.

His memories of Leslie Grade illustrate how thorough he was, giving his attention to the slightest detail however busy he happened to be. 'He was a work-aholic,' Cliff says. 'We got on very well together and he was always very thoughtful. His main aim was that I should be happy when I was working for him. If I found myself in a show where someone was using any blue material I would tell him that I was concerned because of the number of kids in the audience and he would remove whoever it was.'

Leslie Grade died in October 1979, only weeks after the death of Norrie Paramor.

One other member of the entourage for whom Cliff had much respect was Leslie Perrin, without doubt the best-known and best-loved public relations man in show business.

He represented Cliff and the Shadows for many years. Also in his fold for a long time were such diverse luminaries as Frank Sinatra and the Rolling Stones.

His publicity campaign to back up the launching of the Shadows' first big hit, 'Apache', is still recalled affectionately by Cliff. 'Les sent all the record critics and columnists a story with an arrow stuck through it!'

It was a slick way of drawing attention to a group that was trying to make it on their own without Cliff and the critics certainly paid attention.

But Les's task was not only to put his clients' names in the papers. His more important duty was to act as their spokesman – frequently in some difficult situation. On all his Press releases he gave his home telephone number for night calls and there were many long nights when the phone never ceased to ring, often with calls from many parts of the world.

As Cliff said, paying tribute to him, 'We needed a buffer and Les was a buffer, taking the weight whenever necessary.'

He died in 1978 at the age of fifty-seven.

CHAPTER EIGHT

Love and Marriage

By the time you reach this page Cliff Richard may well have surprised us all and married. 'I would like to be married some time,' he told us. 'I hope so. But falling in love is not something you can plan. It's something that happens.'

He has made similar pronouncements over the years, almost since his entry into the big time in 1958 when, barely eighteen, he could only look forward to the great day and repeat that he would not dream of heading for the altar until he was twenty-five at least.

Of course he would like children, particularly a son, he has said. But, as he points out frequently, the problem of whether or not he will marry or why he isn't married is one that seems to concern other people more than himself.

These questions have plagued him for more than twenty years now and in *Which One's Cliff?* (1977), written in collaboration with Bill Latham, his friend and religious adviser, he says that he is really content as a bachelor, although marriage and children around the house are desirable.

'I don't have any great urge to be married. No, I'm not a mass of sexual hang-ups. Yes, I have had girlfriends in the past and, who knows, I may have another in the future and end up married. In the meantime, I'm not pursuing anyone and feel very fulfilled, thank you very much! Perhaps I'll give the next interviewer who starts the well-worn romance routine a copy of this book – it will save a lot of time and a lot of tedium.'

As subsequent interviewers some four years later, we asked Cliff if these sentiments still applied. They did, he said, and repeated that he would still like to be married sometime.

Since he became a star he has always tried to keep his private life private, although this has not always been easy. But in 1968 he did have this to say, 'People were always trying to find out who I was going with, but really I have been in love only three times.

'Once was when I was planning to marry Jackie Irving. We met when she was dancing in my show at the Palladium – but then she went and married Adam Faith. So that was that.'

He went on to say, 'I'm going to get married when I'm ready – and not before. I may not get married at all.'

The Jackie Irving romance blossomed in the early sixties when Cliff was the number one pop and film star and Britain's most eligible show business bachelor.

In July 1963 he said, 'There is one girl I'm very friendly with – dancer Jackie Irving – but she and I know that marriage is out of the question . . .'

Yet he had thought seriously about marrying her, he let it be known some three years later when he said, 'The Shadows had all married and I'd been going around with Jackie Irving for three years and we'd got along very well.

'I did think about marriage then, but I decided I couldn't love her or we'd have been married earlier.'

He was twenty-three when he considered marriage to her and still had some time to go before he reached twenty-five, the age he had designated several times as probably the right one at which to wed.

When he did reach twenty-five he was reminded of this and admitted that 'there have been three or four false alarms which I don't regret. If I meet the right girl then I'll marry straight away . . .

'How can you say that you'll marry at such and such a time? Who can plan for the right girl to turn up?

'Too many of those I do meet are either sarcastic or over-keen. They put me off – it's my job to do the chasing. I much prefer a reserved girl who doesn't do all the talking to the type who charges up and never stops. And I want a girl who is interested in me as a person rather than the pop singer she has read about.'

He did update the marrying age to twenty-seven and later to thirty-two as the bachelor years moved on. After all, he recalled, his father had been in his thirties when he wed Mrs Webb.

Cliff was a few months short of his twenty-third birthday in 1963 – when he was dating Jackie – when he said, 'The girl I marry will be a girl I'm in love with – and that's not likely to happen for some time yet. I don't plan to marry for another four or five years yet. When I do it will be for keeps.

'My wife, whoever she is, will have to put her foot down with me. She'll have to speak her mind and not be afraid to say what she thinks. I can't stand insincerity. There's nothing like a bit of straight talking.'

The romance with Jackie Irving has been the only one that he has talked about at any length and where the name of the girl has been mentioned.

It seems to have foundered while Cliff was in the Canary Islands shooting *Wonderful Life* early in 1964.

Miss Irving, who was then a dancer in the Lionel Blair troupe, lamented, 'I don't see Cliff any more. I haven't heard from him since he went away filming. Not a letter, or a postcard, nothing.'

She, for her part, denied that there had been any romance or that there was any secret engagement. They were, in the time-honoured show business quote, just good friends. They had worked together in Cliff's shows in Blackpool and in South Africa.

'When we were in South Africa we often went out, but with a crowd of people from the show . . .' she said.

'While we were in Blackpool [in the summer of 1963] we went out together quite a lot.'

In fact, she added, 'Cliff and I only seem to have gone out together while we were working together.'

After the Blackpool summer show closed they met only at parties. Said Miss Irving, 'I realize it wouldn't do Cliff's career any good at all if he married. It would only annoy his fans.

'We went out together because Cliff didn't want to be with other fellows all the time. It was just a boy and girl friendship. He doesn't know many girls and he doesn't have a lot of time to go out with them and get to know them.'

Cliff has admitted that he has been 'rather shy' about contact with the opposite sex. 'It takes me a long time to pluck up courage to talk to a girl. If a girl makes the first move – I'm off!'

Some twelve years after the Jackie Irving episode he was more positive about the romance when he recalled in 1975, 'I was madly in love, but I had doubts at the last moment.

'Jackie is the only girl I have ever contemplated marrying. Now I'm glad I'm not married.

'I'm glad I'm not in love with a woman who is going to make me want to come home all the time. My whole life style would have to change.

'What I'm doing now is so valuable for myself as a man, and for the things I believe in, that they come first . . .'

The dimming of his image with his vast following of female fans used to be an important factor to be considered whenever romance was hinted.

One night, during his early appearances at the Finsbury Park Empire, a girl could be seen sitting on his lap in a crowded car as he was driven away from the theatre through a swarm of fans. The reaction was alarming. Several fans flung their autograph books and pictures of him into the gutter in their obvious anger and jealousy.

In those days he often wondered what difference it would make to his career if he did marry. It was a difficult question for anyone to answer, but one adviser thought that maybe some ten per cent of his followers would cease to be counted among his faithful. It was perhaps a conservative estimate. The real answer would never be known.

What was true was that a lot of them really believed they were in love with him and cherished a dream that somehow one day they would become the chosen one who would walk proudly down the aisle on Cliff's arm as his bride.

In 1962 the show business departments of the Fleet Street nationals worked themselves into a frenzy when some watchful tip-off merchant reported that the banns had been called at a church in northwest London for the forthcoming marriage of one Harry Rodger Webb to a Miss Valerie Stratford, who lived in Willesden.

The big day had been set for 10 February. Cars had been arranged to call for the bride and the guests on that date and a present list had been circulated. It all sounded like the real thing.

The only person who appeared to know nothing about the great day was the intended bridegroom, Harry Webb, now trading as Cliff Richard.

Reporters descended on him and some of them took a lot of convincing that he was not planning to wed in secret.

'The story was printed in some papers,' Cliff said, 'and I didn't understand it until I realized that the girl who had made all the arrangements without asking me was a girl who had been following me around so much.

'She had been writing to me and waiting for me outside my office, my home and theatres for a long time. Although I was amazed at her devotion, our friendship never exceeded the "good evening" stage.'

The girl had to admit that the whole thing was a hoax, explaining that three girlfriends had dared her to do it. 'It was just a practical joke,' she said. Her worship of Cliff could be gauged by the fact that she possessed 3,500 pictures of him.

He said at the time, 'I'm not annoyed. Teenagers often do things without thinking. She has apologized to me and I'll forget all about it.'

Valerie still continued to be a fan – and thousands of other girls nursing the same impossible dream of becoming Mrs Richard breathed a sigh and went on hoping that one day their turn might come.

It is easy to understand how a girl fan could be wafted away into a fantasy of believing that she was *the* one who would spend the rest of her life with her idol.

This is the type of letter that nightly awaited Cliff in the dressing room when he arrived at a theatre in those days:

'Dearest, darling Cliff, I know you are basically a shy person, but there's no need to be shy with me. I am deeply in love with you and I know that you feel the same way about me, because you keep singing the songs I like best of all. If you want me to make the arrangements for a quiet wedding, just sing "Living Doll" tonight when I'm in the audience and I'll go straight ahead with all the plans.'

It scared him enough to go through his act that particular night without singing the already scheduled 'Living Doll' – probably to the disappointment of all the audience.

This was not an isolated incident and was a simple method that could be employed by a fan to reach to an idol; to form some secret means of communication that only the two of them would understand. Thus the performance of a requested song could mean only one thing – that the star had understood and was answering in the magic code that only they shared. It was a method not confined only to Cliff Richard fans, and it could spell trouble . . .

The severed romance with Jackie Irving early in 1964 had barely cooled before Cliff's name was being linked with another affair.

This time the girl was actress Susan Hampshire, his co-star in *Wonderful Life*. They had spent three months in the Canary Islands – the shooting had been delayed by unkind weather – and show business gossips wondered how it was possible for them to be together for that length of time without forming some kind of intimate relationship.

Miss Hampshire was livid when she returned to England. 'Of course I'm in love with Cliff,' she said, very much tongue in cheek, 'just like the bulk of the female population of Great Britain. But we are definitely not having a romance.'

She wished that people would understand that the movie life is not exactly a bowl of cherries – even on location on an island. 'It's sheer hard work from dawn to dusk,' she explained. 'Most nights I was in bed and asleep by nine o'clock.'

Although she was his leading lady, she went on, it was Cliff's picture and the life was considerably harder for him. Also, she said, 'He's such a positive person and he knows exactly what he wants – particularly in his choice of girls. He believes in one marriage and one girl in life . . .'

Cliff's first-ever girlfriend, he has said, was one he met in India. A little lady named Joan. It came to nothing. They sat next to each other at school. He was seven . . .

There is little doubt, however, that he experienced the pangs of young love when he was in his teens at Cheshunt. One of the earliest mentions of a girlfriend after making his break into show business was of a damsel named Janet – though it is not certain that this was her correct name. It was reported in an early fan

In the beginning . . . Harry Webb has become Cliff Richard. Shy, a little plump, hair greased Elvis fashion. He is seventeen.

The Elvis twitch of the leg. It was all part of the Cliff Richard act.
Inset: The Richard strut that was to become so familiar, along with black and white stage gear.

The agonized Presley mood . . . while the Shadows kick a leg.

Always the rock'n'roller. And Shadow Hank Marvin is all ears.

THE *FACTS* OF *CLIFF*

HEIGHT:
5 ft. 10½ in.

HAIR: brown.

He's
RIGHT-
HANDED:

SHOE SIZE:
8.

EYES:

dark brown—
        —wears specs
                often.

BIRTHPLACE:

Lucknow, India,

on October 14, 194

HEART:

unattached
        (except to Mum)

WEIGHT:

12 stones.

DRESS:

prefers
casual clothes.

FIRST DISC:

Move It!

POCKETS:

lined to the tune
of £2000
per week (estimated).

SPORT:

badminton,

FAN CLUB ADDRESS:

C/o Jan Vane,
59 Eastern Road,
Romford,
Essex.

BUSINESS CARD

MANAGER:
Peter Gormley

COMPANY:
The Grade Organis

FAMILY TREE:

Mum (Mrs Dorothy Webb),

Donna   Jacqueline   Joa

Above: Of course he's like his mother!

Right: Cliff was an annual 'must' for The Great Pop Prom, staged at the Royal Albert Hall on the Sunday following the last night of the Proms and promoted by the romantic weeklies *Marilyn, Roxy,* and *Valentine.* Here, during the 1961 Pop Prom, he pauses for the camera during an interview with co-author Patrick Doncaster.

JOHNNY and
the HURRICANES

SALVATION

NEW
RECORD MIRROR
6d

116 SHAFTESBURY AVENUE, LONDON, W.1

EVERY WEEK!
BRITAIN'S TOP
50!
AMERICA'S TOP
50!
RECORD CHARTS

No. 58　　　　　　WEEK ENDING APRIL 21, 1962　　　　EVERY THURSDAY. 6d.

★ ★ ★ ★ ★ ★ ★
**GOLDEN
BOYS!**

CLIFF RICHARD together with the SHADOWS went down to Teddington on Friday, to the ABC-TV studios where 'Thank Your Lucky Stars' was being filmed.

But it was no ordinary appearance for the five pop stars because during the programme Cliff's recording manager Norrie Paramor presented him with the SECOND Gold Disc for million plus sales of his latest single - 'The Young Ones'.

Cliff is seen (left) holding up the golden master (ABC-TV photograph).

The Shadows also had their Gold Disc presented to Hank. It was for sales of 'Apache', the first record that put the Shadows in the charts as a recording team.

Below (left to right), we see Brian Matthew (host on the programme), Norrie Paramor, Brian Bennett (drummer with the Shadows although he didn't play on 'Apache'), Jet Harris, Hank Marvin and Bruce Welch. (NRMP Pics).

April 1962 . . . Cliff notches up Gold Disc No.2 for selling a
million records of 'The Young Ones'. 'Living Doll' won the first.
In the lower picture recording manager Norrie Paramor hands
over a gold disc to the Shadows for 'Apache'.

Above: Show time! The girl on the left is Jackie Irving. Cliff confesses that at one time he planned to marry her. Eventually she wed Adam Faith.

Right: You get to meet the nicest people in showbusiness. The armful is singing star Millicent Martin.

How the Germans billed Cliff and company on the street kiosks. Also on the bill, organist Cherry Wainer.

publication that he fell in love with her but was 'in despair' when he discovered that she already had a boyfriend.

In a 1963 interview in a now defunct magazine he said, 'Just before I had my first big break in show business I was courting a girl steadily. We'd been going out for about a year and I guess she was the most serious girl I ever had.

'My career took an upward leap when I signed a record contract and her mother saw a few snags about our association, with me entering show business on a full-time basis.

'Anyway, she called us both together one afternoon. We talked about the situation – which wasn't helped because my recent stage appearances had prevented me from seeing her for three weeks. The result was that we went our separate ways.'

He said in the same interview that he 'wouldn't marry a girl in show business'.

As his fame grew he had only to be seen in the company of a girl – however innocent the reason – to raise questions about romance.

In October 1960 he accompanied American singing star Connie Francis to a midnight supper at the White Elephant, a renowned show business rendezvous in Mayfair – chaperoned by manager Tito Burns.

It was fun. 'But it wasn't really a date,' Cliff had to explain, adding that he didn't have much time for dates, working six nights a week at the London Palladium as he was then, rarely leaving the theatre before midnight. His free Sundays he spent with his parents and sisters and managed to watch some television or gather round the table for a family Scrabble tournament.

He appeared to be extremely cautious in those days.

When he was conducting *Sunday Pictorial* columnist Jack Bentley on an inspection of the new family home at Winchmore Hill the same year, they stopped off at Cliff's bedroom, where three walls were 'painted in a lemon colour and the fourth papered in an animal design'.

Cliff revealed that he was going to put on one wall 'a pin-up picture of Carol Lynley, who starred in the film *Blue Jeans* . . . I think she's terrific.'

Wrote Bentley, 'Cliff caught the look in my eye.

' "Oh, no!" he said. "I have no serious romantic ideas about any girl." '

Again in 1960, still showing caution, he had this to say, 'If I had to choose between marriage and my career, I'm afraid I would put my career first. You see, so many people depend on me.'

He had just reached his twentieth birthday . . .

Pairing or attempting to marry Cliff off has been fair game through the years. Even in 1974 he was still denying that any romance existed, this time with the delightful Miss Olivia Newton-John, whom he had known for many years. So much so that 'people think I discovered her,' he said. 'But I didn't. My agent did. We are great friends, but I haven't asked her to marry me.'

As his involvement with Christianity became more apparent the evergreen question about marriage needed more studied replies.

'I happen to be a Christian,' he said in 1967, 'and I wouldn't live with someone to whom I wasn't married. If you throw marriage out what do you put in its place? The whole point of marriage is that it keeps people stable. Marriage is binding and living with someone isn't.'

On another occasion he said, 'If you're a Christian like I am you need a real spiritual affinity with someone.'

He once defined wedlock: 'Marriage is the public commitment of two people who are free to marry, who want a life together, who cannot live without each other and who want to cement their relationship.'

He will know when the right girl or woman comes along . . .

With the stretching of the years towards his thirties and beyond, a new question about the reasons for his continued bachelordom began to arise. Was he gay?

He dealt with it briefly in *Which One's Cliff?* when he said that 'I'm not a mass of sexual hang-ups.' He has indulged himself in a few more words with several interviewers, however, who noted that he showed some signs of irritation and anger when the subject was mentioned.

To *Daily Mirror* columnist Don Short he said in 1969 (one of the earliest references to the question), 'Of course I've heard stories that I must be a homosexual because I've never married. That's terrible, but there's nothing I can do about it.

'People must do and think and say whatever they want to. As long as I know the truth, that is all that matters.

'If it is not God's wish for me to marry, then it is something I must accept. He may feel that my work can be achieved more purposefully by remaining single.

'One day I hope to marry and have children . . . I believe that the girl I marry will be a Christian. It is essential that two people who are going to be together for the rest of their lives should think the same way.'

Asked if he were gay by a London *Evening News* writer in 1976, he replied, 'It's untrue, but I have given up even talking about it because I think nothing I say will change anything. People are very unfair with their criticisms and their judgements. I know I catch the brunt of it, but I don't give two hoots.

'I've got a lot of living to do and I'm not going to spend my life either proving that I do believe something or that I'm not something else.

'I'm not going to get married just to prove it. I'm damned if I am. Of course I've heard the rumours, but I know what I am and my friends know what I am.

'What the mass public thinks doesn't bother me as long as they buy my records.'

In a reference to extramarital sex he disclosed, 'I don't sleep with women at all now – not since my Christian conversion.'

In 1977 he told *Evening Standard* interviewer Charles Catchpole, 'Let people think what they like. I've had girlfriends. But people seem to think that if a bloke doesn't sleep around he must be gay. I've never ruled out marriage. I'd love to marry one day, but I just haven't met the right girl yet. Marriage is a very special thing to me. I'm certainly not going to do it just to make other people feel satisfied.'

He used similar words to *Daily Mirror* writer Alasdair Buchan in the following year, repeating that the accusation didn't worry him any more. Marriage, he felt, would be the easiest thing in the world – 'but I would find myself in a position where I get married to clear people's minds about me and I don't intend to do that'.

He also commented, 'Nothing, I suppose, will take the place of normal sexual relations. But I never feel I've got to get up and rape someone. Maybe I've been given the personality to cope with the fact that I won't get married.'

Cliff's former manager Tito Burns summed up with these words to the authors, 'When anyone asks me if he is gay I say nonsense. He had some little romances during those early days when he was with me – but nothing that amounted to anything. He just wasn't interested in going into a deep romance.

'As I've said, he has a great respect for his body and didn't seem interested in sex, but no – never anything approaching gay. No way. I always felt he was waiting until the right girl came along. He was very close to his mother and he treated women the way he would treat his mother – with great respect . . .'

Undoubtedly Cliff's career and his devotion to it was a major obstacle in the path of marriage for many years.

The show business life of constant travel and upheaval, of new places and new faces, would never have contributed to a stable home life. Even when he felt he did not have to worry any more about losing part of his vast army of fans if he wed, his life style still had not changed. And he had seen many marriages of show business people around him founder along the way.

When asked at a press conference if he were thinking of marrying, Cliff replied, 'No, but when I am you will probably know about it before I do!'

It could happen that way . . .

CHAPTER NINE

Life with the Webbs

There was no escape for the Webb family. The big breakthrough made by Harry while still in his teens would touch them all in some way. They could never be simply ordinary people again, able to live a normal life going quietly about their day to day business while the eldest child was moving towards his peak as a pop and movie star in the swinging sixties.

Fingers would point at them, at both the parents and the three sisters, and voices would whisper, 'That's Cliff Richard's mum!' 'That's one of his sisters!' Fans would beg favours of them. An autograph of Cliff's; a lock of his dark romantic hair.

The family home, when Cliff's father died in May 1961, was still the house at Winchmore Hill, where the siege would never abate. Some nights a handful of girls keeping a round the clock vigil outside would be invited in for a cup of tea brewed in the wee small hours by a patient Mrs Webb, sitting up awaiting Cliff's return from an engagement.

Jacqueline and Joan, the two youngest daughters, were still schoolgirls, but the eldest, Donella, was moving towards womanhood.

Cliff was now the man about the house whenever he was able to be there but still had several months to go until he attained his majority on reaching twenty-one, then the legal age.

Until that time someone else would have to sign all documents on his behalf (it had been his father up to his death). And according to the law he was not yet old enough to enter a pools coupon, which was hardly a burden when his yearly earnings were now estimated to be in the big pools win bracket anyway.

Within twelve weeks of the loss of her father, daughter Donella was married at Waltham Abbey parish church in Essex. She was eighteen. Cliff gave her away.

The date was 5 August 1961, a Saturday, and there were frantic scenes that made acres of picture space in the Sunday newspapers. The fans turned up to scream and mob Cliff rather than Donella, who fainted when they forced their way through a cordon of police to reach big brother and knocked her veil askew.

Cliff did a man-size job, gathering up his sister and carrying her into the church, although hardly getting her there on time. The service was delayed for fifteen minutes.

Donna, as the family called her, looking radiant in white, had her veil neatly arranged once more before Cliff escorted her up the aisle while the bridegroom, a young man named Paul Stevens, waited anxiously.

After the ceremony there was the same frenzied activity as the fans surged forward, many of them with cameras, when the newlyweds tried to leave the church to escape into the wedding cars.

This time Cliff stayed put inside until the rest of the wedding party had managed to drive away. When he did make his exit he was surrounded by six brawny bodyguards.

In November 1963 the remaining Webbs – Cliff, mother and two younger sisters – folded their tent at Winchmore Hill and moved off into Upper Nazeing, just across the Hertfordshire border in Essex, into a spacious, sprawling £30,000 mansion with elegant chimneys.

It was called Rookswood, had six bedrooms, four reception rooms, four bathrooms, a billiards room, a five-car garage, stables, greenhouses and tennis court and stood in eleven acres. Cars crunched along a 300-yard drive to reach the entrance, which opened on to a large hall panelled with oak that had once looked out on history at Hampton Court.

Cliff's bedroom looked as large or even larger than the famous cellar at the 2 i's.

'This house is essentially a family home and that's the way Cliff wants to keep it,' said manager Peter Gormley.

An aunt and two teenaged cousins also moved in to live with the diminished Webb family, now without Donella as well as father.

But the fans found the place all right. They arrived on foot and

102

in cars and it needed the police to clear them from the driveway and grounds where they churned up the turf. Only after the gates had been strengthened, and Cliff departed for his long sojourn to film *Wonderful Life* in the Canaries, did the siege begin to ease.

Sisters Jacqueline, then sixteen, and Joan, thirteen, felt the loneliness of Rookswood at the beginning, set as it was in a comparative wilderness. For them the transition to such splendour was much more wondrous, after the modest semi-detached at Winchmore Hill and the council house at Cheshunt, where the rent had been 30 shillings a week (£1.50) and the residents looked into each other's gardens.

Only Joan was still at school – Cheshunt Secondary Modern, where Cliff had himself been a pupil – while Jackie, as she was known, had already started work, pounding away at a typewriter.

What made them different was that they travelled each morning in a chauffeured car to their respective destinations. And each morning the postman brought them mail – mostly from girl fans of their famous brother wanting to become their pen pals – anything to reach a little closer to their idol.

At school Joan was taking a daily dose of ragging. The Beatles had now truly arrived to challenge Cliff as Lord and Master of the British pop scene and a lot of youngsters were transferring their affections and letting Miss Webb know.

The Webb girls themselves began to take an interest in another fast-rising name in the group business – the Dave Clark Five – who in January 1964 achieved national acclaim by unseating the seemingly immovable Beatles from the top of the charts with Dave's smash hit 'Glad All Over'.

The Webb sisters became such admirers of Dave and the Five that they became their fan club organizers and were even pictured at their task. It's a free country, they might have said . . .

Some two and a half years later the calm of Rookswood made way for some new excitement in the Webb family saga.

On Monday 20 June 1966 the *Daily Mirror* broke the news at the top of page three with bold black headlines, CLIFF RICHARD'S MUM WEDS HIS EX-DRIVER.

The text ran, 'Pop star Cliff Richard's mother, Mrs Dorothy

Webb, forty-five, has married his 24-year-old former chauffeur Derek Bodkin.

'Last night Dorothy and Derek were on a touring honeymoon in Cliff's white E-type Jaguar.

'Their wedding was such a well-kept secret that not even Cliff was told until AFTER the register-office ceremony on Saturday.

'Mrs Webb telephoned Cliff, twenty-five, from a call-box at Epping, Essex, and broke the news.

'Then she and Derek drove back to Cliff's £31,000 [sic] Tudor-style mansion at Upper Nazeing, Essex, for an impromptu champagne reception.

'It was strictly a family affair,' the story went on to say, with daughters Jackie and Joan present along with Derek's parents, who had also been present at the wedding ceremony.

At some stage Cliff arrived and took photographs of the newlyweds on the lawn. After waving them goodbye on the first stage of their honeymoon he was reported as saying, 'I'm not worried by the difference in their ages. Derek is an old friend.

'Mum has told me that the reason she kept it all secret was that she didn't want it to be a showbiz wedding with lots of people there.

'She wanted to be married quietly and this was the only way she could do it.

'She wanted to be just plain Mrs Webb getting married, not Cliff Richard's mum.'

Cliff had been missing from the family home because he was filming *Finders Keepers* at Pinewood studios in Buckinghamshire with Robert Morley and new leading lady Viviane Ventura.

The journey from Rookswood to Pinewood at daybreak would have meant an hour and a half drive, Cliff explained later. Bill Latham – who had been a master at his old school and one of the people whose advice he had sought about Christianity – lived with his mother Mamie in North London, midway along the route to Pinewood. To save Cliff time he suggested that Cliff should stay with them during the six-week filming, to make the hard movie life that much more bearable.

Cliff accepted the offer and it was the beginning of an enduring friendship.

Today, as this book is being prepared fifteen years later, he still shares a home with Bill and his mother at Weybridge in Surrey. *Which One's Cliff?*, the book co-authored with Bill, is dedicated 'to Mamie, "Mum" Number 2!'

On that Monday in June 1966, when the news of Mrs Webb's secret marriage came out, Cliff held a Press conference at Pinewood between filming at which he announced that he was going to buy a house as a wedding present for his mother and new stepfather, who was younger than himself. He referred to him as Derek and smiled, 'I can hardly call him Dad!'

He added that on the wedding day he had gone out and bought some wine for a celebration with them and that they would continue their honeymoon at his villa in Portugal.

Discussing plans for the future, he said that the house he would buy for his mother and her new husband would be in Essex and not far from Rookswood.

'My sisters and I naturally want our mother and Derek to build a happy life.'

The plans also included a new home for his two sisters and a third for the aunt and cousins who were living with them. He envisaged a smaller home or flat for himself.

'We all met Derek,' he went on, 'when he applied for the job of chauffeur with us years ago, though he has not worked for us since my father died. We all regard him as a friend.'

The first contact with Derek had been when Cliff frequently booked vehicles from the car-hire firm for which Bodkin worked. Later he became Cliff's personal driver for a period.

Within three weeks of the marriage Cliff had sold Rookswood for £43,000. The buyer was a director of the London Rubber Company. At the same time it was announced that Cliff had bought a detached house at Broxbourne, only a few miles from Nazeing but in Hertfordshire, for his mother and Derek, plus two other houses in Broxbourne for sister Jackie and the aunt who had been living at Rookswood.

Six months after the wedding, Bodkin went on record to say that Cliff did not know about the marriage until after the ceremony but that he *did* know 'we were going to get married'.

He also said that he didn't treat Cliff 'like a son'. And he now had his own car-hire business.

Some years later Cliff stressed that the marriage had not upset him. 'It was the nicest thing that could have happened, both to her and to me. My father's death was a great loss to her and although she married someone very much younger, he has been a stabilizing factor.'

Cliff is still very close to his family and his mother, spending the last few days with her before he set off in 1981 for his seven-week American tour.

All his sisters married, but one lives in Norfolk 'and I don't see her as much these days', he told us.

'I have eight nephews and nieces,' he added with some pride . . .

CHAPTER TEN

A Few Slipped Discs

E.M.I. Records had a pleasant problem in 1977. They had decided they would release an album of Cliff Richard hit singles encompassing his complete record-making career.

Usually such compilation albums have anything from twelve to twenty tracks. The eventual figure is arrived at after long discussions on what are fondly called the prevailing winds of the market place at the given time of record release. The agreed total may, though, not entirely reflect what is claimed on an album cover. Few artists have had twelve, let alone sixteen or twenty hit records. Yet the companies have deemed that a sixteen-track album is most acceptable to the public. So these record companies indulge in the practice of padding and a few non-hit but generally popular tracks of the particular artist become included. Joe Public rarely notices he is the subject of a minor sharp practice. As the record companies well know, Joe Public likes to think he has a large number of songs by a popular artist at a fraction of the price he would pay if he bought each song on a single record.

Cliff, though, is different from anyone else bar Elvis. Prior to 1977 he had achieved sixty-eight chart hits!

E.M.I. Head of Marketing John Cabanagh ruefully told us it meant one big headache.

'Well, it was obvious Cliff had too many hits for one LP. Half the number could span his career but even then we had to decide which tracks should be included and I suppose more important in terms of the buying public which would be excluded.'

In the end E.M.I. issued a *40 Golden Greats* collection. It was given a major TV promotional push and a special trade launch at the Carlton Tower Hotel, London. Its release followed extensive market research.

'We really wanted to know what the public wanted and which numbers they knew and remembered.'

The market researchers questioned male and female groups from two age groups – sixteen to twenty-four and twenty-five to forty. The sample groups all thought the project was a good one but in true British fashion, exercising both caution and a reticence towards actually committing themselves, they were less sure whether they would buy the record. Some of them felt a single record would be enough.

Among the final conclusions came statements that for females aged twenty-five and over the appeal of Cliff lay in his early material. Interest in the middle period was low and even nonexistent. Cliff's golden era was identified with the Shadows.

The group samples said his music changed from approximately 1964 onwards, as did his image and also his interests. The gradual diminution of the Shadows' association with Cliff was one of the reasons for a drop in popularity but this decline was also blamed on his becoming religious, adopting 'preachy' attitudes and a 'safer' style.

Other reasons for the so-called low key middle period in Cliff's recording career included his becoming a definite solo singer without a group and the fact that the music scene of the middle and late sixties moved and changed so fast, leaving Cliff unfashionable.

There was a positive reaction towards his singles of the mid-seventies. It seemed that those hit songs – 'You Keep Me Hangin' On', 'Miss You Nights', 'Devil Woman', 'I Can't Ask for Anything More than You Babe', 'Hey Mr Dream Maker', 'My Kinda Life' – had indeed revived and rejuvenated his appeal and made him acceptable to the young.

E.M.I. had another problem and that was image. 'To the committed Cliff may not appear to have altered,' said Cabanagh. 'But when E.M.I.'s planners looked at pictures of Cliff over the years it was clear that the hair, the glasses and clothes were not the same. It was very important to get the right Cliff there on the front cover, the one to whom people respond.

'It took a year of planning – you have to plan when you're

108

spending a great deal of money and also when the project involves a major artist like Cliff.

'E.M.I. put the album into the top spot and that was no mean feat. Outwardly the whole exercise looked easy but when you look at the possible complications then it's not by any means that simple.'

A music critic might not agree with the kind of divisions the public suggested were applicable to Cliff's career although it should be said that a division was made for them when they actually listened to extracts of the proposed running order for a double-record album.

The sample heard records from the periods 1958–61; 1962–3; 1964–7; 1968–77. The length of the last division illustrates Cliff's lack of releases and success compared with previous years.

The first division naturally includes the very first hit 'Move It'. This remains a classic. David Winter, author of the early Cliff biography *New Singer, New Song*, writes an appreciation better than any other attempted: 'It is pure primitive rock 'n' roll. It builds up in the traditional way; a few sharp chords from the lead guitar, then the whole thing is transferred to its rhythmic foundation, an insistent, vibrating bottom E on the electric bass, which, apart from half a dozen B's in the central section, is plugged relentlessly all through. Upon this foundation the drums and rhythm guitar build the fast, pulsing tempo of rock 'n' roll, the lead guitar links the vocal sections, and the voice, inescapably young, tops the whole thing with its emotional appeal.'

The voice hovers around middle C for most of the time but as Winter also noted the whole technique is the introduction of sudden trills or runs above and below the note, where it drops a full fifth and does so rather surprisingly.

It was an excellent record and an amazing start for an unproven seventeen-year-old. Even nearly twenty-five years after its release 'Move It' still possesses an impact which allows a contemporary DJ to segue* it into any current recorded hit without embarrassment.

Looking back on it today, Cliff says, 'It was great at the time.

*Segue is the process in which a DJ will play two records consecutively without his vocal interruption. Generally he picks up the mood and musical note and feel of the first with the second.

We were over the moon. I've a different version for the American tour and when I compare now with then I know I've progressed.'

Several attempts have been made at re-creating the hit feel via another artist, but without success. One of the best-known attempts came from Alvin Stardust in 1975. Cliff at the time said, 'Yeah, it's all right. I love the backing but I don't like his treatment of the lyric. It lost something. I did a version of the song live in Japan two years ago.

'It was really heavy and funky. I prefer that live version even to the original. I sing it better.'

It was the first recording of 'Move It' which made the music critics sit up. Many of those who now write books and are DJs were young at the time like Cliff. 'Move It' has stayed with them. When it first came out it helped Cliff to gain critical acceptance during a period when, for most people, the only good music came from America.

One of rock's most respected chroniclers, Charlie Gillet, wrote in his classic book *Sound of the City* of the times after 'Rock around the Clock': 'The most accomplished and successful British singer was Cliff Richard, with a style and image originally modelled on Presley but subsequently located somewhere between Rick Nelson and Paul Anka. Compared to the other British rock and roll singers, Richard had good vocal control, access to writers who provided competent and suitable material and an unusually capable and disciplined rhythm group.'

Another well-known rock chronicler, Nik Cohn, admired the early Cliff for the way he dominated British pop for years, but Cliff did not achieve this through raw and rugged rock 'n' roll. Reflecting on 'Move It' and its follow-up Cliff says, 'There was an immediate need for a follow-up. We had no background. We didn't write our own material, "Move It" was written by Ian Samwell and he'd written this other song, "High Class Baby", but when we went into the studio the magic didn't happen, and I thought, "Oh no, it's gonna be the end of a great career," and I went home and cried.'

Of course it wasn't the end but his music changed during this early period rather than in 1964 as the market research sample group appeared to believe.

110

Within a year Cliff had passed from the rock-for-the-kids class into singing ballad-style material. This gained him an audience which spanned the generations. It did lose him the kids who wanted a music and a star adults could not relate to. The record which heralded the new era was 'Living Doll'.

There were of course fans who loved the records Cliff made – whatever the style. Typical of these is Cliff Marshall of the Cliff fan club in Southend. 'In 1958 I was fifteen years of age and like most fifteen-year-olds in those days an ardent rock 'n' roller and mad about Elvis. Here in Britain we had nothing to compare with the then king of rock . . . but in August "Move It" was released and immediately I had to sit up and take note of the best rock record I had ever heard.'

Marshal heard more of Cliff's material and after four singles and two albums he decided he would rather hear Cliff than his childhood idol.

Cliff's early album material maintained his touch with rock 'n' roll. His second LP saw him singing 'Blue Suede Shoes' (which Elvis sang) and 'Twenty Flight Rock' (Eddie Cochran) and to fans like Cliff Marshall it was Cliff who won hands down. The singles differed. They became more polite, even wholesome.

Writer Peter Jones saw that Cliff had introduced something new. 'Before Cliff all pop singers sounded what they were, solidly working class – but Cliff introduced something new, a bland ramble, completely classless.'

He sees 'Living Doll' as the most influential British pop single of the sixties.

'He's been followed through his long career by a positive horde of imitators, copyists and plain apes.

'That's why he's a great one. He's lasted the pace, pleased millions, offended only a few – and he's still producing hits. Not as from a mass-production line, but in a variety of styles, moods and atmospheres.'

Nik Cohn is less reverential. He talks of Cliff as akin to a magic slate, 'a pad on which almost everyone could scrawl their fantasies and rub them out and try again. He was the nice boy that girls could be proud to date, the perfect son that

111

mothers could be proud to raise, the good nut that schoolboys could be proud to have as a friend.'

Cliff merely responds to such comments with a cryptic, 'I'm hysterical about it . . . if someone thinks I'm goody-goody I think, well, whey whey, I'm winning out – at least I'm achieving an end.'

In the early sixties Cliff hit the charts with records like 'I Love You', 'Theme for a Dream', 'Gee Whizz It's You', 'Please Don't Tease' and 'A Girl Like You'.

'One thing I remember about it was the way my dad loved it. My dad died not long after and he missed all the success that was to follow on from the films like *The Young Ones* and *Summer Holiday* but whenever I think of "A Girl Like You" I always remember how he said that was the best record I ever made up until that point.'

'A Girl Like You' charted in June 1961. Six months later another major happening in Cliff's disc career occurred. It centred around the single 'The Young Ones'.

The headline in the music paper *Record Mirror* for 13 January 1962 ran,

'CLIFF BEATS ELVIS.

'British singer Cliff Richard is now the holder of the record for advance sales with his new disc "The Young Ones".

'He beats the previous record holder Elvis Presley.

'Official figures released by E.M.I. state that the advance orders by day of release reached an all-time peak of 524,000 copies.'

The Young Ones as a film was equally a stupendous box-office success. What thrilled Cliff was that he and the Shadows had the chance to write songs for the film. The Shadows wrote several numbers.

The only sour note from *The Young Ones* took place across the Atlantic. In the United States Connie Francis recorded Cliff's U.K. number three chart smash from the film, 'When the Girl in your Arms'. Cliff's management felt release of the song should have been held up until the film had been screened in the States. The resulting row saw Cliff leaving A.B.C. Paramount and signing with Big Tree. Needless to say Connie had a big hit with the song and Cliff badly needed a major U.S. success.

Films and hits went together and with *Summer Holiday* Cliff emerged as a songwriter. He wrote 'Big News' with Mike Conlin and his co-writer on the massive hit 'Bachelor Boy' was Bruce Welch.

'It was always an ambition of mine to write and I thought I would keep on just as long as the tunes would keep coming,' said Cliff.

The hits kept coming. In 1963 there were four hits, and in 1964 the total was a staggering six. The following year it went down to four and that set the pattern for every year until 1970. It meant Cliff was rarely out of the charts. He was never missing from the public ear.

Cliff comments, 'All through my career I have always had pretty much the last word on what I record, although I don't lay down the rule.

'Peter Gormley still tells me if he thinks that I am wrong and if he is forceful enough about it, then I usually succumb. When I worked with Bruce as producer he also had a big say. If everyone is against what I feel, then I give in willingly.'

The prolific hit period from 1963 onwards saw chart-toppers like 'The Next Time', 'Bachelor Boy', 'Summer Holiday', 'The Minute You're Gone' and 'Congratulations'. Somehow Cliff could sing in the familiar way and manner when the rest of the pop scene was raging with the Beatles of *Sergeant Pepper*, the Stones, Who, Animals, flower power, acid rock, West Coast sounds, blues, the birth of Pink Floyd and Led Zeppelin. Though they all made the news he continued with the hits.

He says in reflection, 'I know a lot of people hated me for doing the Eurovision-type numbers, particularly "Congratulations". They thought it was a terrible compromise, but the fact is that there were 400 million viewers when I performed that song and you just can't argue with those viewing figures.

'I've never considered recording something because I think the style or the trend is paramount. For me the song itself counts. Actually I don't know if you've heard how I'd heard "Love Me Do" from the Beatles in the early sixties. Now that was a good song. I really liked it. I never dreamed that the Beatles would be a hit, particularly with a name like that. I thought "insects!" Anyway I took "Love Me Do" to South Africa with me. I took it to all the studios and every time they said "Can we play the record for you?' I said, "Yes, please", and I'd hand over "Love Me Do". And I'm sure it didn't help their career in general but I always think that I had a part in it in South Africa!'

Cliff's Christian commitment may have hastened his split from the Shadows, but whatever the market research group may say it didn't really change the kind of song he sang. Norrie Paramor remained his producer and was so until 1973. His song lyrics did start to change from the time of 1969 – 'Throw down a Line' was more socially conscious though quite polite when compared with other rock scene material coming from people like MC5, Jefferson Airplane and Doors.

However the research sample group is right in suggesting Cliff's momentum was running down, but in terms of actual chart and sales achievement Cliff still ran strongly. It was not until midsummer 1971 that one of his songs failed to reach the top thirty.

The dubious honour for this belongs to 'Flying Machine'. In relation to other songs it hardly deserved the fate!

There was still life left in the old but ever young man! 'Living in Harmony' reached number 12 in 1972 and thanks to a return visit to Eurovision circles there was a number four placing for 'Power to all our Friends'. But just before this real calamity had occurred when 'Brand New Song' failed to chart. It was the first record made without Norrie Paramor.

Norrie commented in 1978, 'We'd had a lot of fun and a lot of success, but I felt Cliff had reached the stage where he should work with a younger producer. I knew that it was time for me to move on, although I was sorry to see the end of our partnership.

'I remember the day when I decided to put Cliff in a studio with an orchestra instead of with the Shadows. I can still remember his face when he walked in and there were about forty-five musicians sitting around waiting for him to arrive! However, he enjoyed the experience.

'The first song we did was "I'm Looking out of the Window" – and after that he liked the idea of using strings on his recordings. We also started doing the same thing with the Shadows' records.'

The period from 1973 until early 1976 was not happy from the point of view of hits, high chart placings and sales. For a time Dave Mackay produced and the partnership came up with the very much underrated album *Thirty-first of February Street*. That album actually laid the foundation for Cliff's return to major contemporary prominence via 'Devil Woman' in February 1976.

There was another slipped disc in 1975 when 'It's Only Me You've Left Behind' missed out on the charts. The 'Honky Tonk Angel' fiasco followed and certain sections of the Press, general and music, had a field day. There were those who said they could not believe Cliff would one day record a song about loose-living girls. And now he had. Naturally they were not saddened. Obviously from their oceans of copy they were happy but alas, they did not say so.

Quite what happened remains in doubt and there are a number of conflcting accounts and statements. However it seems Cliff was not conversant with what the term honky tonk could mean. The major upshot of the affair was a definite cooling towards the record. It was another slipped disc in the U.K. while in the world at large it did rather well.

Fortunately the dark days appeared more or less over with the charting of the spine-chilling 'Miss You Nights' in February 1976 and the album *I'm Nearly Famous* in May of the same year.

Said Cliff, 'It was really up for grabs who produced me around this period. Peter said that the first person to come up with the right songs could produce me.'

The producing angel of mercy and release was nearby. It was Bruce Welch of the Shadows.

'Cliff wasn't averse to a change of musical style, what was important was the fact that he should love all the songs,' said Bruce.

'When we first went into the studios it wasn't with the idea of making an album at all. On the first session we put down three songs and they were all successive hits – "Miss You Nights", "Devil Woman" and "Can't Ask for Anything More". We were looking for a single but ended up making an album.

'I think the great thing which came from our sessions when we were making *I'm Nearly Famous* onwards was that Cliff became much more interested in his career.

'For a long time he had just been going into a recording studio and putting down the vocals to a pre-recorded track and then going home again. He realized recording techniques had changed and started sitting in throughout the entire recording sessions.

'After all Cliff had been making records for more than sixteen years. My object was to make him see that he had started as a recording star, and take him back to those roots.'

Cliff was so excited with 'Miss You Nights' that he postponed his planned trip to Russia. Rock star Elton John was reported to be quite crazy about the record. He released the single in the States on his own Rocket label.

The album's self-deprecating title was another positive plus. E.M.I. records man Brian Southall thought *I'm Nearly Famous* was memorable and E.M.I. staff seemed just as revitalized and excited as Cliff was.

Cliff waxed eloquent and talked miles of tape on his *I'm Nearly Famous* spectacular. 'It's the best thing I've done for years. It may be the only hit album I'll have had in years.

'And I was excited. It was like a new thing. I would meet students and they would actually talk about music to me, whereas before it was like a joke. "Oh," people said, "didn't know he did that sort of stuff." All kinds of people were knocked out by this album.'

Even the International Cliff Richard Movement caught this sense of 'didn't know he did' for in the July 1976 issue of *Dynamite* they began their review of the album and of the first track with, 'If you walked into a party while "I Can't Ask for Anything More than You" was on the turntable, you'd just laugh if someone said it was Cliff. The funky super-cool, high-pitched vocals belong to our Cliff. This, and most of the other songs too, really stretch Cliff's vocal range.'

'Devil Woman' followed. It was a monster hit, giving Cliff another market, the disco world. The media buzzed with Cliff. He appeared on all the major TV and radio pop promotional outlets. A new day was dawning.

The following year saw release of the album *Every Face Tells a Story*. Brian Southall of E.M.I. wrote, 'While Cliff Richard was achieving even more fame and fortune with his truly memorable

I'm Nearly Famous album and his string of hit singles, it mustn't be forgotten that E.M.I. were also rewarded handsomely for their efforts during the last year.

'In addition to the satisfaction of reestablishing Cliff as a major force in British rock music, David Munns, marketing manager of the Group Pop, Repertoire Division, and his team, deservedly won the *New Musical Express* award for the best marketing campaign in 1976.

'We had great music supported by a great marketing campaign – virtually an unbeatable combination, and now we are gearing ourselves into that position again.

'Cliff has done his bit . . .'

You could hear the grunts of support for miles from the huge record company's headquarters in London's Manchester Square.

The music press loved it. So did the public. Yet the euphoria of this period was slightly misplaced for the old times of hit after hit were not forthcoming. Dark days still remained. There was another lurch and it was worse than the previous one.

'My Kinda Life', a Cliff and Bruce song from the *Every Face Tells a Story* album, reached number 15 in the singles chart. The follow-up was a touching ballad 'When Two Worlds Drift Apart'. It reached a mere 46. Then came real disaster of a magnitude which Cliff had never previously known. It was a cruel finale to the hopes and joys which had been raised since the late winter of 1975.

Cliff wanted to release a religious song as his next single. It came from his album *Small Corners*, issued in November 1977, and was an excellent gospel record. 'Yes He Lives!' was the title. It had the authentic beaty pop feel. It was ignored. It didn't chart. Cliff was hurt, more so because he badly wanted the world to hear the record's message.

He says, 'I tried to do an album that is in exactly the same bag as *I'm Nearly Famous* and *Every Face Tells a Story*. I tried to find some really good songs. The fact that they happen to have depth of meaning is I think a plus factor.'

He knew there were problems. 'All I have to do is get past the DJs, because I believe the DJs say to themselves, "oh well gospel format, not for my breakfast show", but they haven't heard "Why Should the Devil Have all the Best Music', "Hey Watcha Say" or

"I Wish We'd All Been Ready", or any of the songs, and they're just great songs. I'm so overboard about them . . .'

However the DJs quaked and the producers pretended not to know.

In his London office Cliff told us, 'I think you could say all my religious records have been failures – when issued as singles.'

He smiled momentarily and then laughed. 'Life is short and there is no point in forcing things. But the response to say "Yes He Lives" was really disappointing. I mean look at "Brand New Song", "When Two Worlds Drift Apart" and "Throw Down a Line". I felt like screaming about their being ignored. After all God sent Jesus, the most important fact in the world. I want to tell people of that.'

He does; but in the form of hit pop singles the message was not for telling.

Green Light was issued in October 1978. It produced if nothing else headlines like 'Green Light for Success'. It was the third album produced by Bruce. It hurled Cliff once more back into the general musical fray. Well, so the reviewers said. The public remained unmoved. The singles disaster area continued. There were slipped discs all over the place.

'Can't Take the Hurt Anymore' didn't chart. 'Green Light' spent three weeks in the then extended industry chart of the Top 75 and went no further than 57.

Yet again however there was light at the end of the tunnel. A whole series of media happenings took away the sting of the singles failure. Cliff and the Shadows reunited for a season at London's Palladium which was an instant sell-out. An album followed. E.M.I. issued the *40 Golden Greats* with a superb marketing campaign. No one waited for Cliff's twenty-first anniversary in the music business. His twentieth year in 1978 released an avalanche of tributes from the music press.

Cliff and the Shadows were honoured by Europe's most influential music trade paper *Music Week* at their yearly dinner at the Dorchester. The media queued for interviews and Cliff told the history of his years.

'I was back. "We Don't Talk Anymore" was a five million seller. I was number one in Britain for the first time in eleven years. Marvellous.' So says Cliff and there were beaming smiles everywhere. The media ran a solid barrage of articles proclaiming, 'Cliff does it again'. And it was now 1979. Bruce produced the single. In every way it was how quality pop should be, with the right touch of commerciality.

Cliff was the perfect white rock 'n' roll singer. He had excellent pitch and purity of tone. He showed consummate skill in handling words and tune.

Melody Maker editor of the time, Richard Williams, spent half a page extolling the record's virtues and from the more hardened punk, new-wave quarters there was grudging approval.

Williams pointed out the superb nature of the backing track with the on-the-beat drums and the haunting synthesizer, and felt the delightful sparse production was one of the best pieces of work in the history of pop.

Cliff told B.B.C. Radio One's *Newsbeat* man of the time Richard Skinner (now a fully-fledged Radio One DJ rather than a reporter) that although the song had become a disco hit, as well as a pop smash, it wasn't intended for that market in the first place.

He says, 'It appears on my album *Rock 'n' Roll Juvenile* but that wasn't intentional. I'd started recording the album, which I wanted to go in a specific direction, and when they said to me, "We need a single now," Terry and I said, "Don't rush us, we're not ready. We don't have one ready for you." Then Bruce found an Alan Tarney song. I listened to it and got goose pimples, which is a good sign. Bruce had them as well, so we both went into the studios and recorded it in about forty-eight hours.'

It was inspired spontaneity but then this process has brought into being many great records.

As Cliff says from his vast experience of records and recording, 'You can't really plan a number one. I'll be singing "We Don't Talk Anymore" for ages, maybe not in the same style but the song is good. It's going to be here for a long time.

'I'm not sure though that it's my best record. I think that "Devil Woman" is going to remain my favourite.'

So the stopgap single brought Cliff his biggest sales success ever. He sang the song at Greenbelt, the now massive Christian music festival which covers a wide range of subjects and idioms. It seemed right that Cliff the Christian should celebrate the best thing in the singles market for eleven years in such a gathering. The 17,000 audience agreed.

'I consider myself a current Christian singer who sings songs like "We Don't Talk Anymore" but I also have in my repertoire a few more overtly Christian songs. The religious world, for want of a better phrase, has some really fantastic singers and musicians who are denied worldwide fame because the world is not as free as we are musically. They still think that rock 'n' roll is something and gospel is something else . . . It's the Christian world which needs to come out and say, "Look we're rock 'n' roll singers and we want to sing about God in our own way." '

Naturally *Rock 'n' Roll Juvenile* was a success. Alan Tarney was the bass player and he produced the next Cliff album, *I'm no Hero*. 'As for the title,' Cliff commented, 'I tried to find another anti-title. I liked *I'm Nearly Famous* because it was tongue in cheek and I thought there aren't many heroes in the world, and I'm certainly not one of them. And I thought it's just a nice title so I had an idea for a boxing motif and there I stand with my knock knees with boxing gear on — Lonsdale shorts and stuff. I tried to make the sleeve describe what the album's like, just a fun album . . .'

It too has been a major seller and from it have come the massive-selling singles 'Dreamin' ' and 'A Little in Love'. Those two tracks plus 'Suddenly' (with Olivia Newton-John) from the *Xanadu* film sound track gave Cliff three records at one time in the *Billboard* Hot 100, and paved the way for his 1981 U.S. success story.

Cliff has covered a lot of ground between 1958 and 1981. He dislikes being placed in any particular musical bag. In the beginning he was the lad who was attracted by the rawness and energy of rock 'n' roll. He was a kid without real rebellion for he loved his family and rock 'n' roll wasn't his way of rebelling. Initially his music and stage shows caused some sections of the Press to urge parents not to let their offspring see him, though his appeal was soon wide and the music accordingly became mostly softer.

'I can't say that I actually planned it that way. You can't plan as such. I suppose one could analyse it by looking back at my career but it was a challenge for me – to make sense to all ages. The only way you can do it is to go the whole gamut of rock 'n' roll.

'I think I'm ordinary really. The only thing I do know is that out of my throat comes this noise that people like.'

Cliff these days hopes he can sing 'When I Survey the Wondrous Cross' side by side with other music without it seeming the 'gospel spot'; and there is always the comforting thought that he's seen off most musics and fashions.

'I don't know that I've seen them off, I've joined in with them. I've been having an affair with rock 'n' roll for a long time. I've liked rock 'n' roll in all its aspects and to me it's a musical culture and not just a tempo. For me as a vocalist rock 'n' roll is so wide,' Cliff says. 'I can keep on as long as my voice lasts out.' And of course, provided the hits keep rolling. They have since 1958 with just a few slipped discs.

CHAPTER ELEVEN

International Cliff

The stage suit was carefully handled, neatly folded and hung on a battered coat-hanger in the dressing room wardrobe. He changed into sweater and slacks.

'Wow! you know, I've been eating corned beef like mad recently because it said 240 calories on the outside of the tin and I thought it was non-fattening until I discovered just how fattening 240 calories can be. I think I'll have a quick omelette for lunch.'

Still, as he had said a few moments previously, he had lost three pounds thanks to an instant diet. Pop reporter Ian Dove from *Record Mirror* was less concerned with Cliff's midriff than with how the 22-year-old looked so fresh. After all, Cliff had only been back from the United States for a day or so and since then he had had long consultations with Peter Gormley and had rehearsed, with his usual zeal and professionalism, his coming stage present-ation at London's Palladium. It was October 1962.

'Coming home is as good as a rest. We've been working hard in America. I've done about seven cities in two weeks, and that means starting at breakfast and meeting the press, doing radio and television shows from nine a.m. until nine p.m.

'I believe our American visit is paying dividends – which is unlike what happened when I first went over, when I was right down at the bottom of the bill.

'I am satisfied with my home country. There's nothing in America that I want. It would just be a feather in my cap, a kind of challenge.'

His expression of satisfaction with dear old Britain was doubtless felt but it was also a good public relations comment. Cliff's home-based fans were not too keen at the thought of their artist being taken over by others – across either the Channel or the Atlantic. They wanted Cliff for themselves.

With some successful pop groups and artists fans have little cause to worry. Cliff though, like the Beatles, was different. Almost from the start he was international property. America was just one of the markets clamouring for his records and his presence. One album and six singles preceded his first top-of-the-bill foray overseas. Scandinavia was first on the schedule sheet. The tour took place in October 1960 and was not without immediate problems. Tony Meehan had to have an appendix operation. Laurie Joseph took his place.

There was one week in the early sixties when Cliff topped the charts of six overseas countries. 'Lucky Lips', released in May 1963, gave him the number one spot in Israel, South Africa, Sweden, Holland, Norway, and Hong Kong. The magazines called him, with slight generosity, 'The World's Most Wanted Man – in the pop world that is', and asserted that he was 'the greatest INTERNATIONAL British singer – and certainly as big in the world ratings as any American – including Elvis!'

Cliff fans purred assent.

These days the tall and imposing Peter Jones is U.K. News Editor for *Billboard*, the trade paper of the giant U.S. music industry. In 1963 he was a pop paper reporter. He remembers Cliff in South Africa and looking back after all this he still radiates enthusiasm and incredulity that a mere twenty-year-old should achieve such world prominence so soon.

'I remember Cliff in South Africa. He caused more mob-gathering, more riot-raising, more honest to goodness noises of appreciation than most political revolutions. He took the place by storm. He could have stayed for a lifetime.

'And what's more, he did more good for British pop music than anyone can imagine. He waved a flag. He took over a whole country.

'Do you ever read anything derogatory about Cliff? Have you ever heard of him being off-handed? Or big-time? Or indulging in the favourite show business pastime of running down competitors? Or even throwing a tantrum? Of course a lot is due to the excellent and understanding management.

'I remember Cliff appearing in the office just after his first-ever record had hit the shops. I remember him coping with a massed Press conference at the time. In between these two meetings, one so informal, the other so charged with formality, he had nothing but success. Worldwide success.

'From £20 per week to more like £2,000 – and the brown-eyed, dark-haired bachelor boy hadn't changed at all. I once said "I don't know if you like oysters Cliff, but the world's your personal oyster." '

It was this image which guided various persons to suggest Cliff might give a very special concert in the East African country of Kenya on 11 February 1963. It was held in Nairobi and was in aid of Kenya's under-privileged children. It received the imprimatur of Kenyan leader Tom Mboya.

Cliff, at the time, was extremely popular in this African country. Months later the Kenyan *Sunday Post* said Cliff had topped its Kenya Top of the Pops poll. Largely instrumental in furthering Cliff in Kenya was the British Forces Broadcasting Service, normally known simply as B.F.B.S. A DJ of the time (now Programme Director of South Yorkshire's very successful commercial radio station Radio Hallam), Keith Skues, says Cliff achieved his East African success because nothing was too much trouble for him.

'He didn't have too much time while in Kenya but he gave B.F.B.S. his special attention and of course we were heard throughout the country. I remember four Nairobi teenagers – Gillian Duncan, Valerie Flatt, Karen Bell and Valerie Maskell – being absolutely knocked out by him. They interviewed him for one of our shows and I did my stuff with him earlier in the day at the concert.

'We received many complimentary phone calls about its success and in response to numerous requests it was repeated the following Sunday afternoon.'

Skues, now years later still slimly built and maintaining a DJ's rapidity of speech, says Cliff was one of many stars who came out with the hope of finding African success. Cliff, he still feels, was different from most others.

'He looked good. He was polished. He had a varied offering.

124

He had a genuine air about him. He had professionalism, everything had to be right. And then he had time for everybody. That matters when you're overseas. I mean here he was a major world star, he could have had an arrogant air but he didn't. People liked him. There was time for everybody whatever the work load.

'I remember a few years later. I was walking down London's Savile Row, the street which had Cliff's management offices. He was on the other side of the road from me and he saw me. He let out a yell, "Cardboard Shoes!" I've met up with him subsequently. He makes friends. It's an invaluable asset, really is.'

In those early days Cliff recorded many of his songs in foreign languages. Nowadays he remembers this with some amusement. Between words he chuckles.

'I used to record my hits in German, French, Italian, Spanish – even some Japanese crept in. I couldn't speak the languages. I sometimes wonder what they made of them! But then they bought the records, amazing really.'

He laughs at the memory but he knows it helped. It gained him respect. People felt that he had gone out of his way to communicate on their level. He wasn't just a show business foreigner out for every penny he could get.

'I did it all by phonetics – you know where you learn to imitate the sounds of the lyrics. French and Spanish were the easiest ones to come to grips with.'

Not surprisingly German with its many throat-clearing gutturals provided him with most difficulty. No matter, struggle or no struggle, Cliff's attempts at foreign languages were the best commercial plus for him at the time. They gained him air play. They pitted him against the locals. He wasn't an ordinary damn foreigner. They served him well.

'I reckon it's fairly easy to make hit records once you have the formula but it's the individual who has to make something of himself. Since quite early in my career I did have a definitely long-term attitude.

'It's a problem, though, keeping all the countries happy. They all want you and from early times I was popular all over the place.

'It's easy to lose territories. For a time you can sell records but in the end you have to go and let yourself be seen and heard. I lost

125

the German market. I stopped going there, not for any particular reason, but it was difficult to fit things in.

'I stopped going to Germany for nine years. I've regretted that. It just seemed that every time I wanted to go something else would happen.

'So in 1977, maybe 78, I said to E.M.I. that I wanted Germany to happen for me. I suppose it was a good time, with some strong records coming out. Well, it has happened and I'm knocked out. I'm back in the *Award* listings and at the age of forty-one in the top three with the young stars of today.

'I'm glad those early days gave me this world base. It wasn't easy. It was hard work. You know the routine of flight, airport, car, hotel, rehearsal, concert, hotel, car, airport and off to somewhere else. Still, we had some great times, we really did.

'Japan is another place I've a little neglected. But what do you do when so many things happen? Places like Hong Kong, South Africa, Holland and Australia have always remained loyal.'

He could have added some less likely places – Korea, the Eastern bloc countries nd amazingly Russia, the massive country which has played host to a mere handful of Western pop artists.

Year in and year out Cliff has sung for his supper somewhere other than the U.K. and with his Christian interests increasing from 1966 onwards some territories have fought for either a secular or religious tour. In 1964 he toured Europe along with the Shadows, including a week at the Paris Olympia. In 1965 there were visits to Spain, Switzerland and France. The next year he toured behind the Iron Curtain, and in 1968 Turkey, Hawaii, Israel, Australia, Japan and Spain saw Britain's top pop star.

Before the sixties had come to an end Cliff had visited Germany, Japan, Norway, Israel, Rumania, Czechoslovakia, South Africa, Scandinavia and Holland once more. That he should go anywhere at all was amazing, considering that the last half of the sixties saw him involved not merely in hit records but a plenitude of TV and radio shows, films, plays, gospel lectures, media presentation, general cabaret including various seasons at London's Talk Of The Town and the London Palladium, and the time-consuming activity of the Eurovision Song Contest.

Russia was the event of the seventies, though there was a

sudden splurge of interest from the United States just past the halfway mark which for a time looked as if it might be Cliff's long sought-after breakthrough.

Some 91,000 Russians heard Cliff via twelve concerts in Leningrad and eight in Moscow, with several matinees in both cities. At Leningrad the stage and orchestra pit were level and therefore accessible to the audience. Such was the hysteria on the opening night that the orchestra pit was dropped by some feet for subsequent performances.

'It went fantastically well, amazing reception. I think it certainly proved rock 'n' roll is an international language. It was a marvellous opportunity,' says Cliff.

Peter Gormley was stunned by the reception given Cliff. 'It was just fantastic – Cliff was absolutely knocked out. It was even more amazing considering his records were not even on sale in Russia at that time.'

The £8 tickets fetched £40. It was a case of 'comrade' Cliff rocking the Reds, though one song was removed from the tour programme. It was 'Love Train'.

The major objection to this seemingly harmless bland homage to universal togetherness came because the lyric mentions the state of Israel with which Russia has no diplomatic relations. It might be argued that Israel is speedily dispatched as are most other named places in this song, which was popularized for the Western hit parades by the black Philadelphia group the O'Jays. This and other arguments were put to no avail. 'Love Train' did not run in Cliff's Russian shows.

Cliff's visit had been requested by the Russians. They had seen him perform in Copenhagen and they liked his style. He was considered the most acceptable of Western artists.

'It's only because I don't smash up hotel rooms,' is how Cliff sees it, though he didn't look too serious when saying this.

So there he was on the late August evenings of 1976 on stage as the first invited Western pop artist in the Soviet country. He wore his white suit which looked a dream as he still sported a Barbadian suntan handily acquired some weeks previously. He moved in his usual fashion.

One Russian girl told a British pressman, 'It's the way he moves that's so exciting.' It was like yesteryear, only then the audience was British and it was 1958, with Cliff eighteen, not thirty-six.

Payment was mostly in roubles. Hard currency was limited but everyone agreed the tour was not for money. It was an experience and it opened the possibility of record sales. For the general Western music business the Cliff visit suggested promising sales days ahead.

While Russia for its very uniqueness stands out as the international event for Cliff and perhaps the British music business as a whole during the seventies, Cliff himself seems more affected by the short tour he made the same year in Asia.

At first it took him back home to the sprawling and heavily populated land of India. There he soon knew that many young Indians who are familiar with Western pop culture fervently claim him as part theirs. He was born on their soil.

Public appearances were made in Kalamandir Stadium, New Delhi, on 7 and 8 December 1976. The show bore the advertised title 'A New Message, A New Song'.

For much of the time he was involved in Tear Fund activity, outside the musical sphere, but what he saw in Bangladesh had an indirect effect on his career. Appropriately enough the chapter in his religious autobiography which deals with this visit is titled 'I'll Never Be the Same Again'.

He says he felt at one moment that it seemed almost a cheat that he should return to Britain and resume his career as Cliff Richard – the International Pop Star.

'It was all so easy. I would go ahead and do my twenty concerts for Tear Fund and raise £25,000 and I'd enjoy every minute of it. Compared to what others were contributing it seemed so puny.

'I see now that that was illogical but it took one of the girls to help me realize it. "Without you and other Christians at home," she said, "we wouldn't be here! We need each other." That was real consolation at the time and the words stuck.'

Cliff says he learned the simple fact that in real cold terms he had nothing to contribute in Bangladesh. Yes, he could sweep floors. So can others. True, he could hump materials around but then it's a task most can do. Few though can command the kind of audience and respect which he has in show business. Cliff decided

128

to remain in the world of popular and gospel music and he continues contributing and raising large sums of money for Tear Fund.

For E.M.I. Head of Marketing John Cabanagh worldwide Cliff is a precious possession.

'He's one of the few whom you can speak of anywhere in the world and they know the name. No discussion. No questions. They know Cliff.

'We have what we call local companies virtually everywhere and if we do not have a specific office then someone represents us.

'The marvellous thing about Cliff from a selling point of view is the number of markets which can be tapped. He has fans right across the musical board.

'He's been with us at E.M.I. since he began and the same is true worldwide save for a few years in America. He had some success just after the mid-seventies with Rocket – Elton John's company – but when he signed a new deal with us it was an international deal.

'He's always relevant. There's a constant cry from overseas for a Cliff visit. His records are always being released and foreign licensees can choose their own way of issuing material.

'Internationally he's big. Actually these days he sells more units in Germany than the U.K. I'm not saying he's a bigger artist there, merely in sales terms.

'Japan and France are big. His best-selling single in France has been a record which was never issued in that form in the U.K. – "Early in the Morning".

'The States have always been tricky, it takes an eternity to come big there. But look at the last four or five years and you'll see quiet but growing record market penetration by Cliff. He can sell in millions over there. He had three records in the early 1981 U.S. *Billboard* Hot 100 charts.

'Then again he's someone who can capture the feel of other homegrown culture. I mean when you hear "The Minute You've Gone" you realize he could be an acceptable country singer. He doesn't sing another idiom badly. He has a Latin feel which the continentals like. Let's face it, Cliff's appeal is astronomical. It's amazing really and a lot of people use that adjective but who else makes sense to Japanese, Koreans, Germans, Italians, Australians? What diversity!'

With Cliff it's not so much a question of where he has been, rather where he has not. Where would he go next?

'China, it would be interesting,' he says.

So it would, if international Cliff could find the time.

CHAPTER TWELVE

Religion – Ode to Billy

The gulf between Church and people in Britain had been widening for more than a generation. Church attendances were declining. The drift from the Church was touching all sections of the community.

Clergymen wrote increasingly of their amazement at the indifference to religion expressed by the young and their ignorance of the Christian faith.

Others were complaining of a sharp decline in the observance of moral standards, and they instanced a growth in crimes against the person, in juvenile delinquency and in sexual laxity.

Some of course blamed the impact of two great wars for the disintegration of religious life in Britain. Others said that the aloofness of the working classes from church life was hardly the consequence of two wars, however terrible they had been in terms of loss of human life. They traced the problem's beginning back to the industrial revolution.

So the arguments raged in the British Christian community in the early fifties and in fuller form they found their way into a book by C. T. Cook, *London Hears Billy Graham.*

Billy was a young American of unimpeachable record. He was known for his strict morality. Why, he even said, he didn't kiss his wife Ruth until they were engaged. Billy was a solid evangelical. He knew where he stood. It was with the Bible. He believed he taught what the Bible said. When he preached his long sermons he would continually say 'the Bible says', for it was his authority.

He was an orator, not exactly of the old school, more akin to, though not quite like, a super-salesman. He was charming. He was eloquent. The cynical said he was just like some of the old-time preachers who made converts and took their money. These critics said Billy sold Jesus as a product and took himself a mighty salary from the free-will offerings which flowed from those who had made their decision for Jesus.

Most of the Christian leaders and writers of the fifties spoke differently. They saw that he was a man of God with a definite calling for this age. They saw him as a man of dedicated spirit, with a passionate desire to make people face up to the reality of Jesus's claims and the consequences for their lives, their families and the country at large.

They welcomed him when he arrived in Britain and conducted a massive campaign of revivalist meetings. These gatherings were simple in outline. There was a huge choir which led the singing of noisy and boisterous hymns. There was a soloist named George Beverly Shea, a man equipped with a rich baritone voice which could silence the cynic, at least as long as George sang. There were people who came on stage and spoke of how their Christian faith meant everything to them. And there was Billy, good-looking, suave, cultured, with a resonant voice and radiating conviction. He didn't roast the listeners over the fires of hell like preachers of old, but he posed life and death questions.

It was in the spring and early summer of 1954 that Billy conducted his first Christian campaign in Britain. Rock 'n' roll was just beginning to breathe. Bill Haley was emerging and Elvis would soon come on the scene. Harry Webb was thirteen at the time. He didn't hear Billy this time around. He was more concerned with playing football and being an ideal son for his hardworking parents.

'There was a Bible about the house. I don't remember my father talking to me about faith. I was conscious of Christian things but that was all.

'I had been baptized and brought up as an Anglican. I had been taught my religion in school but I remember when I was fourteen refusing to go to confirmation classes.

'I had rejected religion, or rather I had rejected what most people take for religion but which to me seemed no more than lip service to the Christian code.

'I was, I suppose looking back, a kind of dormant Christian. It's funny really – I say now in the 1980s that many kids do not give Christianity a chance. They say it's a stupid staid thing. But I don't know if I gave things a chance when I was younger!'

He didn't dream that one day a pop writer called Jan Iles would in a flight of racy journalism write, 'From Living Doll to Living Legend? Rebel to Christian? Raunchy, Risqué Baby-Faced Rock 'n' Roller to Mature Balladeer.'

Or, of course, that one June day in 1966 he would stand next to American Billy Graham as he conducted a further series of revival meetings, this time at Earls Court. Or that he, the one-time Harry Webb, would bewail the ungodliness in British society.

Cliff did at least grow up aware of religion. It was through several members of his family and his group the Shadows that his dormant interest in Christian things wakened, so much so that at one point he considered joining the heretical Christian body who call themselves Jehovah's Witnesses.(They, of course, would deny any charge of hereticism and would call into question the beliefs of orthodox Christendom.)

Cliff's sister Jackie is a Jehovah's Witness. Donna almost became one. Cliff's mother was baptized into the movement. Within the Shadows interest in the movement came from Liquorice (Brian) Locking and then from Hank Marvin.

Hank says, 'I'd always been a fairly directionless person and didn't need a path, but like everyone else sometimes I sit down and I wonder what I'm doing here. I always felt that life went on no matter what but that there had to be an answer to it all.

'Jehovah's gave me that answer . . . Jehovah's believe there are things that are totally wrong – they don't have the confusion most other churches have.'

Cliff says, 'What attracted me to the Jehovah's Witnesses was Liquorice Locking leaving to join the movement. It made me think.

'And then there was the time when with the Shadows I was touring in Australia. Dad had died and I had this desire to make contact with him. I thought I would go to a spiritualist seance.'

Liquorice thought he was making a mistake and said so clearly, and it was the way he explained his reason which made Cliff take notice.

He asked whether Cliff had ever bothered to find out what the Bible said about this. Cliff had not. He was then shown a number of Bible passages, some of which suggested dire consequences for those consulting mediums.

Not surprisingly this discussion about spiritualism veered into general religious questions of belief. Informal Bible studies became frequent amongst the touring Shadows and Cliff. They were joined by some of Liquorice's friends. It was 1961.

Cliff was now an established international star. Outwardly he had everything which any kid who dreamed of fame and riches could imagine. Yet something was wrong. The *Daily Express* caught the scent of personal upheaval beneath the outwardly smiling pin-up pop star.

On 14 December 1964 they headlined: Cliff Richard Thinks About God.

The *Express* staff reporter described Cliff standing near the gate of his £30,000 home in Nazeing, Essex, and reported his saying, 'I am thinking about God. This is a very personal thing. It was Liquorice Locking who set me thinking. I am not considering joining the Jehovah's Witnesses. Do you know what that means? It means being baptized in the faith. No, at the moment, I'm just thinking a lot about God. That's all. It's very important to me.'

And with that Cliff drove off in his American car ready for a day's filming on *Wonderful Life*.

'I became dissatisfied with things generally, and if you're upset in life, then it affects everything you do,' says Cliff. 'It was beginning to get me down. My whole career was affected.

'I spent two years with the Witnesses, listening to them. After a while I felt I was a Jehovah's Witness but for some reason I held back from baptism.'

It was now that another group of people came on the scene. It began by accident. Towards the end of 1964 Cliff visited his old English teacher Mrs Jay Norris. Cliff couldn't resist speaking about the Jehovah's Witnesses. Mrs Norris seemed unimpressed, though worried. She was a Roman Catholic whose ideas of God, Jesus and the Holy Spirit differed from the Witnesses'. She suggested Cliff should meet a bright young religious instruction

134

teacher from her school. Cliff agreed and a meeting was arranged at his house.

Jay came, together with the religion teacher, Bill Latham, and a friend of his on the school staff, Graham Disbrey. Cliff was not convinced by their arguments but was impressed with them as people.

David Winter in his book *New Singer, New Song* recalls what Cliff said about his feelings that evening. 'They were the first real Christians I had met, talking about the real thing, appealing only to the Bible, but interested in me as a person, not a scalp.'

Jay invited Cliff to a party where he met Bill once more. The upshot was an invitation given by Bill and a nod of assent from Cliff. The world pop star said he would come and look at the Christian activities which took much of Bill's time.

What followed next almost lies in the bizarre and its very eccentricity speaks volumes for the genuineness of Cliff's later orthodox Christian commitment.

There are those who constantly, even now, suggest that Cliff's Christian interest is merely a promotional gimmick. If so they must ask themselves why it was that a pop millionaire with millions of fans across the globe should begin a so-called promotional con by spending days, even weeks, with a bunch of teenagers, learning from them and their leaders of Christian things.

Cliff recalls that his former mates were struck numb with cold and awkwardness. It wasn't what they expected of a superstar. And the younger element – the people who bought his records and imagined from afar that he had all life's answers – what did they make of him drinking coffee from cardboard cups and sitting in a circle of intent Bible students?

Days and weeks stretched into months. Cliff had many questions needing answers. He had spent two years exploring the Jehovah's Witness faith within his own close circle of friends and it was most unlikely that he would commit himself without another thorough investigation. In any case, his busy, crowded career continued with its many engagements.

This time though there was a definite response. He had been appointed an assistant leader of his local church's branch of the Crusaders and when he could he would spend hours there with his new-found mates – schoolboys who had ceased wondering at the astounding fact that a pop and film star was around the place without expecting trumpets and fanfares.

Life was changing fast for Britain's long-lasting pop star. He took less and less interest in show business activities. He was noticed for his absence. He spent his time at Crusader meetings and sharing in their various social activities. David Winter says he even sang at St Paul's (his church) a version of 'Blowing in the Wind' and the older members hadn't a clue they were hearing someone who could fill stadiums as far away as the Far East, Australasia and the Americas. He recalls in his book how Cliff toured the local hospital wards at Christmas and one lady kindly remarked that he ought to take up singing full time.

In the sixties David Winter was a schoolteacher and a prominent member of St Paul's church. He became a journalist and eventually edited with considerable success a Christian monthly called *Crusade*. These days he's a senior religious producer for the B.B.C. He has always maintained a great personal friendship with Cliff.

'It was quite staggering really. Can you think of another star who was up to this kind of thing or anything remotely resembling it?

'Remember this was an artist who had done it all. Here he was, so casual, at the church with, if you like, ordinary folk, they didn't have to pay! He was so utterly genuine. It was quite remarkable. Don't mistake Cliff, he's a very determined person. He makes up his own mind.'

Cliff decided he would become a Christian. He felt he could say Jesus was his personal saviour. However the scene was not yet right for the appearance of American evangelist Dr Billy Graham. Cliff had heard the evangelist when he attended a Graham meeting incognito with his youth group. Like many Londoners at the time they wanted to know just what made this famous evangelist tick.

Somehow this activity was missed by the Press. They certainly did not miss out on the eventual public meeting between Billy and Cliff at Earls Court on the evening of 16 June 1966.

On that evening the 25-year-old pop star who was dressed

casually and soberly in his brown corduroy jacket told 25,000 people, 'I have never had the opportunity to speak to an audience as big as this before but it is a great privilege to be able to tell so many people that I am a Christian.

'I can only say to people who are not Christians that until you have taken the step of asking Christ into your life, your life is not really worthwhile. It works – it works for me!'

After he had finished his testimony which told of his new life and his commitment Cliff sang the familiar gospel song of personal witness 'It Is No Secret' which has the added punchline of 'what God can do'.

Outside Earls Court countless thousands of fans had gathered but they had been unable to gain admittance, for there were 'house full' signs everwhere. Cliff told them how he found Christian faith so utterly relevant.

Though Cliff's past Christian explorations and expeditions had escaped much attention the following morning's daily press and ensuing interest from weekly and monthly journals certainly made up for it.

But not everyone had been caught napping. Maureen Cleave in London's *Evening Standard* had remarked in December 1965 how Cliff's friends were mostly teachers and were interested in religion. Cliff had told her of his own Christian base.

'It's a kind of a way of life, it's a moral way of life. I've always tried to be a bit moral, a bit Christian and not ashamed of it.'

He spoke of reading the Bible nightly and of taking his Crusader group to Whipsnade, for trips in his Cadillac, and for a week the previous April sailing on the Norfolk Broads.

'It's a new way of life for me. I came into show business when I was seventeen and when you come in you lose your childhood immediately. I find all this specially fun because I never did youthful things.

'At the moment I feel dissatisfied. I don't get the same kick out of my life as I used to. I always said that if I didn't feel completely happy I would retire. I feel I could do more with my life.

'I would have to go to college for two years because I only got English Language in G.C.E. but then I would be equipped to teach English and Religious Education.'

The night after the Earls Court meeting much of the press picked up on the observations Cliff had made to Maureen Cleave. They wondered aloud whether Cliff the pop star had run his course. They saw the end. They shouted of possible retirement. Cliff fans frothed at the mouth. It was dreadful news for them. They wrote pleading letters. They bombarded the music press with anguish.

The fans had cause to ponder and wonder and shed some tears. In the *Daily Express* of 20 September 1966 writer David Wigg said, 'It is now generally known that Cliff Richard wants to retire from show business and teach religion in a school. These days he regularly telephones his office to say which days he must have off for either religious studies or religious work of some kind.'

Cliff said, 'I have always believed in God and always prayed, but that doesn't make me a Christian. Being a Christian, to me, has been a step I didn't realize I had to take.

'I've enjoyed every second of show businesss but now I've found something else I would like to get into.'

He told journalist Rhona Churchill, 'I was thrilled to be invited to sing and give my testimony at Earls Court, thrilled by the size of the audience, but scared to death. You see I couldn't rehearse my testimony. If I had it might have sounded like an act. So I went forward knowing what I wanted to say but not how I would say it.

'I steadied myself by gripping the lectern. Then when I tried to move my arms I found I couldn't. I had pins and needles.

'At church one day someone said to me that if I wanted to be a real Christian, I must go to church, testify to my faith and set aside a fixed time every day for Bible reading and prayer, as they did.'

Rhona Churchill concluded her feature by saying, 'But his faith is real. It is no publicity stunt. He merely feels it's his duty to testify to it when asked to do so.'

Later, a few years on, Cliff had put behind him thoughts of giving up show business and becoming an R.I. teacher. 'I'd like to be a successful evangelist. I would love it. But I don't think I could make it, I am not a leader.

'Show business is the only thing I can do properly. It is certainly the only thing I've succeeded at. It's good for me – I can sing a bit, and act a bit, and in show business all I have to do is what I'm told.

138

'I make the most of my career to do Christian things. I'm not just a pop singer. I'm a Christian pop singer. I don't like the permissive society. I am not shocked by it, but as an individual I am allowed to show my distaste.

'Before I became a Christian who knows what I was heading towards, greed, sexual lust, who knows . . .'

Reveille magazine writer Jan Reid says she found Cliff at that time the epitome of the man mothers would like their daughters to marry. 'Handsome, gentlemanly, well-groomed. To many young people Cliff is a bit of a square . . . Despite his religious fervour, Cliff must be one of Britain's most eligible bachelors.'

Cliff's association with Billy Graham led him into making the film *Two a Penny* for the Billy Graham Organization. It was not without immediate controversy.

'I didn't want paying. I saw it as an evangelistic effort. Union regulations compelled me to accept a fee, which I have returned to Dr Graham.'

The fee was £40 per week for ten weeks. Billy was proud of Cliff. He talked of Paul McCartney and Cliff. Paul disturbed the evangelist by proclaiming he had taken L.S.D. and that he had seen God through taking the hallucinatory drug.

Billy said, 'Cliff has found what I think Paul is looking for. My heart goes out to him. He has reached the top of his profession and now he is searching for the true purpose in life.'

Cliff's announced conversion led to numerous offers of Christian witness and work. For a brief period he appeared on television arguing for his faith. In A.B.C. TV's *Looking for Faith* series Cliff engaged in a dialogue with Paul Jones, former lead singer of Manfred Mann.

Jones said Cliff was letting himself be exploited by the Church. The programme itself had an opening sequence which stressed Paul's point. Jones had been in the film *Privilege* where he had acted a pop star cynically manipulated by the Church. An excerpt from this film began the programme and this was cut into a shot of real-life Cliff singing a hymn at a Billy Graham meeting.

Intellectually it was an unfair situation. Paul Jones had attended university. Robert Kee the interviewer had a similar background and was regarded at the time as one of television's most knowledgeable and perceptive interviewers. And there was Cliff, bright and verbally cogent but with no training in the finer points of semantics and debate. As it was he came through. His genuine witness won him respect even if in the battle of words he did not win the final comment.

Cliff was a guest on a number of similar programmes. Some might have argued it was often placing him in invidious situations, particularly when he talked at universities and colleges where there was always someone who could outwit him for words. Yet he survived and there are those who maintain that whatever the situation Cliff's basic sincerity would always win through and make a lasting impression on many.

Magazine interviews were easier for Cliff to handle. There was a situation where he could plainly say how he felt without intellectual riposte coming his way. Indeed the Christian message was heard in all kinds of quarters where previously it might have been regarded at best as quaint but possessing no relevance to the teenage girl whose greatest concern was with cosmetics and clothing.

His diary soon read quite unlike that of any other pop star. There were the expected items like routining, recording, photographs, the occasional press interview, radio and television and basics from time to time, the doctor, dentist and hairdresser. Then there were evening meetings – showing that Cliff was making forays into churches, schools and youth gatherings. Somehow he managed to pursue a pop career and witness at the same time.

Soon came invitations to speak at a variety of meetings and adult conferences, his involvement with Tear Fund, and gospel tours where the proceeds went towards the named charity.

He recorded several albums and cassettes during the seventies where he sang or put across the Christian message. He took part in a Japanese religious crusade and earned from Mary Whitehouse the comment, 'In my view he is precisely the type of young Christian one wants to see.'

It was the kind of remark which, while approved by some, did little to enhance Cliff's standing in the rock world, where it's never been too fashionable to express Christian sentiments. Much more in keeping is the profession of faith in some obscure cult.

By and large Cliff has escaped criticism but there have been a few problems. Sometimes he has deliberately courted the angry riposte.

He had hard words for those he termed 'Gay Lib banshees' who disturbed religious meetings in London and Lancaster University.

'They came in camping about and screaming and there were almost fights. The public hated them. I really prayed hard and said, "Please, God, don't let this turn into a fiasco."

'I wrote to them and suggested we had a meeting on neutral ground and no publicity. I said they could bring twelve of their thinkers and I would bring six of mine. I approached some friends and a couple of Christian workers but never had a reply to the letter.

'Everybody knows homosexuals exist, but I don't think an honest homosexual wants to be known as gay for a start. The homosexuals I've met – and I haven't met hundreds of them – are different from the Gay Lib people who come crashing in dressed as nuns or something.

'Don't think those people who take pills or who smoke marijuana are being tough. That's not toughness. It's weakness.

'Pop stars should show a greater responsibility for what they say and do.'

Such comments brought verbal comebacks but Cliff seemed perfectly happy to deal with whatever came. Less easy to deal with was the carping from some extreme quarters of Christian evangelism.

The Christian monthly *Crusade* has in its time carried some very bitter letters about the pop, gyrating Cliff.

For some Christians pop is anathema. It is the kingdom of the devil. They see its system perverting the minds of youth and encouraging immoral behaviour leading to eventual destruction of the spirit. They see rock music as ungodly. They regard dancing as one step towards worship of the flesh.

These days Cliff is far better able than he was at the outset to deal with carving knives from within the camp. He takes it all with a shrug of his shoulders but admits it gives him no pleasure and at times does cause him some distress. This is made worse by

141

the fact that in general his attackers are people who have never met him face to face and are not even prepared to declare their identities.

'You can only do what you feel is right and what they say doesn't add up to me,' Cliff says. 'I don't know what God has in mind for me in the future but at present I am sure I am doing His will where I am. I can only say, "here is me, this is what I am", but really in the end what matters is how people respond to Jesus.

'Through being in the pop world I believe I've brought the Christian message to masses of people who otherwise would have heard nothing. And, of course, on a very practical level I've been in part responsible for founding and ensuring the success of the Arts Centre Group where Christians in the media can talk and pray together, compare notes and gain strength.

'I am constantly thrilled by the Christian faith, and what we offer. Christian faith doesn't depend on your emotions. It's a stable solid factor. It gives us ground to feel confident and positive whatever happens.

'What we have is a reality, there are roots in the Christian faith. You can't live up there on some high plane, you have to come down to reality and survive in the world as we know it. I'm worried by some young people who think everything must be high all the time and they get so down when they find you can't shout hallelujah all the time. You have to work for a living and so on.

'I'm not trying to be high and mighty but I mean it, I know what I believe. If some people feel I've sold out or whatever then OK, they've sounded off but I'm confident.

'Some of the criticism comes because there are Christians who are genuinely frightened of all this media stuff. But I've used my career to further Christian things and books have been one of the recent means. There's my *Which One's Cliff?* and I've started Christmas annuals.'

Of course meeting the criticisms of rock fans on the pop level is another thing but since the album *I'm Nearly Famous* there has been a much more healthy regard for his music. He has become more contemporary and the sing-along days have to a great extent been pushed into the background.

Cliff frequently says he's a singer and that his whole object is providing entertainment. This attitude has resulted in the uncanny ability with which he has successfully courted up to five generations of fans. People come and they assume they will receive a wholesome show. It's not a sentiment which would necessarily be shared by the rock-oriented young. They expect some spice and a few verbal fireworks. They want the music and the presentation to give them a solid smack in the guts. And some expect their hero to take a definite political or social stance.

The Christian attitude to stage presentation does no more than expect the artist to be sincere and not misuse or exploit the audience for dubious ends; but as far as politics is concerned a definite concern for society and the individual is an intrinsic part of the Christian faith. It may well be that if Cliff wishes to make a late major impact upon rock-oriented kids he must dig for radical roots in the Bible. Certainly the evangelical Christian world is very conscious these days of social and political matters. It is true of an evangelist as persuasive and powerful as Billy Graham.

As it stands at the moment Cliff will never capture rock adoration and commitment as John Lennon did. Cliff has never dug as deeply into the ways in which people respond both to themselves and the world at large.

He may never trot out stirring sentences on major social issues but in the end that is his choice.

It seems churlish for some people to write off Cliff Richard as anaemic. Such criticisms are the product of condescending, spiteful minds. Cliff may not wax eloquent on racism or nuclear misuse but the time he gives to charity, the money which he donates to causes, is considerable. No other star of his stature devotes so much time to non-musical activities, and it is not totally his fault that he attracts some well-wishers who find scant sympathy among today's young people.

He has probably addressed more young people than any other Christian speaker of the past decade. Certainly his work is highly valued by Maurice Rowlandson who leads the continuing ministry of the Billy Graham Organization in Britain.

'I've known Cliff now for a long time. He's matured a great deal over the years. There is no one like him. For many youngsters he is good news. My two youngsters said to me one day that since I knew Cliff, why couldn't I get him to the house one day? He kindly agreed. There was a whole crowd of youngsters. He came and he stayed an hour and a half and he had them totally spellbound. The answers he gave to the many questions asked were fabulous.

'His whole contribution has been fantastic. He's always been ready to do what we've asked. He's always kept close contact with Dr Graham and although they come from different generations they have a rapprochement. And there's been all this work he's done for Tear Fund. I said jokingly once to Billy, "You needn't come back, we've Cliff." '

It's an assessment shared by people like David Winter, who also observes quite rightly, 'Cliff is a professional in everything he does. He's never casual when it comes to work. Gospel concerts have never been an extra to his so-called secular activities. He spends days with a band rehearsing those gospel programmes.'

Of course Cliff could easily stroll on stage with a guitar, serve up some three-chord magic, sing a few songs and, with a word of witness, depart. In fact he spends hours perfecting those concerts. The only real difference between gospel and secular according to many fans is the informality of the former. He chats and talks rather than presents.

Billy Strachan is the principal of Capernway Hall and is responsible with Cliff for one of the cassettes in the Scripture Union *Start the Day* series. Both were at Eurofest and Spree 73.

He is one of Cliff's admirers and says, 'People criticize the rock 'n' roll side of Cliff, but what have they got to offer in its place? You see, the people who say "We prefer the old hymns" little realize that when the hymns were written, they were in the music which was popular.

'So all Cliff is doing in the media is to satisfy what people want today. If you can't appreciate the new generation, don't enter it. You'll never satisfy everybody.

'Many Christians are critical of him but they don't know anything about him. Their criticism is from a distance, they don't know what he is achieving for Christianity, because he never tells anybody, so they are wrong. They condemn a man without giving him a hearing, and just because he does not do exactly what they

144

expect of him, to have their approval of him as a Christian or Spiritual person, they don't give it.

'Then Cliff Richard, like any Christian, has to learn to leave it between himself and the Lord and not between himself and the churches, and I think he is doing that.

'I have observed in him a strength of character and Christian growth that is lacking in many people.

'Watching his various appearances on television, I find he never has to bring up his faith, they always bring it up, and he is very open and honest in his response to the commentators.'

Ron Palmer of *New Christian Music* says Cliff is someone who sees his career as part of God's ordained plan for his life.

'It is clear that Cliff has a very healthy understanding of the Bible, which he has been able to translate into a well-balanced view of life.

'He, in turn, has been an encouragement to others in similar situations to express their faith and to develop it within the crucible of their own professions.'

Cliff himself is reticent about accepting the praise heaped on his shoulders. 'What I really want is to be seen to actually be this Christian that I claim I am – not so that people will say "What a sincere bloke Cliff Richard is", but simply so that Jesus will be noticed. What other people think of me is becoming less and less important; what they think of Jesus because of me is critical.'

This is how he ends his book *Which One's Cliff?* On stage one evening for a gospel concert he said, 'No Christians own Jesus. He belongs to absolutely everyone – anybody who is willing to say, "Jesus I know, you're there – I would like you to come into my life."

'I didn't know how he was going to come into my life, I asked him to do it, because I believed he could somehow. And he did. So it hurts, it upsets me sometimes when I meet people who know a great deal about Jesus, they know a great deal about the Church and yet somehow they just hold back. They hold back, because they will not step forward and say HELP – the magical word . . .'

He told us, 'My career comes second to Jesus. Nothing would really disappear if it all ended tomorrow. I don't think it *could* collapse, mind you, *that* quickly!

'No, it all depends on how you view life. I can survive without stardom. I like it but I have other things to do if it disappeared.

'I feel God is with me. If He said tomorrow that I should go and do something else, then I would whatever the pain. I've no ultimate fears. I don't fear for my career.'

The cynic will give a wry smile. Others will shout hallelujah! Whatever the case all this makes him a pretty unusual star.

Oddly enough, when E.M.I. Records researched for their *40 Golden Greats* Cliff Richard album they found that all groups spontaneously mentioned his Christian beliefs, and it was an aspect of which most people disapproved.

Some males resented his 'preaching' attitude. It was felt that post-conversion he had a much 'safer' style in his singing.

In the meantime he marches on and Billy is proud.

CHAPTER THIRTEEN

Fans – We Love You Cliff

Mrs Williams, a pensioner from Denton near Manchester, read her way through the Sunday newspaper. There was nothing particularly interesting until her eye caught the headline 'Cliff Scores a Big Hit with the Young Ones'.

The article described how forty-year-old Cliff was mounting a final campaign to conquer the United States. Mrs Williams knew her daughter would enjoy hearing about Cliff's adventures across the Atlantic.

Memories came back and she recalled, 'Cliff's not only *my* "special" but also my daughter's one and only star. She was fourteen when he was at the Apollo, Ardwick, and his film *Summer Holiday* was also showing.

'So Joan, that's her name, and her friend Mary had a beautiful cake made in the shape of a bus. I worked at the cinema at the time, so the manager arranged a meeting and was she pleased!

'The girls had photos taken with Cliff as he accepted the cake and from that day onwards his career has been followed with more than passing interest.'

Not all of the newspaper copy about Cliff's U.S. tour was pleasing. There was mention of how a truck containing £40,000 worth of guitars and sound equipment had been stolen.

It distressed Mrs Williams. She knew just how upset Cliff would be. He had arrived in good spirits and then he had this kind of greeting.

She let a few minutes slip by before saying, 'I would send him replacements if I could afford them but then I'm a pensioner. We think the world of him. I say *God bless Cliff*, so sincere and so kind to so many in so many countries.'

It's not the kind of comment you would hear said of many stars. Mrs Williams is typical of a great many followers of Cliff – there's almost a family feeling in their attitude, as if they would think nothing of it if he just popped in for tea. He would be Cliff. It sounds a trifle sentimental but that's the way it is.

Cliff is one of the few contemporary music stars whose fans range from pensioner to teenager. Also there is the strange hold he keeps on his fans, the majority of whom, at least in Britain as for example opposed to Germany, are female.

Joy Dyer of Stratford-on-Avon is thirty-three and she feels just as uplifted by him now as she was at eighteen. Year in and year out she's steadily built a Cliff record collection. In all that time there have been only two records which have not endeared themselves to her – 'Congratulations' and 'A Brand New Song'.

She met Cliff once, before a gospel concert in Reading. She felt that he was 'genuine' and it's a sentiment shared by many.

Linda Inman talks of being a fan since the age of nine and comments, 'No other entertainer has ever meant half so much to me. The point about Cliff is that he has always seemed so accessible, no big "I am a superstar" fuss . . . When you meet him he does appear to be genuinely nice, a silly word but it's hard to express it any other way . . .

'Despite all this ordinariness, he does have a magic which reduces one's knees to rubber.'

It's an effect which afflicts unmarried and married women. Indeed a great percentage of members of a Cliff fan club or meeting house seem happily and loyally wed. Nevertheless they retain more than a passing affection for this unmarried star who seems ageless and timeless. One cannot help wondering just how their husbands feel.

There are some fans who, when Cliff takes the stage, suddenly feel they are sixteen again, in mind and body. He makes time stand still for them and for some he may be 'considerate, helpful, reserved, talkative, charming, gentle, handsome' but he is still, simply, 'sexy'.

Viviane Mees of Belgium says quite simply that Cliff Richard 'is music, is faith, is a way of living' and quotes with approval his remark, 'God is only a prayer away'.

She adds, 'If it hadn't been for the faith I refound thanks to Cliff, I don't know what I would have done . . . He doesn't need scandals, sex, drugs, etc. to make headlines. His O.B.E. proves it. His music has lived for over twenty years: rock 'n' roll, ballads, gospel. His personality and voice convince. May God bless him and his loved ones.'

Jennifer Chatten of Harrogate, North Yorkshire, says, 'When Cliff received his O.B.E. it was an accolade richly deserved. While other stars reach their peak Cliff just gets better and better and never once has he let down his fans. In fact he has had a good influence on two generations of teenagers. Cliff is a very special person, loved and respected by everyone.'

Jennifer is thirty-six, mother of Sally Ann aged fourteen and Lynne aged eleven. She teaches part time and then spends a considerable part of her week running the affairs of the Cliff Richard Fan Club of Yorkshire.

She enjoys the global aspect of her activities.

'I am in touch with Cliff fans all over the world, e.g. Australia, New Zealand, Korea. In 1977 I held a soft toy competition with several records, autographed by Cliff, as prizes. Fans from all over the world sent me beautiful hand-made toys and I later took them to the local children's home for Christmas.'

Maureen Suykerbuyk from Belgium talks of Cliff's warm and beautiful voice and says disarmingly, 'He's mine No. 1 for eighteen years now and I really hope he's stay this for ever.'

Obviously her view of Cliff's voice is one shared by many. R. S. Witchell heard Cliff in 1979 at the Trust Arena, Johannesburg, and commented, 'The sound was superb and Cliff's five-piece Australian backing band and three vocalists were right on their job – not to mention Cliff who never seems to age and could teach John Travolta a thing or two about dancing.

'Neither has his voice aged. He spent close on two and a half hours on stage without hitting a bum note.'

On 9 May 1978 Cliff and David Bryce slipped quietly into Hong Kong and drove straight from the Kaitak Airport to an undisclosed destination. Fans had no inkling, on this (Cliff's fourth) visit, when he would arrive. It was far from quiet after Cliff had visited E.M.I.'s Music Centre at Causeway Bay for an interview by Commercial Radio which was broadcasting live from the store. The size of the crowd outside afterwards was such that he was sneaked out through the rear entrance of the shop.

In the sleepy Middlesex town of Ashford the Record Scene store managed by John Friesen was engulfed on all sides when Cliff arrived for a sign-in of his book *Which One's Cliff?* The queue sprawled for over a mile and a half. For Ashford it was a sight not previously seen. Fans came in one door and having met Cliff they disappeared out the other! Even Bill Latham, Cliff's friend, who thought he had seen most things, was somewhat dazed.

Cliff has strong views on fan behaviour. In February 1979 he landed at Jan Smuts Airport, South Africa. Girl fans from Pretoria University were there at the ready with screams of 'Welcome Cliff'.

Harry De Louw attended the ensuing press conference and Cliff was asked whether he was influenced by anyone or anything particular at that time.

'Yes, the enthusiasm and energy found in punk and new-wave music is exciting. I find ninety per cent of this music useless but the remaining ten per cent is very good.

'My fans are pretty vocal at concerts. They wait respectfully for me at the stage door for autographs. No hair-pulling, chair-smashing mobs. The fever has been cured. I find these destructive crowds most unhealthy. It smacks of anarchy, and that philosophy is so childish. I'll be glad when people grow up and realize that. Scream for more, yes, but basically enjoy yourself and leave in a sane frame of mind.'

Certainly there was the right form of restrained behaviour when he sang at the Rossiya Concert Hall, Moscow. Hundreds of applauding fans swarmed towards the stage when the encore period arrived. Cliff sang some rock 'n' roll classics but there were no wild scenes outside the stage door.

It wasn't entirely like that when Cliff began his career, but there weren't the scenes which have accompanied some stars, with fans leaving a trail of destruction in their wake.

Yet there was a definite air of hysteria. Some of it may even have come from those fans, now well into their thirties, who these days appreciate the poised, polished and totally professional Cliff.

150

In 1958 and 1959 he was raw and packed with energy. Oddly enough initial disruption at his concerts came from Teddy Boys who objected to their girl friends swooning over this good-looker in preference to their own hardened features.

The girls threw their kisses but on more than one occasion the boys pelted the stage with rotten eggs and tomatoes. Police protection was necessary on several occasions.

Several music papers found his act objectionable and a thoroughly bad influence upon the morals of young virgins. A few years later in the mid-sixties those, and other sources, saw Cliff as British, Pat Boone-ish, endowed with good looks, a constant toothpaste smile and a casual immaculate look.

Writing in 1963, Colin Frame claimed, 'The adulation, crazy, vociferous, hysterical, followed him – still follows him – like a pack of baying hounds.

'And he knows how to handle it – the thousand eyes adoring him, the thousand hands held out to him, the thousand voices calling his name.

'He knows when to please, when to tease, when to disappear.'

On his twenty-first birthday Cliff received 30,000 birthday cards. He had presents galore, 'ranging from sweaters to the key-of-the-door, five feet long, worked in satin and lace and garnished with roses and soaked in perfume'.

Writer Colin Frame called it 'orgiastic self-release' for the girls and perhaps he had in mind the more extreme fans.

There was the girl who sent Cliff a piece of chewing gum and asked him to chew it and then return to sender. Another girl, showing a certain creativity, had herself posted as a parcel. Inevitably there have been those who have gate-crashed theatres and television dressing rooms, or shinned up the drainpipe and appeared at the window.

From time to time the various Cliff Richard magazines and journals ask fans not to bother Cliff and if they find where he lives then not to encamp outside and generally make a nuisance of themselves. They are reminded that Cliff deserves privacy as much as anyone else.

The fan groupings busily rack their brains for a suitable present when his 14 October birthday date approaches. Recently several have given up the task, maintaining Cliff has or could buy whatever he wants, but one would have thought the task was not impossible. Starting with the premise that one should search for the unusual, the countless craft shops of one kind or another would seem to be good places to look.

Fans of course keep scrap books, photos, programmes, autographs, press cuttings, calendars, posters, records and all kinds of mementos – even, according to one Cliff fan, Sheila McAvoy of Coventry, Cliff Perfume. John Friesen has 278 Cliff albums and a mass of singles and EPs, all different or at least different in country of origin if not always in title. Danish Cliff fan Bo Larsson is another major collector.

From time to time the more involved Cliff fans have put together special collections for Cliff. In 1976 Eileen Edwards thought it would be a good idea to celebrate Cliff's eighteenth anniversary in show business by constructing an Encliffopedia.

She suggested that fans should pick a particular year and then describe it in terms of Cliff with suitable photos and anything else which might be relevant.

The Hong Kong branch of the I.C.R.M. issued in 1974 *Cliff's Collections*. It comprised 100 pages, words of 112 songs, a crossword puzzle, some coloured pictures and of course endless bits and pieces about their hero.

London member Janet Johnson has published three Cliff annuals, the first issued in 1979. These comprise reports on another Cliff year, tributes, Christmas and New Year greetings, poems and quizzes.

Obviously many of the activities of Cliff fans are not dissimilar to those of other stars' fans. And oddly enough there is no official Cliff Richard fan club. There was one once. It was organized by a girl called Jan Vane. She ran it from her house and somehow managed to keep a reputed 40,000 fans continuously happy with news of their man.

She had known Cliff for some time, even before his first taste of stardom with 'Move It' in 1958. These days she's a married woman. She says she doesn't think too much about those early days unless someone broaches the subject. Jan follows Cliff's activities but she does so as his friend rather than a fan.

'They were fantastic days, the early ones. Everyone was so taken up with the success. We just enjoyed every moment without really thinking too much.

'I was just part of the family. I would go shopping with Cliff. I remember once they threw me in the swimming pool for laughs. Fortunately Johnny Foster realized I couldn't swim and he pulled me out.

'We never had much money. I can remember sometimes forking out the taxi bill! But they were great times. An official fan club was necessary because all sorts of people were trying to jump on the Cliff name bandwagon and fans were powerless. There were many fans in those early days.'

There were several attempts later on to organize fan clubs, in one instance with dire consequences. Eventually Cliff and his management had to step in and sort things out, ensuring that no one had been financially deprived. There were simply too many fans and the whole operation ran out of control.

Since the late sixties there has been the International Cliff Richard Movement which is run from Holland. Various branches exist throughout the world and in many countries there are meeting houses. Although not official, it seems to be well respected by Cliff's management. A more recent movement is Grapevine which is run by members who broke away from I.C.R.M. In Denmark is the headquarters of The Christian Friends of Cliff Richard which concentrates on Cliff's religious activities.

What distinguishes Cliff fan clubs and meeting houses from those of other stars is the time and effort spent on raising money. Most of the proceeds go to Tear Fund, the Christian relief agency which has received an enormous amount of time and support from Cliff himself.

Many societies in the United Kingdom run the inevitable raffle and jumble sale. The Coventry branch has also held Cliff film and disco nights, and a Tearcraft party where goods produced by this offshoot of Tear Fund were on sale.

The meeting house at Bognor has held sponsored walks, and jewellery and clothing parties. The Weybridge meeting house raised enough money in 1980 to sponsor a child for a year through Tear Fund's child care programme. It took the meeting house in

Poole, Dorset, just two years of small but obviously effective events to raise £250. Even the smallest meeting house raises money well into three figures and sponsored activities can take in the world Cliff following.

Maureen Powell of West Bromwich says, 'I myself have sponsored a child for seven years. I signed a covenant for Tear and this was through a picture I saw in a gospel concert programme, of Cliff and children in Bangladesh, although Anna (whom I sponsor) lives in the Dominican Republic.'

During 1980 and into 1981 the Cliff Richard Fan Club of Leicestershire took part in a sponsored knit. Angela Barcock says, 'By knitting squares and sewing them together we managed to make a total of ten full-size blankets to be distributed by Tear Fund and we've also raised at least £121 through the sponsoring.'

The Waterlooville Meeting House near Portsmouth, like the London branch, holds yearly Cliff days; 1981 was their eighth Cliff evening. All profits from the evening and the inevitable raffle go to Tear Fund. During the evening only Cliff music is played for listening and dancing.

A film show with *Two a Penny* and *A Day with Cliff* drew 100 people to the Yorkshire meeting house while a later showing of *Summer Holiday*, together with slides and taped commentary by Cliff about Bangladesh, a bring 'n' buy sale, and a raffle for a belt and scarf from Cliff, brought in a valuable £150 for Tear Fund work.

Karen O'Neill and Alan Elliott of the Manchester Fan Club are among a number who give to charities other than Tear Fund. On Good Friday of 1981 they organized a sponsored walk to raise money for a baby unit. The Yorkshire Fan Club has given considerable sums to the National Spinal Injuries Centre at Stoke Mandeville. The latter occasioned a letter from Jimmy Savile, who thanked the fan club and remarked how he was a Cliff fan.

The same Yorkshire group, via its president Jennifer Chatten, has been involved in a special appeal for hand-made toys and gifts for disabled people. Other groups raise money towards Cliff's Charitable Trust Fund which regularly donates to worthy causes.

The brief descriptions given illustrate just a few of the extremely impressive fan club and meeting house charitable works. All these groups are associated with the International Cliff Richard Movement. The other organization, Grapevine, is also involved in raising money, and it sponsors a child called Wasana in the Tear Fund child care programme.

The fan clubs and meeting houses ask no kind of Christian allegiance from their members although not surprisingly, in view of Cliff's gospel tours, some groups do stress his Christian side. The Grapevine organization mentions its Christian concern in its own write-up and Bill Latham speaks of a definite Christian response to the gospel tours.

One Christian who has been converted through the gospel tours and general fan club activities is Shirley Urand. 'Obviously Cliff's Christian beliefs have had a strong influence on his career and in fact I became a Christian four years ago as a result of hearing him talk and sing about his faith. Being a Cliff fan has obviously made a difference to my life.'

Another glowing word comes from Linda Gilmour of the Blackburn Meeting House. On the question of whether Cliff's Christian beliefs have harmed his career she comments, 'A lot of people said he lost a lot of his fans when he stood up and said he was a Christian but since then he has gained a whole lot more. It is harder work now than ever before to obtain tickets for his concerts.'

There are doubtless some sycophantic fans but generally speaking Cliff fans seem level-headed. They can even be critical, though constructive in their criticisms of what he does. The London Cliff Richard Fan Club which raised £400 for a special charity in 1980 is one such example. Members do not see themselves as stuffed parrots nor do they unquestioningly accept what is offered. In common with all clubs they have one insatiable request of Cliff – that he should visit them. In the meantime they hear records, watch videos, organize trips to concerts and discuss Cliff the person and his future.

Cliff himself tells a fan story. 'There was a girl I heard about. She spent an hour putting on her best clothes and make-up to watch me on TV. At the end of the programme she went and took it all off again.'

Such is the fan. Such at any rate is the Cliff fan. They seem a loyal good-to-have-around bunch.

CHAPTER FOURTEEEN

Nearest and Dearest

'What caused that reporter to hate me so much? I do not know,' muses Cliff with a look of concern momentarily ageing his young features. He waves his arm in an expansive gesture which almost dislodges one of a thousand or so record awards which hang from the walls of his immaculate house.

'I'm as human as the next person when it comes to criticism, and I don't mind admitting that I find it hard to take when I feel it's unjustified.

'I'm not a complicated person and I don't think I should pretend to be anything else. I was described in the interview as "mechanically charming" and really what stings me is the realization that somebody is trying to knock me for being friendly.'

He shakes his head and finds solace in his always effervescent and energetic dogs, Kelly and Emma. He recalls another article which appeared in the music weekly *Melody Maker*. Cliff's management had agreed that the paper should send a reporter who would move around with the band.

'I suppose to some people I don't fit in. I don't fit the bill and it bugs them. This reporter was disturbed that I, and the band, didn't do all kinds of outrageous things. We did the show, we came off, sat down and chatted. And then, as usual, it was off for a good meal somewhere.

'I mean with us you do not get dressing rooms wrecked. There are no drugs, no brawling and actually I quite like the way we do it. I expect it will become a cult thing one day.'

The thought amuses him. He draws back his shoulders and lavishes some more attention on Kelly and Emma. He sighs and continues with his obvious preoccupation of the moment.

'I really don't think I'm so benign as these papers make out. I do say outrageous things but when I do no one listens. I criticize the music press but it never gets reported!

'I'm an avid walker up in the woods, I suppose it helps me relax. And I manage swimming. I've said sometimes that I hate being alone but I do find comfort in just me being with me. I'm not a recluse, don't think that.

'I remember years ago I had a flat in Marylebone. Well, it was years ago, not long after I started. I just didn't like it. I'm a family, a home-loving kind of person.

'I have my own house, with Bill Latham and his mother also living there. I see a lot of my family. I spend a great deal of time with other people who are close to me.

'I don't think I would be as stable as I am if it wasn't for a closely-knit bunch of people around me. There's Peter my manager, there's Pat and Di in the office, David Bryce, Bill.

'They've been with me for ages. I guess it's a family affair. There's also been a long-term commitment of people which is fantastic. They worry about me. There's this marvellous solidarity behind me.

'I'm not a complicated person. I have this love for sticking things in the ground and watching them grow. Well, it excites me but I suppose some music papers would find all that amusing.

'This career of mine has gone on a long time. There have been a few moments when I have thought, should it end? I know people debate for ages, wondering how my career can go on and on.

'I remember saying to you in the dressing room at *Top of the Pops* how I was on the verge of saying it's the end, just before I bounced back with "We Don't Talk Anymore". For I felt I had to be up there and winning over all the new bands.

'I guess I am a work-aholic. I dig the stage. The final challenge is the stage, the record is just the beginning of everything. You have to perform and it takes a great deal of time and effort.

'I have this perfectionist thing in me and it applies to everything I do. I suppose I was a pioneer in the gospel scene. All that has required even more time and thought, but I still get excited over what is happening.

'It's all an attitude of mind. Isn't it?' .

Cliff stops talking. There is silence. When he talks, he talks. The words flow.

He's a different person though from the rock 'n' roller of early times. Gone is the early turbulence, the freneticism of youth. No one these days writes about the one-time famous snarl which in reality was a grimace because Cliff didn't want people to see a bad tooth! He dresses smartly, with a contemporary trend but without looking an aged teenager. He still knows that there are writers who would describe him quite cheerfully as of old as Britain's No. 1 Bachelor Boy.

He never did agree he was deliberately provocative in those early times.

'I've never tried to be either vulgar or sexy, consciously. Nothing I did at that time was shameful. But rock and beat, rhythm and blues, need movement.

'Do the negroes in the jungle, dancing to their drumbeat, think they are being sexy? Of course not. The music gets into their blood and each movement they make is forced out because it expresses the music.'

So Cliff wrote in *It's Great to be Young*. These days he doesn't face a barrage of press accusation although his penchant for tight trousers and even leathers does not go unnoticed amongst some fans. However the pressure still exists. It comes from the kind of press coverage he does not relish, or bitching of certain religious extremists, from constant secular and religious work, from endless engagements and in the end from those post-midnight wonderings about self and the meaning of existence.

Obviously the stability of his management team has contributed a great deal towards both his success and his ability to withstand the snares and temptations which frequently reduce other major stars to insignificant music personalities.

Peter Gormley has been with Cliff for over twenty years. He is very much someone who keeps in the background. Any collector over the years of Cliff interviews will know there has been precious little comment from Peter.

He says simply, 'Why have me chattering? It's Cliff who matters surely?' Well, of course it is and then on the other hand it isn't!

Peter travels the world. He is the person who arranges the tours and decides where Cliff goes. Sometimes his is the delicate task of choosing from a number of competing and perhaps flattering invitations which one suits Cliff best and will advance his career. He keeps a close watch on contractual and recording matters. He takes a check on media and promotional activities but will leave some matters to others. In the eighties this has meant the efficient and dedicated Brian Munns of E.M.I. press office liaising with the Gormley management over any possible Cliff interviews.

Cliff says Peter is the ideal manager. There is obviously a great affection between the two. In the land of pop and show business the manager who can stay even five years with someone at the top is a rarity – an outstanding testimony to Peter Gormley's quality and professionalism. He is known as one of the straightest persons in the pop business, which can be a land of sharks.

It should also be remembered that Cliff's Christian activities have severely eaten into his general musical career and consequently into his availability. They have added an extra stress upon management.

Peter Gormley has the unenviable job of weighing up the pros and cons of the needs of these two worlds. He must be continually aware of the fluctuations of the pop market with its umpteen variables, of his need to sustain Cliff as a major force and of the importance of serving the needs and aspirations which spring from Cliff's Christian commitment. It cannot be an easy task.

Not everyone likes David Bryce. It would be surprising if they did. This important person in the Cliff setup has a way of describing himself as a mere employee in the Gormley management.

'Originally I worked for what was then Lew and Leslie Grade – which later became London Management. I was handling tours for them and I came into contact with Peter. My general background is work in theatres. I handled tours years ago for artists like Bill Haley and Buddy Holly.

'I became involved with Cliff in the autumn of 1959, on the second Arthur Howes tour. We did all the security ourselves. There was another boy who worked with Cliff at the time, Mike Conlon. There was Sid, myself and then Peter.

'We were the security people. We used to work things out about the way we could get Cliff in and out. We went through kitchens and courtyards . . . We knew most of the places we were going to play on the cinema and theatre circuit and there were all kinds of ways of doing it . . . Sometimes you'd have a stage door with a crowd and there'd be another door and we'd arrange an obscure car to be there and he'd just walk out quietly. I remember once we put an overcoat and cap on him to walk him out, but a fan apparently told him that he looked silly in the cap!'

David Bryce drives Cliff to many of his engagements. He operates the much-praised light show at Cliff's gigs. He runs his eye over tour schedules and looks into even apparently minor detail. For example he took the trouble to find out whether Cliff's band, on the 1981 American tour, had any particular food wants on their Atlantic flight, and even their choice in toothpaste. It's a cliché perhaps but a happy band is the one which gives the best result.

David Bryce courts unpopularity in his role as Cliff's protector from the endless people who want his time and who in numbers could easily fill a fortnight of Cliff's time within the space of a normal week.

He can be tough, for this is a prerequisite of dealing with situations which can quickly shoot out of control. On the other hand there is a gentle, reflective and quiet side to his nature. He has a quick sense of humour. He is a family man and is known amongst his close associates as rather given to bestowing large glasses of gin and tonic upon guests. The recipients are often surprised by the small amount of tonic water.

He is a tower of strength behind the Cliff success story. Less obvious but none the less vital are the two office members, Pat Bermer and Di Sanders.

Pat says with humour, 'Having worked for Cliff's office for the best part of seventeen years, how do I feel about it? Well *old* for a start! Still haven't figured out the secret of Cliff's youthful looks. However, maybe I'll discover the secret in the next seventeen!'

Di is tall and extremely good-looking and she is, as is Pat, fond of a good clean story. The two work in a happy office. Running off from their central work section, which looks straight down the hall towards the main entrance of Gormley Management, is a

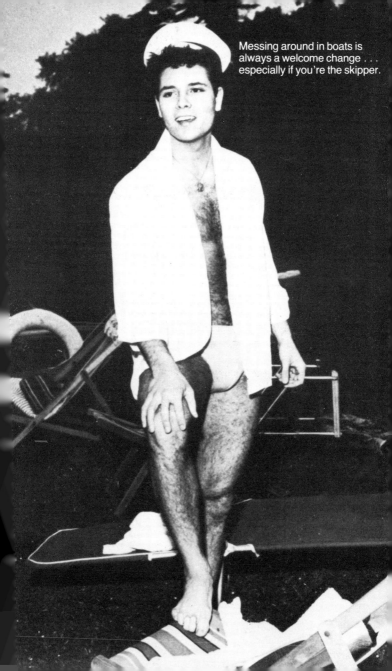

Messing around in boats is always a welcome change . . . especially if you're the skipper.

Top: Playback . . . Cliff and the Shadows hear the results of their labours in the recording studio. At left behind the telephone is rarely-photographed manager Peter Gormley. At extreme right is the late Norrie Paramor, recording manager.

Above: Studio rehearsal. The Shadows pay attention.

Right: One-man recording session – in his dressing room.

A seat in the stalls during a rehearsal.
Inset: Well, you can't go round smiling twenty-four hours a day!

Up, up and away! But the rural setting is only a backdrop.

Above: With the vivacious Una Stubbs, who featured in *Summer Holiday* and *Wonderful Life.*

Right: The strawberry blonde is the late Jayne Mansfield, pictured with Cliff during her British tour not long before her tragic death in a car accident.

Above: Film time! Cliff turns the camera on to Susan
Hampshire, his co-star in *Wonderful Life.*
Below: 'Cliff! Meet Cliff!' Shaking hands with a puppet of
himself created for the *Thunderbirds* T.V. series. There were
puppet Shadows as well.

Above: With Peter Gormley,
the man who prefers the
background. 'It's Cliff who
matters, surely?' he says.

Right: David Bryce, protector,
aide, lighting expert – 'a tower
of strength behind the Cliff
success story'. He is a brother
of the late singer Dickie
Valentine.

The 1970s Cliff, rockin' on to the forty mark.

Inset top: Rockin' on to the eighties. Still he sings 'Move It', the song that began it all more than twenty years ago.

Inset bottom: And still he's happy in his work!

whole series of rooms which deal with matters relating to Cliff, the Shadows and whoever else may be managed at the time.

They deal with the day to day affairs relating to Cliff, operate a central switchboard, act as hostesses to the many callers, and when Peter and David are away there are often essential matters and enquiries to deal with.

For all its closeness and commitment to the central figure of Cliff the management team does not spend evenings and weekends with him. Cliff has acquired his own small circle of friends, though he spends a considerable amount of time on his own. Obviously the most intimate people in his life outside of his mother and family are Mrs Latham and Bill.

Bill and his mother Mamie came into Cliff's life from his early days of religious exploration and a number of other close acquaintances come from the same background. Three of these are David Winter, Nigel Goodwin and Cindy Kent.

It is from his Christian faith that Cliff finds his basic motivation and value as a human being. David Winter chronicled Cliff's early sixties career with sensitivity and insight in his book *New Writer, New Song*.

In his book Winter spends a number of pages concentrating on a remark of Cliff's: 'The moment I became famous I lost most of my friends. Suddenly they became awkward, withdrawn, as though some invisible barrier had been erected. They couldn't talk sensibly to me . . . pretended they didn't know whether to call me Harry or Cliff. Being well-known didn't alter my attitude to them – I value my friends – but it altered their attitude towards me, I'm afraid.

'Even our relatives were affected. It's crazy, really, but when Mum would ask them why they hadn't been to see us lately they'd say, "Oh, we felt you wouldn't want to see us now"!'

Isolation is bad for anyone, more so for stars since they live off their enthusiasms, their nerves and their dependence on being liked by the public, in a manner and to a degree which few others can appreciate.

Cliff told David Winter, 'People treat show business artists with awe, but it's not the artist's doing. Most of us don't want it that way. I'm always glad when people say I'm ordinary. I don't care how they mean it.'

Of course in the fifties and into and through much of the sixties, Cliff had his regular mates the Shadows. When they left he had various backing musicians and back-up singers. Sometimes these have lasted and been with Cliff for a considerable time but they hardly fulfil the need of most human beings to share their deepest thoughts. Women seem to find this easier. They can meet another of their sex and within a short time converse on a personal level. Most men seem weak at this with fellow males, and so Cliff has found a great source of strength and comfort in David, Bill and Mamie Latham.

Cliff and David Winter meet on a spiritual level but there is also a mutual admiration. Each is good at his job. Both are professionals and there is an undisguised delight in sharing biblical truth. Winter smiles broadly when he recalls how years ago he gave Cliff around five years in popsville. On normal reckoning such a time scale might seem generous in the fast-moving days of the early to middle sixties.

'Well, I was aware of his vast reservoir of fans and now it's colossal and worldwide. Still, when you look back to the music scene around 1967 it seemed reasonable to question the future of an artist like Cliff.

'He survived. He is talented, of that there can be no doubt. He also likes hard work which is useful. Offstage he's not too happy. I don't really think he would have taken to the teaching profession and I'm really thinking of the teacher's life rather than the actual teaching in the classroom.

'I keep saying to him, "Less and less work, Cliff." He's good at a lot of things. I really think he could have become a professional football player.

'There's nothing casual about Cliff when it comes to serious things. He's had very good management. I doubt if he could survive a change there.

'He's always been prepared to do things. His activity rate is staggering. And through everything he's always suffered from a dodgy throat and a back which used to play up a great deal. My word for everything is astonishing.'

Nigel Goodwin is Director of the Christian Arts Centre Group. He, with David Winter, Ronald Allison (who at one time was the

B.B.C.'s Court correspondent, Press Secretary to the Queen and then in the eighties went back into the world of television), Cindy Kent and other well-known figures of the evangelical world, were responsible with Cliff for establishing that influential centre. Nigel has a varied background which has included RADA, some stage and television (including a small part in *Expresso Bongo* and *Two a Penny*), broadcasting for the British Forces Broadcasting Service and getting to know some of the best Christian evangelical writers of the seventies including Dr Francis Schaeffer.

These days he works from an office at the top of the A.C.G. headquarters in Short Street, a stone's throw from the Young Vic and a mighty heave with some height from the Old Vic.

He and Cliff have been buddies for years. Cliff was best man at his wedding with Gillian and is godfather to the Goodwin offspring. Some say Nigel is Cliff's spiritual adviser *par excellence*. Certainly the two discuss the pros and cons and implications of being a Christian in show business.

'Cliff is a very unselfish person. He's very vulnerable. I think he needs protecting from those who see him as the answer to their particular want and who do not consider him and his feelings along the way.

'The A.C.G., which is for people in the media, is one place where he can be himself and that's vital for someone who lives with his stresses and strains.

'When he comes here he doesn't come as a speaker and one who must have an audience. Here he can speak and listen as an individual. And he is not being used.

'Obviously the A.C.G. owes a tremendous debt to Cliff but I've always tried to say that the group is not Cliff's alone. I don't think it's a good thing tying the whole thing around one neck, it's not good for God, nor for us.

'The thing is of course, and this makes him vulnerable to everyone with a want, he can raise thousands of pounds just by doing a concert. Well, he has done specials for the A.C.G. and he did give a great deal in the first place.

'To me Cliff is a great ambassador for the good side of the music business. In private he has problems like we all have. For him it's harder to share them. With someone who is well-known there is always the problem of someone saying something in the wrong place and then it's there in the newspapers, even when it's trivial.

'I hope I will see him married one day. It's not an easy path for him. It's not easy for someone who travels, who is on view, to find a private life style. There are people who would tag along with him, who would love to marry him but they may be in love with the image, the star and not the real inner Cliff.

'He has to contend with all this chatter about whether he is homosexual or not – sometimes from people who should know better and doubtless wouldn't like it if they were the subjects.

'These days he's a Baptist, Millmead Baptist Church in Guildford, where David Pawson exercised a ministry. And he gets on with Billy Graham.'

Cindy Kent achieved public notice for her work as lead singer in the Settlers, a group in some ways similar to the Seekers and even the New Seekers. The Settlers played numerous concerts, had endless TV and radio spots, played gospel and secular music with Cliff, without exactly becoming a major force. Cindy also gained press coverage for a believed romance with Richard Barnes and, for some more important, whispers of deep romance with Cliff.

'The story of me and Cliff was a put-up by a journalist. He was one of those who asked a lot of questions and some simple things like "would you like to have tea with Cliff or go to the theatre with him", all that kind of thing. He even rang up my Mum and asked whether she approved of Cliff. Anyway all the bits and pieces were thrown together into a major splash on me and Cliff and apparently marriage. I was livid. I rang Cliff and explained.

'I met Cliff through the church. A friend of mine got me into his company. I was very much someone who had been a Christian but then dropped away. I always made excuses and said I had no time to go.

'Cliff said he was a Christian. I felt guilty and thought about things. Anyway, the outcome was a definite commitment to God from me. I just said I'm sorry, let me do things for you.

'Within two or three weeks Cliff, who had heard reports about my singing and heard me, said, "Come with me to Europe," and off went the group!

'I also said to Cliff I had found it a problem finding the right sort of church. So I said I would go to the church where he went. St Paul's, Finchley, was a weak church. It had enormous potential though which was never realized. In some ways you might wonder what I or Cliff found there. Oddly enough it gave us what we didn't have – it was not very full and we were used to audiences – so, strange as it may seem, it provided the contrast.

'I liked the drama of the whole thing. I had been a Congregationalist and there you do not find much colour. These days I'm fairly high church.

'Cliff obviously got fed there, that's important when you're always giving out.

'He rehearses everything. Everything matters and I admire that very much. He's easy to work with. He does take advice. He isn't arrogant. He's very aware of what he wants and even if no one else says anything he knows when he does something not exactly the way it ought to be done.

'He has a great sense of discipline. He was never much good at the guitar – a few chords and not too well-played either – but he's persevered through the years and now he's quite a respectable player.

'His singing is something different. I mean, he's a natural.

'I took him home one day. We were rehearsing at A.T.V. in Birmingham and we had time to spare. So, he said what can we do? I said we could go to Mum's and I swore her to secrecy. He liked egg and chips and that's what we had. He just fitted in.

'But then there are the knockers. Cliff in the beginning had this lovely innocent fervour about his Christian experience. He wanted to pass this experience on. A lot of people heard it, still hear it, but of course there is always the question, do people come for Cliff or something deeper? But then how can you escape the dilemma? If he wasn't who he was they wouldn't come – at least by coming they've a chance of hearing.'

Apart from show business friends like Mike Read, Tim Rice, Elton John, Andy Peebles, Una Stubbs, B. A. Robertson, Richard Skinner and many others, there are also the many who have met and entertained Cliff, particularly through the gospel tours where he comes closest to people.

John and Elaine Horner are just two who remember their meal

with Cliff before his gospel concert at the Nottingham Methodist Central Hall.

'He was unassuming, unflamboyant. He was prepared to listen to what I suppose must have seemed a rather trivial conversation. Sometimes one's experience of the great is that they're only interested in their greatness! He really seemed interested. It's that sort of behaviour which helps him to make friends so easily.'

The Horners may never meet Cliff again. Others who have been in similar situations have found the same but what unites them is that, however corny it may sound, Cliff is the sort of person you would enjoy as a friend, and would like to know more about. They are not the nearest and dearest but they help in small ways to give him the support he needs. At very least they keep Cliff's feet on the ground.

Then there are the Lathams. Cliff has described Mamie Latham as a second mum. Bill is the schoolmaster who came to a special party thrown by English teacher Mrs Jay Norris who was worried by Cliff's excursions into Jehovah's Witness territory.

Their care and concern is continually evident. Bill, after a lengthy period with Tear Fund, has become concerned with gospel work via Network Three and Garth Hewitt. He manages Cliff's religious affairs and arranges the gospel tours. The two for many years, and often in the eighties, have toured churches and schools. Bill poses Cliff with the questions and Cliff answers. If in the early days questions from the audience seemed a bit much for the new-into-the-faith Cliff, then Bill held forth. Their ministry has proved extremely fruitful.

It was the influence and guidance of Bill Latham which was largely responsible for the subtle but increasing change in Cliff's whole attitude as performer and artist from the post-Billy Graham, 1966 period.

Bill Latham, like Peter Gormley, is someone content to remain off-stage. He has never courted publicity. He is a quiet and friendly person who, despite these characteristics, has considerable push.

Of course it might well be insisted by Cliff fans that there is one important group of friends which has so far been omitted – the Shadows. This is true, and in fact they are worthy of their own book. During their time together Cliff and the Shadows were great friends.

Cliff sums up the way he felt years ago, 'We decided to make it or break it together and in those days of the early sixties we felt that was the way it would stay. We travelled everywhere. We appeared together in films and on stage and we spent endless days and nights recording.'

It meant a deep loyalty and friendship. It was a relationship which caught the attention of perceptive journalist Colin Frame in 1963. He said, 'In 1961 the Shadows won the Novello award for the best contribution to popular music. A formidable group. But it is as Cliff's friends, filling with horseplay, legpull and good company the lonely moments he finds at the top, that the Shadows play a part in his story.'

Yet the Shadows-Cliff friendship only went so far. The group's members married and Cliff was left, the bachelor boy. The Shadows-Cliff Jehovah's Witnesses period also ended the same way. Cliff was left. He did not commit himself. These days he's disappointed that Hank and Liquorice should have done so.

Notwithstanding all this there is still the obvious fact that the Shadows and Cliff had some great times. Hank believes Cliff was largely instrumental in their basically good relationship. He was also the one who gave them their chance.

'We had our first hit with "Apache", a record which established that we weren't just a backing group,' says Hank. 'A lot of credit for that goes to Cliff because he was so unselfish, he pushed us as individuals. Anyway from a business point of view it made us a much stronger force.'

Cliff acknowledges the compliment and with a smile says that as far as he was concerned a great deal of his early motivation came from a simple straightforward desire.

'I just wanted to be a pop singer. I just wanted to put on my pink jacket, sing their songs [the Shadows' compositions], and get all the glory. And that was it.

'I loved those days, really did. We started off by feeling we could be millionaires. We had no particular plans, not until *The Young Ones* came along, though we had no intention of being like most stars – here today and gone tomorrow.

'Now my career has gone on and on. Too long they say, but I'm not complaining!'

Bruce Welch remarks on how the early financial arrangement eased and cemented a friendship. 'The very first tour we did, Cliff just split the money with the group – five ways. I think we got twelve quid each. Then in 1959, when he was big, we got twenty-five quid a week. But for twenty-five quid a week in those days I had a flat in the West End. I was married and I still had money left at the end of the week.

'We travelled everywhere together and that is how the song-writing developed. Coaches, cars, trains . . . we just used to get our guitars out all the time . . . that's how all the music came, just from that sort of atmosphere.'

Hank Marvin talks of the life style which has afflicted every up and coming band since pop began. It's a world of bad food and little sleep but, in their case, no drugs. Groupies exist.

He says, 'When we got high then it was on our music. Groupies to us were birds or chicks but I don't want to talk about it.

'I remember the first time I met Cliff. He looked at us and thought we were yobs. Mind you, he was right.'

Hank recalls how Cliff brought back from the States a special-sounding Fender guitar which gave the group a very American sound. Critics remember how Hank's use of the treble arm allied with the Shadows' twanging made them special.

In those early days a mutual respect was brought into being, a respect and cooperation which gave Britain her top singer and top group.

Cliff says, 'We did have our arguments, fierce ones. In fact there were times when we had violent arguments. To an outsider these displays of disagreement could easily have been misinterpreted but we were five of the closest friends I know.'

It wasn't easy for the Shadows and Cliff, for from the early sixties the pop press endlessly debated when they would split. Facts and figures were constantly wheeled forward. Chart statisticians merrily talked of how particular Shadows records raced up the charts faster than some of Cliff's

In September 1961, with the release of their album *The*

Shadows imminent, an E.M.I. spokesman said, 'Advance orders are pouring in. It's going to be a big one, one of our biggest.'

Events proved his comment correct but the critics did not have it their way. Cliff and the Shadows stayed together for many more records, shows and films.

In 1967 Cliff's religious plans threatened their relationship. Yet in an interview Hank admitted that they were partly to blame for whatever consequences might follow a move out of show business on Cliff's part.

'Cliff was always interested to a small degree in religion. But it was latent until he met Liquorice.'

Bruce picked up the thread of Hank's speech with the comment, 'In the five years we knew him before meeting Liquorice, we never saw Cliff touch a Bible. After Liquorice, Cliff took to carrying a caseful of religious material around with him.'

Cliff stayed with show business but his increasing gospel load meant a gradual drifting apart from the Shadows. Cliff, though, could point out that the Shadows were also busily pursuing their own career with work abroad and the inevitable British tour. The separation became painfully evident at the end of the sixties. Cliff's basic pattern in 1969 and 1970 was a new single every few months, a film in Israel for the Billy Graham Organization, the usual run of television shows and interviews and the odd concert or two. He began a TV series which involved thirteen programmes and meant a considerable portion of the year was taken up.

In 1978 long-lasting fans of Cliff and the Shadows had their time of joy. They were reunited at London's famed Palladium for a season which lasted from 27 February until 11 March. The Shadows comprised Hank, Bruce, Brian Bennett, Cliff Hall and Alan Jones.

Bruce said in 1976, 'The Shadows were three-chord wonders.'

Cliff disagreed. 'The Shadows were the motivators of myriad instrumentalists. Hank was the only guy who could play Buddy Holly's solos note for note. That made you stardust.

'Hank was the king. In Italy they said that without the Shadows there would've been no pop music. After we started there there were Italians up and down the country wearing pink jackets and doing the goose step in the background!'

Many a famous rock musician has said that the Marvin style gave him his first thrill and his grounding in rock. Among those who have acknowledged his influence are Pete Townshend, Jeff Beck, Eric Clapton and Peter Green.

Bruce says there was no one else but Hank in the early sixties.

The eighties see the Shadows very much alive with a number of late seventies hit albums and singles ensuring their future for many years. Cliff experienced his recording revival of the seventies as a result of Bruce's producing finesse. Bruce produced Cliff's chart-topper of 1979, 'We Don't Talk Anymore', his first number one since 1968.

Cliff and the Shadows may not see each other very often, but they remain near and dear to each other.

CHAPTER FIFTEEN

The New Columbus

Some of the natives were anything but friendly when Cliff Richard arrived in the United States late in February 1981 to try once more to conquer the New World – his last frontier.

His first attempt twenty-one years earlier in 1960 had been, as we have seen, something of a hurried, slapdash rock 'n' roll tour featuring a bunch of recording stars among whom Cliff was a mere fledgling. His inclusion was due to the fact that 'Living Doll' was beginning to bite in America.

Since then he has made several promotional visits to the States, but not until 1981 did he return to the challenge and set forth to tour again with the hope of winning what was for him virtually uncharted territory.

It was a different story this time. There was nothing hasty about the preparation. The much-experienced Peter Gormley, in his usual wisdom, had gone ahead to smooth the path. This time it would be Cliff's own show plus a few supporting acts. There would be six extremely competent musicians behind him and a trio of professional back-up voices.

Three successful Cliff Richard recordings which had found their way into the charts had ensured that a lot of North Americans knew the name and no doubt would like to see Cliff in the flesh. ('Devil Woman' alone had sold 1,300,000 copies in America – without even reaching number one. Its highest placing was fifth.)

It would be a lengthy visit of seven weeks with thirty-five concerts scheduled in a coast to coast venture taking in Canada.

The party flew out from England on 27 February after long days of rehearsal at Shepperton Studios and made landfall in Los

Angeles where, before the tour wagon could even begin to roll, some West Coast natives went into the attack.

A lorry loaded with £40,000 worth of Cliff's equipment – guitars, keyboards, sound gear – was spirited away by thieves from outside his hotel in Hollywood. The haul included three of his favourite guitars.

It was a hit below the belt that shook every one in the touring party. The opening date in Seattle was only three days away. What was the point in trying to carry on?

Said Cliff, 'The temptation was to say "to hell with it". But then an inner voice – that of God – told me, "Cliff, you have to do it. You have a responsibility." '

That the thieves showed something of a sense of humour was little comfort. They left behind a note that said – in typical Californian fashion – 'Have a nice day!'

Cliff and company recovered and hustled around buying or hiring new equipment. By the time they reached the east coast early in April, with several successful concerts now behind them, they were in good cheer.

'Everything's going well,' David Bryce, Cliff's Man Friday and lighting expert, told us when they arrived in New York.

'But nothing has been seen of the truck,' he added, 'and chances are that we'll never see it again.'

Saved was Cliff's stage wardrobe – much of it leather – and there was no repetition of the 1960 foray when he landed in the States with only the one white stage suit.

After the initial shock of the robbery, the party had set off undaunted for Seattle on the first leg of the tour.

The theatre was only something like half full for this opening shot in the campaign to conquer America. Nevertheless, 1,200 young people had handed over their money to see this new Columbus of rock 'n' roll looking much younger than his forty years.

They screamed and squealed like the fans of yesteryear and Cliff was both grateful and somewhat amazed by the size of the audience. He had genuinely not expected that many to buy tickets.

Modest, as always, he told us when he reached New York, 'I wouldn't have been surprised if nobody had turned up. I'm not known here. It has been like starting again, going back to square one and all those years ago.'

At this stage of the tour he had given three concerts in the States and worked his way from west to east across Canada.

The excursion was showing definite signs of success.

'The reaction has been fantastic,' he told us, 'and the reception better than we ever dreamed of. The audiences have been alive and vibrant. I'm staggered.'

He particularly recalled the one-nighter in the Chester Fritz Auditorium at Grand Forks, North Dakota. 'The reception was so deafening that the band were sticking their fingers in their ears!'

One of the songs that had audiences screaming for more was 'Move It' – the Ian Samwell number that was planned as a modest B-side on Cliff's debut disc back in 1958 but was turned over to become the smash hit that put him firmly on the stardust trail.

Strangely, it had been omitted during the abortive attempt to capture North America on the 1960 tour.

Wrote a Canadian critic, reviewing one of the 1981 concerts, 'A version of his very first record, "Move It", almost sounded like it could have been written this year . . .'

And it was noted in Canada, where Cliff is certainly better known than he is in the United States, that audiences ranged 'from teeny-bopper to grandmother'.

There were those present as well who knew what they wanted of Cliff. 'One fellow kept calling out "sing 'Lucky Lips'!" Right, I said to myself, if he calls it out once more we'll have to do it. He did. There was no music and the band had to busk it.'

Proving that the customer is always right. He pays his money and is entitled to make his choice, it seems. The object of the tour was not, however, to return home with sackloads of dollars.

Cliff himself felt from the start that financially it would be a failure and anyway, he didn't need money. What he needed most was to be recognized as a true star of rock 'n' roll in America – its birthplace. 'It's something I want badly,' he said. It was an ambition that he had achieved almost everywhere else in the world . . .

The party travelled from venue to venue in a luxury bus or, where distance demanded, by chartered aircraft.

'The bus was very comfortable,' David Bryce reported. 'We had video aboard and could watch concerts or movies.'

Headlines in the Canadian newspapers reflected the ecstatic reception given to Cliff wherever the tour bus halted. Some typical examples: 'Reception proves Richard still rock's most durable icon.' 'Cliff wows 'em.' 'Pop's perfect prince.'

But still there was the odd snag, such as industrial trouble reaching out to take the shine off slightly, as the *Vancouver Sun*'s music critic, Fiona McQuarrie, wrote. 'Cliff Richard's latest album may be called *I'm no Hero,* but you would have a hard time convincing the devotees who came to see him Thursday night. It was Richard's first ever Vancouver appearance, in a career that's covered almost twenty-three years, and although the show concentrated on his more recent material, it was slick enough and clean enough to satisfy fans of every age.

'The show was switched from the strikebound Queen Elizabeth theatre to the Italian Cultural Centre; the big losers, besides the audience members at the back who had to crane their necks to see anything, were Richard and his band. Ten musicians were crammed into an area the size of your standard high school gym stage. One could imagine only too well how stunning the skilful lighting and effects would have been in a proper theatre.

'Richard, who at forty doesn't look a day over twenty, is a spirited singer who infuses finely crafted pop songs with feeling and life. At times, his dramatic poses and karate movements become hammy, but generally Richard puts his songs across sincerely.

'Where he really shone, though, was in his departure from the pop fare. He went back into the mists of time for a driving version of his first hit, 1958's "Move It", and he obviously enjoyed performing two gospel rock numbers, "Why Should the Devil Have all the Good Music" (by gospel rock pioneer Larry Norman) and "The Rock that Doesn't Roll".

'Richard is a professional who knows how to pace a show and how to present a song, but if all his material was performed with the joyous energy that he puts into his gospel rock numbers, he would be truly outstanding.'

In the *Winnipeg Free Press,* critic Glen Gore-Smith certainly backed up Cliff's description of his reception as fantastic. 'You could almost call it Richard-mania,' the writer reported.

'The Centennial Concert Hall stage wasn't stormed by swarms of screaming, barely nubile bodies, but Richard's fans skirted the outer edges of Beatle-era madness.

'Just about everything Richard did touched off a ringing hallful of applause, hoarse shouts, stomping feet, and the kind of screeches and screams that rock 'n' roll fans supposedly desposited in a time vault along with video tapes of the Ed Sullivan Show.

'Fans didn't want the British superstar to quit the stage, even after four standing, leaping ovations had exhausted his current repertoire.

'Cliff Richard was a legend in the U.K. before the Beatles started playing The Cavern, and he's managed to ride out The Fab Four, folk rock, art rock, heavy metal, punk and new wave.

'Richard stands virtually alone as a first-generation rocker who hasn't become a relic, and last night, he showed why he is pop music's most durable icon . . .

'Richard's stage savvy was evident in special effects, like rolling, colored fog banks spilling off the stage, sci-fi and Vegas touches with a glitterball, and in his unerring control of body language . . .

'Cliff Richard has lived on the edge of North American superstardom for two decades. Judging by the reception here last night, it would appear that he is close to conquering his final frontier.'

Then there was the critic who could only accuse him of being too good!

'Watching Richard in concert,' he wrote,' 'is more like an I.T.V. Celebrity Concert than a typical pop show. Every turn is calculated for effect. Every phrase his six-piece band and his trio of back-up vocalists add has been measured and remeasured, until the final tracking is perfect . . .'

Observed Cliff, 'If that is the worst thing anybody can find to say about us this is going to be a great tour!'

Like his Canadian concerts, his New York appearance at the Savoy, a former Broadway theatre that has been turned into a 1,000-seater club something like London's Talk of the Town, was a sell-out.

Not only the box-office take impressed him. He was the first star to perform there following the completion of its transformation.

'It was a great honour opening it,' he told us.

There is no doubt that Cliff was pleasantly surprised at the warmth he generated during this most recent tilt at America.

Even the natives of Los Angeles eventually demonstrated how friendly they could really be. When the box office opened for bookings for the last concert of the tour there on 18 April the queue stretched round the block.

The new Columbus had arrived at last . . .

Facts

DIARY OF EVENTS 1959–81

February 1959: elected Best New Singer by readers of *New Musical Express* in their annual poll (in those days the *N.M.E.* was pop and chart orientated).

February 1960: *N.M.E.* readers vote Cliff Top British Male Singer.

February 1961: Cliff continues where he left off in 1960. In the *N.M.E.* poll he is voted Top British Male Singer.

March 1961: Peter Gormley becomes Cliff's manager (and he still is!). A note in the diary for 1961 says the two met for talks in Peter's office on 20 January.

May 1961: Cliff's father dies.

11 May 1961: Cliff goes to the Variety Club Awards at the Dorchester, London.

13 May 1961: with the Shadows Cliff attends a special event organized by the Variety Club at the Festival Gardens, Battersea, London.

26 May 1961: Cliff presents awards at the Methodist Association of Youth Clubs' annual national get-together at the Royal Albert Hall, London. He sings 'Living Doll'.

January 1962: the press report seventeen-year-old Valerie Stratford saying she is going to marry Cliff. Claim dismissed.

February 1962: *N.M.E.* readers again vote Cliff Top British Male Singer.

13 March 1962: Cliff receives award from Variety Club of Great Britain as Show Business Personality of the Year. Presentation is at the Savoy in London.

24 April 1962: Cliff dines with the head of E.M.I., Sir Joseph Lockwood.

11 December 1962: Cliff attends London Home Counties Cinematograph Exhibition's annual dinner.

10 January 1963: Cliff with the Shadows at *Summer Holiday* premiere, Warner Theatre, London.

11 February 1963: appears in a charity concert in Nairobi which is organized by Kenya leader Tom Mboya.

August 1963: top-selling U.S. magazine *16* votes Cliff Most Promising Singer in annual poll.

19–21 August 1963: Cliff records in Nashville, backed by Elvis's Jordanaires.

27 September 1963: Cliff's rumoured romance with Jackie Irving hits the headlines.

20 October 1963: Cliff appears on the top-ranking U.S. T.V. *Ed Sullivan Show*.

2 July 1964: attends premiere of *Wonderful Life* at Leicester Square Theatre, organized by the National Association of Youth Clubs. Princess Alexandra and Angus Ogilvy also attend.

November 1965: Cliff and the Shadows at the Royal Variety Show.

4 December 1965: Cliff in a show at his old school, Cheshunt Secondary Modern.

3 April 1966: appears in the Stars' Organization for Spastics concert at Wembley Empire Pool.

16 June 1966: on stage with Billy Graham at Earls Court, London.

3 July 1966: Cliff makes a radio appeal for Westminster Homes for Elderly People.

20 August 1966: news of Cliff purchasing a house for his mother at Highfield Drive, Broxbourne. Two other houses also bought within easy distance of Highfield Drive for his two sisters and aunt.

24 October 1966: newspapers say Cliff is heading for concerts behind the Iron Curtain.

8 December 1966: attends premiere of *Finders Keepers* at Leicester Square, London.

12 December 1966: with the Shadows attends premiere of puppet film *Thunderbirds Are Go!* Cliff and the Shadows are the puppets!

14 February 1967: *Disc* votes Cliff Best-Dressed Male Star.

23 September 1967: *Melody Maker* readers vote Cliff Top Male Singer.

14 February 1968: Cliff at *Disc* Valentines Awards.

9 March 1968: sister Joan Webb marries and Cliff gives her away.

28 June 1968: Cliff lends aid to the National Society for the Prevention of Cruelty to Children projected Christmas card.

Late 1968: the Shadows split up.

10 December 1969: Cliff represents the pop world at a special gala midnight performance at the London Palladium in aid of the Royal Society for the Prevention of Cruelty to Animals.

14 February 1970: Cliff receives *Disc*'s Mr Valentine award. He is also voted Best-Dressed Male Star, comes second as Top British Singer, and third in the World Singer stakes.

3 May 1970: Cliff is voted second Top British Male Singer, Top British Vocal Personality, and third World Male Singer in the 1969 *N.M.E.* readers' poll. Cliff's personality award is presented by Malcolm Roberts at the *N.M.E.* Poll Concert.

5 July 1971: Antibes-Juan Les Pins. Eighth Festival of the Rose d'Or. Cliff receives Ivor Novello Award for outstanding service to British music from festival organizer Claude Tabel. With Olivia Newton-John, Cliff charms the music delegates. The duo sing together on each of the three festival nights and are filmed by the B.B.C. The festival is also filmed by French T.V.

14 April 1972: *The Sun* presents Cliff with its award for Top Male Pop

Personality for the third year running. He is out of London on a Gospel tour at the time and receives the award in Liverpool, the first location on the tour.

1974: Cliff is a awarded a Silver Clef for outstanding services to the music industry at the second annual Music Therapy Committee luncheon. He receives his award from the Duchess of Gloucester.

3–11 April 1974: London Palladium season. Cliff falls ill with throat and chest problems. Rolf Harris deputizes for three nights.

9 July 1974: headlined as an 'All-time First', the International Cliff Richard Movement gathers members together at the United Reform Church, Crouch End, London, for a day of Cliff with material about Tear Fund, the film strip *Love Never Gives Up* (made during a visit by Cliff to Burundi), a 'Portrait of Cliff' competition, a short concert from Cliff, the chance to ask him questions, and a screening of the film *A Day in the Life of Cliff Richard*.

4 September 1974: Romsey Abbey Appeal. Cliff gives support and meets Lady Janet Mountbatten.

27 October 1974: Cliff at the London Palladium with the Shadows, who re-form to appear with him there in a charity concert for the widow of former B.B.C. T.V. producer Colin Charman. The Shadows on this occasion are: Hank Marvin, Bruce Welch, Brian Bennett, with John Farrar replacing the late John Rostill who had died on 26 November 1973. Cliff sings 'Willie and the Hand Jive', 'Bachelor Boy', 'Don't Talk to Him', 'A Matter of Moments', 'Power to All Our Friends'.

21 February 1975: lunch with the head of B.B.C. religious programmes John Lang.

1 May 1975: at the offices of the World Record Club (affiliated to E.M.I.) Cliff receives a presentation from Managing Director Derek Sinclair to mark the sale of 40,000 of the six-record boxed set, *The Cliff Richard Story*. A gold presentation soon follows, on 8 June, for double that amount.

5 June 1975: Cliff headlines a special charity concert at Manchester's Free Trade Hall promoted by Radio Piccadilly. Proceeds are for the families of Sergeant Williams and P.C. Rodgers, two Manchester policemen who had died on duty.

22 July 1975: attends Variety Club luncheon honouring Vera Lynn at the Savoy, London.

1976: A record deal is announced by E.M.I. for the release of Cliff recordings in the U.S.S.R.: *I'm Nearly Famous* and *The Best of Cliff Richard*. Cliff is the third E.M.I. artist given record release in the Soviet Union. The others are Wings and Robert Young.

March 1976: Cliff's visit to the Soviet Union is postponed. In the States, 'Miss You Nights' gives promise of the long-awaited Cliff record triumph across the Atlantic.

8 June 1976: Cliff is back at World Records for a gold disc presentation for *The Cliff Richard Story* six-record boxed set.

15 September 1976: Cliff begins his visit to the Soviet Union via Copenhagen and Stockholm, from where he proceeds to Leningrad.

25 September 1976: reception at the British Embassy, Moscow.

December 1976: Cliff in India, the country of his birth. Meets Mother Teresa of Calcutta and her Missionaries of Charity. Cliff spends an hour singing carols and visits the Home of the Destitute and Dying. Two major appearances at the Kalamandir Auditorium, New Delhi, on 7 and 8 December. Visits Tear Fund projects in Bangladesh.

10 February 1977: obviously appreciated by World Records, Cliff is guest of honour on its twenty-first anniversary.

6 June 1977: Cliff speaks at a Youth Rally, part of the Queen's Silver Jubilee celebrations, in Windsor Great Park.

5 September 1977: publication of Cliff's book, written with Bill Latham, *Which One's Cliff?*

18 October 1977: to celebrate the coinciding events of the Queen's Silver Jubilee and the centenary of the gramophone, the British Phonographic Institution in its Britannia Awards names Cliff Best British Male Solo Artist.

28 October 1977: Cliff receives the Gold Badge Award from the Songwriters' Guild of Great Britain.

27 February 1978: appears at the London Palladium reunited with the Shadows. Season ends 11 March.

6 March 1978: special dinner with E.M.I. at Rags restaurant.

7 March 1978: dines with Elton John.

29 June 1978: Music Therapy Committee luncheon.

1 September 1978: presents budgerigars to pensioners in Weybridge.

6 November 1978: is photographed, with others, for the front cover of the *Guinness Book of Hit Singles*.

1 February 1979: E.M.I. throw a special luncheon at Claridges to celebrate their twenty-one-year partnership with Cliff, who receives a gold replica of the key to E.M.I.'s Manchester Square offices, and a gold clock.

13 February 1979: *Music Week* annual awards. Cliff and the Shadows receive an award for their twenty-one years as major British recording artists.

27 February 1979: Cliff lunches at New Scotland Yard.

1 May 1979: attends Local Radio Awards at Grosvenor House Hotel, London, organized by *Radio and Record News, Radio Month*.

5 July 1979: Variety Club of Great Britain lunch, Dorchester Hotel, London. Cliff presents the Sunshine Coach, which has been given

by the organization to children in the Club's homes. Cliff is guest of honour in celebration of his twenty-one years in show business. The Shadows, Joan Collins, and the Duke of Kent are some of the guests.

22 September 1979: Cliff takes part in an anti-racist festival in Birmingham – Hosannah '79.

4 October 1979: Cliff and Kate Bush with the London Symphony Orchestra appear in concert at the Royal Albert Hall in aid of the L.S.O.'s Seventy-Fifth Birthday Appeal.

2 December 1979: Cliff takes part in a concert in aid of the International Year of the Child at Camberley, Surrey.

16 December 1979: Cliff leads a crowd estimated at 30,000 in Carols for the Queen outside Buckingham Palace, part of the International Year of the Child activities.

1980: Cliff voted number one in the Top Pop Star category by listeners of B.B.C.'s high-audience Saturday morning show *Swapshop*. He wins the *T.V. Times* Award for the Most Exciting Singer (male) on television.

6 February 1980: Cliff tops the bill at a special tribute concert at Fairfield Hall, Croydon, to long-time musical mentor Norrie Paramor who died in 1979. The concert, in aid of the Stars' organization for Spastics, is attended by the Duchess of Kent. Cliff, accompanied by the Ron Goodwin Orchestra with aid from Tony Rivers, John Perry, and Stu Calver, sings six numbers closely connected with Norrie: 'Congratulations', 'Summer Holiday', 'The Young Ones', 'Bachelor Boy' (Cliff on guitar), 'Constantly', and 'The Day I Met Marie'.

27 February 1980: *Nationwide, Daily Mirror,* and *Radio One* annual awards. Cliff receives the Nationwide Golden Award as Best Family Entertainer.

16 April 1980: mother-of-two Kim Kayne pays £1,400 for the privilege of lunching with Cliff. Capital Radio (London) listeners were invited to make a financial offer for this meeting with Cliff, with the winning total being donated to the charity Help a London Child. The menu: melon, fillet steak with Spanish sauce, green beans with ham, new potatoes, aubergines in batter, salad, strawberry shortcake, champagne, wine, and coffee. The lunch was held at Cliff's office.

23 July 1980: at 10.10 a.m. Cliff arrives at Buckingham Palace with his mother to receive his O.B.E. Those watching break into 'Congratulations' as he drives through the Palace gates. At 12.30 Cliff leaves, waving a Union Jack through an open car window and holding his O.B.E. high. He then attends a champagne lunch.

2 October 1980: Cliff takes part in a long-lasting Telethon T.V. show organized to raise money for charity.

January 1981: promotional visit to the United States for March tour.

24 February 1981: at the Café Royal Cliff receives the *Daily Mirror*

readers' award as Outstanding Music Personality of the Year, presented by Una Stubbs.

27 February 1981: at 12.30 Cliff leaves London's Heathrow Airport for the U.S. and Canada for a tour which was originally planned to last a month but which extends to seven weeks. Cliff regards this as a most important tour. The locations were: 3rd March, Seattle; 4th, Victoria (Canada); 5th, Vancouver; 6th, day off; 7th, Calgary; 8th, Edmonton; 9th, Saskatoon; 10th, Regina; 11th–12th, Winnipeg; 13th–14th, days off; 15th, Minneapolis; 16th, T.V. programme *Solid Gold*, Los Angeles; 17th, Grand Forks; 18th, day off; 19th, Thunder Bay; 20th, Sault St Marie; 21st, day off; 22nd, Sudbury; 23rd, Ottawa; 24th, Hamilton; 25th, day off; 26th, Kingston; 27th, Kitchener; 28th, London; 29th, day off; 30th, Toronto; 31st, Montreal; 1st April, Boston; 2nd, New York; 3rd, Philadelphia; 4th, Baltimore; 5th, day off; 6th, Cleveland; 7th, Cincinnatti; 8th, Columbus; 9th, Chicago; 10th, Milwaukee; 11th, day off; 12th, Kansas City; 13th, day off; 14th, Denver; 15th, Salt Lake City; 16th, day off; 17th, San Francisco; 18th, Los Angeles.

1 May 1981: Cliff Richard Rock Special at Odeon Theatre, Hammersmith – one show, filmed by B.B.C. producer Norman Stone. Audience in fifties-style gear.

Spring 1981: voted Top Pop Star in the *Sunday Telegraph* readers' poll of major personalities in British life.

3 May 1981: Cliff is filmed at London's Hardrock Café. The press is invited. He relives the early rock 'n' roll days. He wears black leather drainpipes, lurex tie, crepe shoes, white jacket plus a wig combed into a greasy teddy boy quiff. He sings '"D" In Love' and is backed by the Fantoms. The next day the newspapers show pictures of the event. He has been filmed by the B.B.C. for their forthcoming documentary on his life.

27 June 1981: poet and writer Steve Turner weds Mo MacAffety. Cliff attends. The reception is held at Cliff's house.

24 July 1981: Milton Keynes. Shoppers see Cliff being filmed for a video which is for promoting the single 'Wired for Sound' and the album of the same title.

Late July to August 1981: holidays in Portugal and some concerts in South Africa.

30 September 1981: begins two-week U.S. promotional visit.

14 October 1981: birthday celebrations with family.

15 October 1981: hardback edition of this book is published by Sidgwick and Jackson.

2 November 1981: British tour opens at Glasgow and like all Cliff's locations, tickets were sold out within hours of dates being announced.

5 November 1981: begins Edinburgh booking.

11 November 1981: starts four nights at Manchester's Apollo.

18 November 1981: commences concerts at The Centre, Brighton.

23 November 1981: Cliff is one of the invited artistes at the Royal Variety Command Performance.

25 November 1981: starts four nights at the Odeon, Birmingham.

21–27 November 1981: appears on the front page of the *Radio Times* edition for this week.

2 December 1981: the London four-concert booking begins at the Odeon, Hammersmith.

10 December 1981: Cliff makes a public appearance at Woolco, Bournemouth. He signs 1,057 albums and books.

16 December 1981: Coliseum, St Austell, the last tour venue. The last night is 19 December.

23 December 1981: off to Florida for his Christmas holiday.

4 January 1982: returns from Florida.

12–13 February 1982: plays the Queen Elizabeth Hall, Hong Kong.

15–16 February 1982: he is at the Hua Mark Stadium, Bangkok, Thailand.

19 February 1982: in Singapore.

22 February 1982: has a concert at the Entertainment Centre, Perth, Australia.

24–25 February 1982: concert at the Apollo Stadium, Adelaide, Australia.

27–28 February 1982: at the Festival Hall, Melbourne, Australia.

3 March 1982: appears at the Festival Hall, Brisbane, Australia.

5–6 March 1982: there is a booking at the Horden Pavilion, Sydney, Australia.

9–10 March 1982: plays the Town Hall, Christchurch, New Zealand.

12–13 March 1982: Cliff is 'in concert' at the Lagan Campbell Centre, Auckland, New Zealand.

25 March 1982: British newspapers carry story of possible romance between Cliff and tennis star Sue Barker.

31 March 1982: Cliff is in London and launches an appeal for children's hospitals.

1 April 1982: the *Daily Mail* quotes Cliff on his relationship with Sue Barker in a front-page article saying: 'Our relationship has only just started, but I have seen more of her than anyone else for quite a while.'

CHRISTIAN ACTIVITIES

These, as with almost all categories for Cliff Richard, are considerable. This section lists some of the most interesting and important. The many Gospel concert tours are not listed, nor are the endless meetings at which Cliff and Bill Latham engaged in dialogue in schools, colleges and churches, or the many charitable organizations helped by Cliff.

16 June 1966: Cliff proclaims from the stage of Earls Court, London, that he is a Christian. He takes part in the evening meeting of the Billy Graham crusade and sings 'It's No Secret'. 'The most exciting moment of my life,' Cliff says.

24 June 1966: an announcement is made that Cliff is closing down his 42,000-strong British fan club and will begin a three-year divinity course. The following month these retirement plans are denied. Cliff decides on a healthy mix of music and religion.

22 October 1966: Cliff joins the Archbishop of York, Dr Coggan, and the Bishop of Coventry, Dr Bardsley, to mark the twenty-first anniversary of Lee Abbey evangelical training centre.

9 July 1967: Cliff appears on the A.B.C. T.V. discussion programme *Looking For an Answer* with evangelist Dr Billy Graham.

16 July 1967: Cliff appears once more on *Looking For an Answer* and this time is in discussion with Paul Jones, lead singer of Manfred Mann.

6 December 1967: Cliff is confirmed and becomes a communicant of the Church of England. The event takes place at St Paul's, Finchley, London. The Bishop of Willesden, Graham Leonard, presides.

13 June 1968: showing of *Two a Penny* for religious press.

22 September 1968: Cliff attends Coventry Call to Mission meeting.

1 December 1968: Cliff introduces *Songs of Praise* B.B.C. television programme from Manchester.

4 December 1968: Cliff takes part in Christmas cake cutting for the Mental Health Trust at the Carlton Towers Hotel, London.

January 1969: Cliff begins filming a major religious series, *Life With Johnny*, for Tyne Tees Television.

11 June 1969: Cliff goes to the Holy Land where he films *Fire in Zion* for Worldwide Films, part of the Billy Graham organization. Later the film is re-titled *His Land*.

October 1970: E.M.I./Columbia issue Cliff's *About That Man* album.

9 October 1970: Cliff is awarded the National Viewers and Listeners Association annual award for his outstanding contribution to religious broadcasting and light entertainment.

5 March 1971: records with Dora Bryan *Music for Sunday* series for B.B.C. Radios One and Two. Producer is Jack Davies.

16 May 1971: presents prizes at the Methodist Association of Youth Clubs' yearly extravaganza at the Royal Albert Hall.

22 May 1971: opens a fete at St Anthony's Hospital, Cheam, Surrey.

24 June 1971: attends Arts Centre Open Day. The Arts Centre provides a meeting place for Christians professionally involved in the arts.

28 August–4 September 1971: attends the European Congress on Evangelism at Amsterdam.

8 September 1971: attends Festival of Light meeting, Westminster Central Hall, London.

26 October 1971: attends Christian Film Awards meeting.

1 November 1971: press conference to publicize Cliff's cassette series *Start the Day*.

25 November 1971: records another *Music for Sunday* series for B.B.C. Radios One and Two.

11 December 1971: takes part in carol concert at the Royal Festival Hall and sings 'Yesterday, Today, Forever', 'Down to Earth', 'The First Noel'.

15 December 1971: goes to see *Godspell*.

11 March 1972: Cliff gives a religious concert for Tear Fund at New Century Hall, Manchester.

14–15 April 1972: appears in a special Gospel concert at Philharmonic Hall, Liverpool, for charity. He leads a Gospel session.

6 December 1972: a special Cliff concert with Dana, Gordon Giltrap, the Settlers, and Roy Castle is held to raise money for the Arts Centre Group.

February 1973: Cliff releases the song 'Jesus' as a single. The record is ignored by some radio stations and does not become a major hit. Cliff is disappointed.

25 February 1973: Cliff appears in the eight-week series of contemporary Christian and general music concerts being held at St Paul's Cathedral.

12 April–8 May 1973: Cliff aligns himself with an evangelistic crusade with the general title of Help, Hope and Hallelujah, and appears in concerts across Australia. Cliff is backed for his singing by the Strangers, a group reformed by John Farrar and including his wife Pat. The address is given by the Reverend David MacInnes, Precentor of Birmingham Cathedral. MacInnes asks Cliff questions about his faith. Among the songs Cliff sings are: 'Sing a Song of Freedom', 'How Great Thou Art', 'Day by Day', 'Everything Is Beautiful', 'Silvery Rain', 'Jesus Loves You'.

27 August–1 September 1973: Spree (Spiritual Emphasis) gathering at Earls Court, London, for a gigantic teach-in. Johnny Cash, Parchment, Judy McKenzie, and Cliff are some of the musical contributors.

1 January 1974: at Southall Football Ground Cliff plays (for about ten minutes) in his first football game in about twenty years. The charity match is between the Buzz All Stars XI (Buzz being a British Christian youth monthly journal) and Choralerna (a Swedish Christian choir who had been at Spree the previous August). Cliff is sent off for fouling a player, though it looks like a theatrical foul to enable a cold Cliff to leave the pitch.

June 1974: release of the album *Help It Along* in aid of Tear Fund.

17 June 1974: speaks on B.B.C. Radio Two programme *Pause For Thought*.

28 August 1974: appears in a special concert at the New Gallery, Regent Street, London, for Crusaders.

19 November 1974: opens Christian bookshop in Sutton.

1 January 1975: rehearses with Choralerna.

18 January 1975: appears with Choralerna in Manchester.

20–21 January 1975: appears with Choralerna in Newcastle.

22 January 1975: appears with Choralerna in De Montfort Hall, Leicester.

25 January 1975: appears in The Name of Jesus concert, Royal Albert Hall, with Malcolm and Alwyn, and Choralerna. Cliff sings 'Bless You', 'Help It Along', 'Jesus Is My Kind of People', 'Why Me Lord', 'Power' (with Choralerna), 'Amazing Grace'. Cliff speaks of Tear Fund and of his faith.

19 April 1975: attends Way to Life rally, Empire Pool, Wembley, presided over by evangelist Dick Saunders. Bill Latham also sits on the platform. Cliff speaks of his Christian conversion and continuing faith. He sings 'Didn't He', 'Love Never Gives Up', 'Why Me Lord'. Part of this rally is broadcast the following weekend on *Sunday*, the B.B.C. Radio Four religious current affairs magazine programme.

30 April 1975: goes to see *Joseph and the Amazing Technicolour Dreamcoat*.

3 December 1975: records a Christmas Day Special for B.B.C. Radio. Producer David Winter.

4 December 1975: begins recording for a series of *Gospel Road* for B.B.C. Radios One and Two.

15 April 1976: Scope, a religious organization, presents two major charity concerts featuring Cliff and U.S. artist Larry Norman at the Odeon Theatre, Birmingham. The concerts are in aid of Free – The National Institute for the Healing of Addictions. Eric Clapton was the first of several personalities to be cured by the treatment offered. Pete Townshend of The Who was the first person to give a donation.

6 March 1977: the International Cliff Richard Movement magazine *Dynamite* reports, in anticipation of Tear Fund Sunday, that in 1976 Cliff's concerts for Tear Fund raised over £37,000. The money provides six vehicles which go to Argentina, the Yemen Arab Republic, Nigeria, Haiti, and Burundi, a generator for a hospital in India, a rural development centre in Kenya, and a nutritional training centre in Zaire. The same issue carries a commentary on Cliff's recent visit to India, his meeting with Mother Teresa and his visit to some of the Tear Fund projects in Bangladesh.

5 September 1977: Hodder and Stoughton publish Cliff's thoughts on his career, *Which One's Cliff?* in which he tells why he is a Christian and how he relates show business and his Christian convictions.

November 1977: E.M.I. issue *Small Corners*, an album of Cliff's often-featured religious songs.

31 January 1978: Face to Face meeting organized as part of the Booksellers Convention at Wembley Conference Centre. Chuck Girard, Roy and Fiona Castle also take part. Cliff accompanies himself on guitar and among his songs are 'Why Should the Devil Have All the Best Music', 'When I Survey the Wondrous Cross', 'Every Face Tells a Story'.

16 February 1978: Cliff joins Dana, Neil Reid, and Roy Castle at a special concert at Croydon for the Arts Centre Group. Graham Murray provides extra guitar to Cliff's.

April 1978: French single pairs 'Why Should the Devil Have All the Best Music' and 'Hey Watcha Say' (EMI 2C008 06623).

27 June 1978: Cliff attends opening of new Arts Centre Group building, Short Street, London SE1.

2 September 1978: Cliff joins evangelist Dick Saunders on stage and sings, amongst other songs, 'Up In Canada', 'Lord I Love You', and 'When I Survey the Wondrous Cross'. He tells the Crusade audience that his faith daily grows stronger. In an interview prior to the event Cliff tells the magazine *Dynamite* that he thinks the Rolling Stones make great records but their song lyrics are ridiculous; he makes complimentary remarks about Elvis.

9–10 October 1978: Cliff gives two concerts to celebrate the tenth anniversary of Tear Fund. In the first half he sings 'World of Difference' with Garth Hewitt and Dave Pope. In the second half he sings 'Such Is the Mystery', 'Song for Sarah', 'Yes He Lives', 'Yesterday, Today, Forever', 'Up In Canada', 'Night Time Girl', 'When I Survey the Wondrous Cross', 'Leaving My Past Behind', 'You Can't Get to Heaven by Living Like Hell', and 'Why Should the Devil Have All the Best Music'.

January 1979: U.K. Scripture Union launches a series of cassettes which feature Cliff reading the Scriptures.

20 April 1979: Cliff takes part in a special Youth Festival at St Alban's Cathedral.

10 June 1979: Cliff takes part in a chat show at a theatre in Liverpool and speaks of his Christian faith.

12 June 1979: further Bible readings for cassette series recorded at Scripture Union.

28 June 1979: Cliff is involved with both providing entertainment and giving Christian witness at the European Baptist Congress at the Great Brighton Centre, Brighton. He talks of his work for Tear Fund, his visit to the Soviet Union and the Baptist church he visited while there. He sings nine songs – his total singing spot is fifty minutes. At the meeting's completion he leads, with Bryan Gilbert, the general singing of 'God Is So Good'.

Autumn 1979: Cliff launches his own Gospel label, Patch Records, in association with E.M.I.'s export division. The first release is an album from Garth Hewitt with Cliff producing. The album is launched at the Greenbelt religious music festival. On this occasion Garth appears for the first time with a backing band.

26 August 1979: at the Greenbelt religious music festival Cliff is interviewed by poet and writer Steve Turner about his music and faith. Wearing his 'Rock 'n' Roll Juvenile' jacket he sings for one and a half hours during one of the concert sessions. His band comprises Graham Jarvis, George Ford, Tony, Stu and John, Mart Jenner, Snowy White, Mike Moran and Derek Beauchamine.

18 September 1979: attends Filey Christian Holiday Crusade meeting. He participates in four sessions and signs books.

18 December 1979: sings at a special concert to raise money for the Arts Centre Group.

7 February 1980: attends Christians in Sport dinner in London.

10 February 1980: appears with Dr Billy Graham at an evangelistic meeting in Cambridge. In the afternoon Cliff takes part in the meeting and in the evening he speaks at Great St Mary's, the university church.

27 March 1980: Cliff cuts short his American music business trip to appear on stage at London's Royal Albert Hall at the Sing Good News event honouring the top writers in a contest organized by the Bible Society. The audience numbers 5,500, the choir 300, and the orchestra 60 plus a rhythm group. Over 1,300 entrants were attracted by the competition. Cliff sings 'Why Should the Devil Have All the Best Music' and 'When I Survey the Wondrous Cross'.

15 April 1980: Cliff records for the popular Granada T.V. show *Pop Gospel* in Manchester.

1, 8 and 15 September 1980: Cliff contributes his thoughts to a B.B.C. World Service radio series *Reflections* in which he chooses biblical texts that he says sustain his faith.

September 1980: a fun Yuletide volume, *Happy Christmas From Cliff*, is published by Hodder and Stoughton. The book has lavish colour illustrations, stories, poems, puzzles, information and Christmas readings, and looks at how the countries of the world take account of Christmas and the birth of Jesus.

Christmas 1980: Cliff is one of a number of major stars invited to design their own shop window at Selfridges, London. Cliff's window takes a traditional religious theme – Christmas through the eyes of a child.

16 January 1981: Cliff attends the twenty-fifth birthday celebrations of the major British evangelical magazine *Crusade*. Along with Dr Billy Graham, Cliff is interviewed by Ronald Allison. Cliff talks about his recent promotional tour in the States, his forthcoming concert programme, and his thoughts on the death of John Lennon.

28 August 1981: Cliff is with Garth Hewitt, Network Three, at the Youth for Christ concert organized by Kamperland Muziekfestival, Holland.
30 August 1981: Cliff is at the Greenbelt Festival.
1–2 September 1981: tenth anniversary of the Arts Centre Group. Cliff sings at two special concerts, Wembley Conference Centre, Middlesex.
16 November 1981: Tear Fund Gala Night at London's Royal Albert Hall. Cliff is a surprise guest.

CHRISTIAN ORGANIZATIONS

Crusader's Union: the basis of the Crusader's Union is belief in God as the Creator of all men and the Father of all who believe in the Lord Jesus Christ as the only begotten Son of God, Redeemer of the world, and the One Mediator through faith in whom alone we obtain forgiveness of sins. God the Holy Spirit. The fact of sin. The necessity for the Atonement. The Incarnation, Death and Resurrection, Ascension and Coming Again of the Lord Jesus Christ. The whole Bible is the Inspired Word of God.
Tear Fund: founded in 1968, its work has been much furthered by Cliff. Its full title is The Evangelical Alliance Relief Fund. It channels money which has been donated by individuals and groups into relief and development work around the world. Tear Fund has projects in sixty countries in the Third World – in Africa, South-East Asia, and Central and South America. The Fund aims to demonstrate the love of God to needy people all over the world. Apart from Cliff, Tear Fund has received tremendous financial support from the many member societies of the International Cliff Richard Movement, as well as meeting houses associated with the umbrella organization, and those with allegiance to Grapevine, the Cliff fan club movement. Tear Fund has its headquarters in the United Kingdom at Whitfield House, 186 Kennington Park Road, London SE11 4BT.

DISCOGRAPHY

Many of the records listed below are deleted and cannot be obtained by record retailers for customers. They *may* be found in record shops' old stock, but second-hand dealers' shops are more likely to have them. The major U.K. dealer for Cliff and Shadows material is John Friesen of The Record Scene, 3 Church Parade, Ashford, Middlesex, where there is a shop and a mail-order service (telephone Ashford 55322). Friesen deals in worldwide Cliff releases.

United Kingdom

The information given below is record title(s), in the case of singles highest chart position, record number, and release date.

In the early chart days if there was a demand in record retail outlets for both sides of a single then each was noted independently for chart statistics. If this had not been the practice, a number of Cliff's records would have obtained a higher position and would doubtless have increased the total number of his chart-toppers. Where both sides of a single were listed separately in the charts, the position of each is given in brackets after the title. In all other cases except one the number in brackets refers to the first (A side) title. The exception is 'Move It', originally released as the B side, which reached no. 2 in the charts.

SINGLES

Schoolboy Crush/Move It (2). Columbia DB 4178. August 1958. Also 78 r.p.m. release.

High Class Baby/My Feet Hit the Ground. (7). Columbia DB 4203. November 1958. Also 78 r.p.m. release.

Livin' Lovin' Doll/Steady With You. (20). Columbia DB 4249. January 1959. Also 78 r.p.m. release.

Mean Streak (10)/Never Mind (21). Columbia DB 4290. April 1959. Also 78 r.p.m. release.

Living Doll/Apron Strings. (1). Columbia DB 4306. July 1959. Re-entered charts December 1959 (26) and again January 1960 (28). Also 78 r.p.m. release.

Travellin' Light (1)/Dynamite (16). Columbia DB 4351. October 1959. Also 78 r.p.m. release.

Voice in the Wilderness/Don't Be Mad at Me. (2). Columbia DB 4398. January 1960. Re-entered charts May 1960 (36). Also 78 r.p.m. release.

Fall in Love With You/Willie and the Hand Jive. (2). Columbia DB 4431. March 1960.

Please Don't Tease/Where Is MY Heart. (1). Columbia DB 4479. June 1960.

Nine Times Out of Ten/Thinking of Our Love. (3). Columbia DB 4506. September 1960.

I Love You/'D' in Love. (1). Columbia DB 4547. December 1960.

Theme For a Dream/Mumblin' Mosie. (4). Columbia DB 4593. February 1961.

Gee Whizz It's You/I Cannot Find a True Love (export single). (4). Columbia DC 756. March 1961. Demand in the U.K. for this export single was such that it reached no. 4 in the U.K. charts.

A Girl Like You/Now's the Time to Fall in Love. (3). Columbia DB 4667. June 1961.

When the Girl in Your Arms Is the Girl in Your Heart/Got a Funny Feeling. (3). Columbia DB 4716. October 1961.

The Young Ones/We Say Yeah. (1). Columbia DB 4761. January 1962.

I'm Lookin' Out the Window/Do You Want to Dance. (2). Columbia DB 4828. May 1962.

It'll Be Me/Since I Lost You. (2). Columbia DB 4886. August 1962.

The Next Time/Bachelor Boy. (1). Columbia DB 4950. February 1963.

Summer Holiday/Dancing Shoes. (1). Columbia DB 4977. February 1963.

Lucky Lips/I Wonder. (4). Columbia DB 7034. May 1963.

It's All in the Game/Your Eyes Tell on You. (2). Columbia DB 7089. August 1963.

Don't Talk to Him/Say You're Mine. (2). Columbia DB 7150. November 1963. Re-entered charts February 1964 (50).

I'm the Lonely One/Watch What You Do With My Baby. (8). Columbia DB 7203. January 1964.

Constantly/True True Lovin'. (4). Columbia DB 7272. April 1964.

On the Beach/A Matter of Moments. (7). Columbia DB 7305. June 1964.

The Twelfth of Never/I'm Afraid to Go Home. (8). Columbia DB 7372. October 1964.

I Could Easily Fall in Love With You/I'm in Love With You. (9). Columbia DB 7420. December 1964.

The Minute You're Gone/Just Another Guy. (1). Columbia DB 7496. March 1965.

Angel/Razzle Dazzle (export single). Columbia DC 762. May 1965.

On My Word/Just a Little Bit Too Late. (12). Columbia DB 7596. June 1965.

The Time in Between/Look Before You Love. (22). Columbia DB 7660. August 1965.

Wind Me Up (Let Me Go)/The Night. (2). Columbia DB 7745. November 1965.

Blue Turns to Grey/Somebody Loses. (15). Columbia DB 7866. March 1966.

Visions/What Would I Do (For the Love of a Girl). (7). Columbia DB 8968. July 1966.

Time Drags By/La La La Song. (10). Columbia DB 8017. October 1966.

In the Country/Finders Keepers. (6). Columbia DB 8094. December 1966.

It's All Over/Why Wasn't I Born Rich. (9). Columbia DB 8150. March 1967.

I'll Come Running/I Get the Feelin'. (26). Columbia DB 8210. June 1967.

The Day I Met Marie/Our Story Book. (10). Columbia DB 8245. August 1967.

All My Love/Sweet Little Jesus Boy. (6). Columbia DB 8293. November 1967.

Congratulations/High and Dry. (1). Columbia DB 8376. March 1968.

I'll Love You Forever Today/Girl You'll Be a Woman Soon. (27). Columbia DB 8437. June 1968.

Marianne/Mr Nice. (22).
Columbia DB 8476. September 1968.

Don't Forget to Catch Me/What's More (I Don't Need Her). (21).
Columbia DB 8503. November 1968.

Good Times/Occasional Rain. (12). Columbia DB 8548. February 1969.

Big Ship/She's leaving You. (8). Columbia DB 8581. May 1969.

Throw Down a Line/Reflections (with Hank Marvin). (7). Columbia DB 8615. September 1969.

With the Eyes of a Child/So Long. (20). Columbia DB 8641. December 1969.

Joy of Living/Boogatoo, Leave My Woman Alone. (25). Columbia DB 8687. February 1970.

Goodbye Sam, Hello Samantha/You Never Can Tell. (6). Columbia DB 8685. June 1970.

Ain't Got Time Anymore/Monday Comes Too Soon. (21). Columbia DB 8708. September 1970.

Sunny Honey Girl/Don't Move Away (with Olivia Newton-John)/I Was Only Fooling Myself. (19). Columbia DB 8747. January 1971.

Silvery Rain/Annabella Umbarella/Time Flies. (27). Columbia DB 8774. April 1971.

Flying Machine/Pigeon. (37). Columbia DB 8797. July 1971.

Sing a Song of Freedom/A Thousand Conversations. (13). Columbia DB 8836. November 1971.

Jesus/Mr Cloud. (35). Columbia DB 8864. March 1972.

Living in Harmony/Empty Chairs. (12). Columbia DB 8917. August 1972.

Brand New Song/The Old Accordion. (No chart placing). Columbia DB 8957. November 1972.

Power to All Our Friends/Come Back Billie Joe. (4). EMI 2012. March 1973.

Help It Along/Tomorrow Rising/The Days of Love/Ashes to Ashes. (29). EMI 2022. May 1973.

Take Me High/Celestial Houses. (27). EMI 2088. December 1973.

(You Keep Me) Hanging On/Love Is Here. (13). EMI 2150. May 1974.

It's Only Me You've Left Behind/You're the One. (No chart placing). EMI 2279. March 1975.

Honky Tonk Angel/Wouldn't You Know It. (No chart placing). EMI 2344. September 1975.

Miss You Nights/Love Is Enough. (15). EMI 2376. February 1976.

Devil Woman/Love On. (9). EMI 2485. May 1976.

I Can't Ask for Anything More Than You Babe/Junior Cowboy. (17). EMI 2499. August 1976.

Hey Mr Dream Maker/No One Waits. (31). EMI 2559. December 1976.

My Kinda Life/Nothing Left for Me to Say. (15). EMI 2584. March 1977.

When Two Worlds Drift

194

Apart/That's Why I Love You. (46). EMI 2663. June 1977.

Yes He Lives/Good on the Sally Army. (No chart placing). EMI 2730. January 1978.

Please Remember Me/Please Don't Tease. (No chart placing). EMI 2832. July 1978.

Can't Take the Hurt Anymore/Needing a Friend. (No chart placing). EMI 2885. November 1978.

Green Light/Imagine Love. (57). EMI 2920. March 1979.

We Don't Talk Anymore/Count Me Out. (1). EMI 2975. July 1979.

Hot Shot/Walking in the Light. (46). EMI 5003. November 1979.

Carrie/Moving In. (4). EMI 5006. February 1980.

Dreamin'/Dynamite. (8). EMI 5095. August 1980.

Suddenly (with Olivia Newton-John)/You Made Me Love You (Newton-John only). (15). Jet 7002. October 1980.

A Little in Love/Keep on Looking. (15). EMI 5123. February 1981.

Wired For Sound/Hold On. (4). EMI 5221. August 1981.

Daddy's Home/Shakin' All Over. (2). EMI 5251. November 1981.

Reissued oldies, available separately or in a special boxed set:

Move It/Schoolboy Crush. (–). DB 4178. February 1982.

Living Doll/Apron Strings. (–). DB 4306. February 1982.

Travellin' Light/Dynamite. (–). DB 4351. February 1982.

Please Don't Tease/Where Is My Heart. (–). DB 4479. February 1982.

The Young Ones/We Say Yeah. (–). DB 4761. February 1982.

The Next Time/Bachelor Boy. (–). DB 4950. February 1982.

Summer Holiday/Dancing Shoes. (–). DB 4977. February 1982.

Wind Me Up (Let Me Go)/The Night. (–). DB 7745. February 1982.

Congratulations/High and Dry. (–). DB 8376. February 1982.

Miss You Nights/Love Is Enough. (–). DB 2376. February 1982.

Devil Woman/Love On, Shine On. (–). EMI 2458. February 1982.

We Don't Talk Anymore/Count Me Out. (–). EMI 2975. February 1982. (This is not a reissue since it was not deleted, but it is included in the boxed set.)

E.P.s

Serious Charge: Living Doll/No Turning Back/Mad About You/Chinchilla (The Shadows). May 1959.

Cliff No. 1: Apron Strings/ My Babe/Down the Line/I Gotta Feeling/Baby I Don't Care. June 1959.

Cliff No. 2: Donna/Move It/Ready Teddy/Too Much/Don't Bug Me Baby. July 1959.

Expresso Bongo: Love/A Voice in the Wilderness/The Shrine on the Second Floor/Bongo Blues (The Shadows). (24). January 1960.

Cliff Sings No. 1: Here Comes Summer/I Gotta Know/Blue

Suede Shoes/The Snake and the Bookworm. February 1960.

Cliff Sings No. 2: Twenty Flight Rock/Pointed Toe Shoes/Mean Woman Blues/I'm Walkin'. March 1960.

Cliff Sings No. 3: I'll String Along With You/Embraceable You/As Time Goes By/The Touch of Your Lips. June 1960.

Cliff Sings No. 4: I Don't Know Why (I Just Do)/Little Things Mean a Lot/Somewhere Along the Way/That's My Desire. September 1960.

Cliff's Silver Discs: Please Don't Tease/Fall in Love With You/Nine Times Out of Ten/Travellin' Light. December 1960.

Me and My Shadows No. 1: I'm Gonna Get You/You and I/I Cannot Find a True Love/Evergreen Tree/She's Gone. February 1961.

Me and My Shadows No. 2: Left Out Again/You're Just the One to Do It/Lamp of Love/Choppin' 'n' Changin'/We Have Made It. March 1961.

Me and My Shadows No. 3: Tell Me/Gee Whizz It's You/I'm Willing to Learn/I Love You So/I Don't Know. April 1961.

Listen to Cliff No. 1: What'd I Say/True Love Will Come to You/Blue Moon/Lover. October 1961.

Dream: Dream/All I Do Is Dream of You/I'll See You in My Dreams/When I Grow Too Old to Dream. November 1961.

Listen to Cliff No. 2: Unchained Melody/First Lesson in Love/Idle Gossip/Almost Like Being in Love/Beat Out Dat Rhythm on a Drum. December 1961.

Cliff's Hit Parade: I Love You/Theme For a Dream/ A Girl Like You/When the Girl in Your Arms. February 1962.

Cliff Richard No. 1: Forty Days/Catch Me/How Wonderful to Know/Tough Enough. April 1962.

Hits from The Young Ones: The Young Ones/Got A Funny Feeling/Lessons in Love/We Say Yeah. May 1962.

Cliff Richard No. 2: Fifty Tears for Every Kiss/The Night Is So Lonely/Poor Boy/Y'Arriva. June 1962.

Cliff's Hits: It'll Be Me/Since I Lost You/Do You Want to Dance/I'm Looking Out the Window. November 1962.

Time for Cliff and the Shadows: So I've Been Told/I'm Walkin' the Blues/When My Dreamboat Comes Home/Blueberry Hill/You Don't Know. March 1963.

Holiday Carnival: Carnival/Moonlight Bay/Some of These Days/For You, For Me. May 1963.

Hits from Summer Holiday: Summer Holiday/The Next Time/Dancing Shoes/Bachelor Boy. June 1963.

More Hits from Summer Holiday: Seven Days to a Holiday/Stranger in Town/Really Waltzing/All at Once. September 1963.

Cliff's Lucky Lips: It's All in the Game/Your Eyes Tell on You/Lucky Lips/I Wonder. October 1963.

Love Songs: I'm in the Mood For You/Secret Love/Love Letters/I Only Have Eyes For You. November 1963.

When in France: La Mer/Boum/J'attendrai/C'est si bon. February 1964.

Cliff Sings Don't Talk to Him: Don't Talk to Him/Say You're Mine/Spanish Harlem/Who Are We to Say/Falling in Love With Love. March 1964.

Cliff's Palladium Successes: I'm the Lonely One/Watch What You Do With My Baby/Perhaps Perhaps Perhaps/Frenesi. May 1964.

Wonderful Life: Wonderful Life/Do You Remember/What've I Gotta Do/Walkin'. August 1964.

A Forever Kind of Love: A Forever Kind of Love/It's Wonderful to Be Young/Constantly/True True Lovin'. September 1964.

Wonderful Life No. 2: Matter of Moments/Girl in Every Port/A Little Imagination/In the Stars. October 1964.

Hits from Wonderful Life: On the Beach/We Love a Movie/Home/All Kinds of People. December 1964.

Why Don't They Understand: Why Don't They Understand/Where the Four Winds Blow/The Twelfth of Never/I'm Afraid to Go Home. February 1965.

Cliff's Hits from Aladdin and His Wonderful Lamp: Havin' Fun/Evening Comes/Friends/I Could Easily Fall in Love With You. March 1965.

Look in My Eyes Maria: Look in My Eyes Maria/Where Is Your Heart/Maria/If I Give My Heart to You. May 1965.

Angel: Angel/I Only Came to Say Goodbye/On My Word/The Minute You're Gone. September 1965.

Take Four: Boom Boom/My Heart Is an Open Book/Lies and Kisses/Sweet and Gentle. October 1965.

Wind Me Up: Wind Me Up/In the Night/The Time in Between/Look Before You Love. February 1966.

Hits from When in Rome: Come Prima (The First Time)/Nel Blu Dipinto, Di Blu (Volare)/Dicitencello Vuie (Just Say I Love Her)/Arrivederci Roma. April 1966.

Love Is Forever: My Colouring Book/Fly Me to the Moon/Someday/Everybody Needs Somebody to Love. June 1966.

La La La La La: La La La La La/Solitary Man/Things We Said Today/Never Knew What Love Could Do. December 1966.

Cinderella: Come Sunday/Peace and Quiet/She Needs Him More Than Me/Hey Doctor Man. May 1967.

Carol Singers: God Rest You Merry, Gentlemen/In the Bleak Midwinter/Unto Us a

Boy Is Born/While Shepherds Watched/O Little Town of Bethlehem. November 1967.

ALBUMS (all released by E.M.I.)

Cliff: Apron Strings/My Babe/Down the Line/I Got a Feeling/Jet Black (The Drifters)/Baby I Don't Care/Donna/Move It/Ready Teddy/Too Much/Don't Bug Me Baby/Driftin' (The Drifters)/That'll Be the Day/Be-Bop-A-Lula (The Drifters)/Danny/Whole Lotta Shakin' Goin' On. Mono SX 1147. April 1959.

Cliff Sings: Blue Suede Shoes/The Snake and the Bookworm/I Gotta Know/Here Comes Summer/I'll String Along With You/Embraceable You/As Time Goes By/The Touch of Your Lips/Twenty Flight Rock/Pointed Toe Shoes/Mean Woman Blues/I'm Walkin'/I Don't Know Why/Little Things Mean a Lot/Somewhere Along the Way/That's My Desire. Mono SX 1192. November 1959.

Me and My Shadows: I'm Gonna Get You/You and I/I Cannot Find a True Love/Evergreen Tree/She's Gone/Left Out Again/You're Just the One to Do It/Lamp of Love/Choppin' 'n' Changin'/We Have It Made/Tell Me/Gee Whizz It's You/I Love You So/I'm Willing to Learn/I Don't Know/Working After School. Mono SX 1261, stereo SCX 3330, different takes. October 1960.

Listen to Cliff: What'd I Say/Blue Moon/Trust Love Will Come to You Lover/Unchained Melody/Idle Gossip/First Lesson in Love/Almost Like Being in Love/Beat Out Dat Rhythm on a Drum/Memories Linger On/Temptation/I Live For You/Sentimental Journey/I Want You to Know/We Kiss in a Shadow/It's You. Mono SX 1320, stereo SCX 3375, different takes. May 1961.

21 Today: Happy Birthday to You/Forty Days/Catch Me/How Wonderful to Know/Tough Enough/Fifty Tears for Every Kiss/The Night Is So Lonely/Poor Boy/Y' Arriva/Outsider/Tea For Two/To Prove My Love For You/Without You/A Mighty Lonely Man/My Blue Heaven/Shame On You. Mono SX 1368, stereo SCX 3409. October 1961.

The Young Ones: Friday Night/Got a Funny Feeling/Peace Pipe/Nothing's Impossible/The Young Ones/All for One/Lessons in Love/No One for Me But Nicky/What D'You Know We've Got a Show and Vaudeville Routine/When the Girl in Your Arms Is the Girl in Your Heart/Just Dance/Mood Mambo/The Savage/We Say Yeah. Mono SX 1384, stereo SCX 3397. December 1961.

32 Minutes and 17 Seconds With

Cliff Richard: It'll Be Me/So I've Been Told/How Long Is Forever/I'm Walkin' the Blues/Turn Around/Blueberry Hill/Let's Make a Memory/When My Dreamboat Comes Home/I'm On My Way/Spanish Harlem/You Don't Know/Falling in Love With Love/Who Are We to Say/I Wake Up Cryin'. Mono SX 1431, stereo SCX 3436. October 1962.

Summer Holiday: Seven Days to a Holiday/Summer Holiday/Let Us Take You For a Ride/Les Girls/Round and Round/Foot Tapper/Stranger in Town/Orlando's Mime/Bachelor Boy/A Swingin' Affair/Really Waltzing/All at Once/Dancing Shoes/Jugoslav Wedding/The Next Time/Big News. Mono SX 1472, stereo SCX 3462. January 1963.

Cliff's Hit Album: Move It/Living Doll/Travellin' Light/A Voice in the Wilderness/Fall in Love With You/Please Don't Tease/Nine Times Out of Ten/I Love You/Theme For a Dream/A Girl Like You/When the Girl in Your Arms Is the Girl in Your Heart/The Young Ones/I'm Looking Out the Window/Do You Want to Dance. Mono SX 1512, stereo SCX 1512. July 1963.

When in Spain: Perfidia/Amor Amor Amor/Frenesi/You Belong to My Heart/Vaya Con Dios/Sweet and Gentle/Maria No Mas/Kiss/Perhaps Perhaps Perhaps/Magic Is the Moonlight/Carnival/Sway. Mono SX 1541, stereo SCX 3488. September 1963.

Wonderful Life: Wonderful Life/A Girl in Every Port/Walkin'/A Little Imagination/Home/On the Beach/In the Stars/We Love a Movie/Do You Remember/What've I Gotta Do/Theme for Young Lovers/All Kinds of People/A Matter of Moments/Youth and Experience. Mono SX 1628, stereo, SCX 3515. July 1964.

Aladdin and His Wonderful Lamp: Emperor Theme/Chinese Street Scene/Me Oh My/I Could Easily Fall in Love With You/There's Gotta Be a Way/Ballet (Rubies, Emeralds, Sapphires, Diamonds)/Dance of the Warriors/Friends/Dragon Dance/Genie With the Light Brown Lamp/Make Ev'ry Day a Carnival/Widow Twankey's Song/I'm Feeling Oh So Lovely/I've Said Too Many Things/Evening Comes/Havin' Fun. Mono SX 1676, stereo SCX 3522. December 1964.

Cliff Richard: Angel Sway/I Only Came to Say Goodbye/Take Special Care/Magic Is the Moonlight/House Without Windows/Razzle Dazzle/I Don't Wanna Love You/It's Not For Me to Say/You Belong to My Heart/Again/Perfidia/Kiss/Reelin' and Rockin'. Mono SC 1709, stereo SCX 3456. April 1965.

More Hits – By Cliff: It'll be Me/The Next Time/Bachelor Boy/Summer Holiday/Dancing Shoes/Lucky Lips/It's All in the Game/Don't Talk to Him/I'm the Lonely One/Constantly/On the Beach/A Matter of Moments/The Twelfth of Never/I Could Easily Fall in Love With You. Mono SX 1737, stereo SCX 3555. July 1965.

When in Rome: Come Prima/Volare/Autumn Concerta/The Questions/Maria's Her Name/Don't Talk to Him/Just Say I Love Her/Arrivederci Roma/Carina/A Little Grain of Sand/House Without Windows/Che Cosa Del Farai Mio Amore/Tell Me You're Mine. Mono SX 1762, no stereo version. August 1965.

Love is Forever: Everybody Needs Someone to Love/Long Ago and Far Away/All of a Sudden My Heart Sings/Have I Told You Lately That I Love You/Fly Me to the Moon/A Summer Place/I Found a Rose/My Foolish Heart/Through the Eye of a Needle/My Colouring Book/I Walk Alone/Someday You'll Want Me to Want You/Paradise Lost/Look Homeward Angel. Mono SX 1769, stereo SCX 3569. November 1965.

Kinda Latin: Blame It on the Bossa Nova/Blowing in the Wind/Quiet Night of Quiet Stars/Eso Beso/The Girl from Ipanema/One Note Samba/Fly Me to the Moon/Our Day Will Come/Quando Quando Quando/Come Closer to Me/Meditation/Concrete and Clay. Mono SX 6039, stereo SCX 6039. May 1966.

Finders Keepers: Finders Keepers/Time Drags By/Washerwoman/La La La Song/My Way/Senorita/Spanish Music–Fiesta/This Day/Paella/Medley (Finders Keepers/My Way/Paella/Fiesta)/Run to the Door/Where Did the Summer Go/Into Each Life/Some Rain Must Fall. Mono SX 6079, stereo SCX 6079. December 1966.

Cinderella: Welcome to Stonybroke/Why Wasn't I Born Rich/Peace and Quiet/The Flyder and the Spy/Poverty/The Hunt/In the Country/Come Sunday/Dare I Love Him Like I Do (Jackie Lee)/If Our Dreams Came True/Autumn/The King's Place/She Needs Him More than Me/Hey Doctor Man. Mono SX 6103, stereo SCX 6103. January 1967.

Don't Stop Me Now: Shout/One Fine Day/I'll Be Back/Heartbeat/I Saw Her Standing There/Hang On to a Dream/You Gotta Tell Me/Homeward Bound/Good Golly Miss Molly/Don't Make Promises/Move It/Don't/Dizzy Miss Lizzy/Baby It's You/My Babe/Save the Last Dance For

Me. Mono SX 6133, stereo SCX 6133. April 1967.

Good News: Good News/It Is No Secret/We Shall Be Changed/Twenty-Third Psalm/Go Where I Send Thee/What a Friend We Have in Jesus/All Glory Laud and Honour/Just a Closer Walk With Thee/The King of Love My Shepherd Is/Mary What You Gonna Name That Pretty Little Baby/When I Survey the Wondrous Cross/Take My Hand Precious Lord/Get on Board Little Children/May the Good Lord Bless and Keep You. Mono SX 6167, stereo SCX 6167. October 1967.

Cliff in Japan: Shout/I'll Come Runnin'/The Minute You're Gone/On the Beach/Hang On to a Dream/Spanish Harlem/Finders Keepers/Visions/Move It/Living Doll/La La La La La/Twist and Shout/Evergreen Tree/What I'd Say/Dynamite/Medley (Let's Make a Memory/The Young Ones/Lucky Lips/Summer Holiday/We Say Yeah). Mono SX 6244, stereo SCX 6244. May 1968.

Two a Penny: Two a Penny/I'll Love You Forever Today/Questions/Long Is the Night (instrumental)/Lonely Girl/And Me (I'm on the Outside Now)/Daybreak/Twist and Shout/Celeste (instrumental)/Wake Up Wake Up/Cloudy/Red Rubber Ball/Close to Kathy/Rattler.

Mono SX 6262, stereo SCX 6262. August 1968.

Established 1958: Don't Forget to Catch Me/Voyage to the Bottom of the Bath (The Shadows)/Not the Way That It Should Be/Poem (The Shadows)/The Dreams I Dream/The Average Life of a Daily Man (The Shadows)/Somewhere By the Sea/Banana Man (The Shadows)/Girl On the Bus/The Magical Mrs Clamps (The Shadows)/Ooh La La/Here I Go Again Loving You (The Shadows)/What's Behind the Eyes of Mary/Maggie's Samba (The Shadows). Mono SX 6282, stereo SCX 6282. September 1968.

The Best of Cliff: The Minute You're Gone/Congratulations/Girl You'll Be a Woman Soon/The Time in Between/Time Drags By/In the Country/Blue Turns to Grey/On My Word/Wind Me Up/Visions/It's All Over/I'll Come Runnin'/The Day I Met Marie/All My Love. Mono SX 6343, stereo SCX 6343. June 1969.

Sincerely Cliff: Sam/London's Not Too Far/Take Action/I'm Not Getting Married/In the Past/Always/Will You Love Me Tomorrow/You'll Want Me/Time/For Emily Whenever I May Find Her/Baby I Could Be So Good at Loving You/Take Good Care of Her/When I Find You/Punch and Judy. Mono SX 6357, stereo SCX 6357. October 1969.

Cliff 'Live' at The Talk of the Town: Intro (Congratulations)/Shout/All My Love/Ain't Nothing But a House-Party/Something Good/If Ever I Should Leave You/Girl You'll Be a Woman Soon/Hank's Medley/London's Not Too Far/The Dreams I Dream/The Day I Met Marie/La La La La La/A Taste of Honey (guitar solo)/The Lady Came from Baltimore/When I'm Sixty-Four/What's More (I Don't Need Her)/Bows and Fanfare/Congratulations/Visions/Finale (Congratulations). Regal SRS 5031. July 1970.

About That Man: Sweet Little Jesus Boy/Where Is That Man/Can It Be True/Reflections/Cliff tells the story of Jesus in the words of the Living Bible. SCX 6408. October 1970.

Tracks 'n' Grooves: Early in the Morning/As I Walk Into the Morning of Your Life/Love, Truth and Emily Stone/My Head Goes Around/Put My Mind at Ease/Abraham Martin and John/The Girl Can't Help It/Bang Bang My Baby Shot Me Down/I'll Make It Up to You/I'd Just Be Fool Enough/Don't Let Tonight Ever End/What a Silly Thing to Do/Your Heart's Not in Your Love/Don't Ask Me to Be Friends/Are You Only Fooling Me. SCX 6435. November 1970.

His Land: Ezekiel's Vision (Ralph Carmichael Orchestra)/Dry Bones (Ralph Carmichael Orchestra)/His Land/Jerusalem, Jerusalem/The New Twenty-Third/His Land/Hava Nagila (Ralph Carmichael Orchestra)/Over in Bethlehem (and Cliff Barrows)/Keep Me Where Love Is/He's Everything to Me (and Cliff Barrows)/Narration and Hallelujah Chorus (Cliff Barrows). SCX 6443. November 1970.

The Best of Cliff Volume 2: Goodbye Sam, Hello Samantha/Marianne/Throw Down a Line/Jesus/Sunny Honey Girl/I Ain't Got Time Anymore/Flying Machine/Sing a Song of Freedom/With the Eyes of a Child/Good Times (Better Times)/I'll Love You Forever Today/The Joy of Living/Silvery Rain/Big Ship. SCX 6519. November 1972.

Take Me High: It's Only Money/Midnight Blue/Hover (instrumental)/Why (and Anthony Andrews)/Life/Driving/The Game/Brumburger Duet (and Debbie Watling)/Take Me High/The Anti-Brotherhood of Man/Winning/Driving (instrumental)/Join the Band/The World Is Love/Brumburger (finale). EMI EMC 3016. December 1973.

Help It Along: Day by Day/Celestial

Houses/Jesus/Silvery
Rain/Jesus Loves You/Fire
and Rain/Yesterday, Today,
Forever/Help It
Along/Amazing Grace/Higher
Ground/Sing a Song of
Freedom. EMI EMA 768.
June 1974.

The 31st of February Street: 31st of
February Street/Give Me Back
That Old Familiar Feeling/The
Leaving/Travellin'
Light/There You Go
Again/Nothing to Remind
Me/Our Love Could Be So
Real/No Matter What/Fireside
Song/Going Away/Long Long
Time/You Will Never
Know/The Singer/31st of
February Street Closing. EMI
EMC 3048. November 1974.

I'm Nearly Famous: I Can't Ask
for Anymore Than You/It's
No Use Pretending/I'm Nearly
Famous/Lovers/Junior
Cowboy/Miss You Nights/I
Wish You'd Change Your
Mind/Devil Woman/Such Is
the Mystery/You've Got to
Give Me All Your Lovin'/If
You Walked Away/Alright,It's
Alright. EMI EMC 3122. May
1976.

Every Face Tells a Story: My
Kinda Life/Must Be
Love/When Two Worlds Drift
Apart/You Got Me
Wondering/Every Face Tells a
Story (It Never Tells a
Lie)/Try a Smile/Hey Mr
Dream Maker/Give Me Love
Your Way/Up In the
World/Don't Turn the Light
Out/It'll Be Me Babe/Spider

Man. EMI EMC 3172. March
1977.

Small Corners: Why Should the
Devil Have All the Good
Music/I Love/I've Got News
For You/Hey Watcha Say/I
Wish We'd All Been
Ready/Joseph/Good on the
Sally Army/Goin' Home/Up in
Canada/Yes He Lives/When I
Survey the Wondrous Cross.
EMI EMC 3219. November
1977.

Green Light: Green Light/Under
Lock and Key/She's a
Gipsy/Count Me Out/Please
Remember Me/Never Even
Thought/Free My Soul/Start
All Over Again/While She's
Young/Can't Take the Hurt
Anymore/Ease Along. EMI
EMC 3231. October 1978.

Thank You Very Much (with The
Shadows): The Young
Ones/Do You Want to
Dance/The Day I Met
Marie/Shadoogie (The
Shadows)/Atlantis (The
Shadows)/Nivram (The
Shadows)/Apache (The
Shadows)/Please Don't
Tease/Miss you Nights/Move
It/Willie and the Hand Jive/All
Shook Up/Devil Woman/Why
Should the Devil Have All the
Good Music/End of the Show
(Cliff plus Shadows). EMI
EMTV 15. February 1979.

Rock 'n' Roll Juvenile: Monday
Thru' Friday/Doing Fine/Cities
May Fall/You Know That I
Love You/My Luck Won't
Change/Rock 'n' Roll
Juvenile/Sci-Fi/Fallin' in

Love/Carrie/Hot Shot/Language of Love/We Don't Talk Anymore. EMI EMC 3307. September 1979.

Cliff Richard's 40 Golden Greats: Move It/Living Doll/Travellin' Light/Fall in Love With You/Please Don't Tease/Nine Times Out of Ten/Theme for a Dream/Gee Whizz It's You/When the Girl in Your Arms Is the Girl in Your Heart/A Girl Like You/The Young Ones/Do You Want to Dance/I'm Lookin' Out the Window/It'll Be Me/Bachelor Boy/The Next Time/Summer Holiday/Lucky Lips/It's All in the Game/Don't Talk to Him/Constantly/On the Beach/I Could Easily Fall in Love With You/The Minute You're Gone/Wind Me Up (Let Me Go)/Visions/Blue Turns to Grey/In the Country/The Day I Met Marie/All My Love/Congratulations/Throw Down a Line/Goodbye Sam, Hello Samantha/Sing a Song of Freedom/Power to All Our Friends/(You Keep Me) Hangin' On/Miss You Nights/Devil Woman/I Can't Ask for Anything More Than You/My Kinda Life. EMI EMTVS 6. October 1979.

Cliff – The Early Years (this album was scheduled for release February 1980 but its release was cancelled): Please Don't Tease/Willie and the Hand Jive/'D' in Love/High Class Baby/Mean Woman Blues/Nine Times Out of Ten/My feet Hit the Ground/Apron Strings/Livin' Lovin' Doll/Never Mind/Schoolboy Crush/It'll Be Me/Gee Whizz It's You/Choppin' 'n' Changin'/Blue Suede Shoes/Dynamite/Mean Streak/She's Gone/I Cannot Find a true Love/Move It.

I'm No Hero: Take Another Look/Anything I Can Do/A Little in Love/Here (So Doggone Blue)/Give a Little Bit More/In the Night/I'm No Hero/Dreamin'/A Heart Will Break/Everyman. EMI EMA 796. August 1980.

Cliff – Love Songs: Miss You Nights/Constantly/Up In the World/Carrie/A Voice in the Wilderness/The Twelfth of Never/I Could Easily Fall/The Day I Met Marie/Can't Take the Hurt Anymore/A Little in Love/The Minute You're Gone/Visions/When Two Worlds Drift Apart/The Next Time/It's All in the Game/Don't Talk to Him/When the Girl in Your Arms/Theme for a Dream/Fall in Love With You/We Don't Talk Anymore. EMTV 27. June 1981.

Wired for Sound: Wired for Sound/Once in a While/Better Than I Know Myself/Oh No Don't Let Go/'Cos I Love That Rock 'n' Roll/Broken Doll/Lost in a Lonely World/Summer Rain/Young Love/Say You Don't Mind/Daddy's Home. EMI EMC 3377. September 1981.

I'm Nearly Famous: Fame 3010. May 1982.

Take Me to the Leader: expected title of new gospel album, due out summer 1982.

MISCELLANEOUS

The Cliff Richard Story six-record boxed set with booklet featuring the Shadows, mail order from World Records.

Cliff Richard: tape-only compilation. TC EXE 1006.

The Music and Life of Cliff Richard: tape-only compilation, a de luxe set of six cassettes. Apart from music, it has Cliff giving an account of his life. He narrates his story from 'schoolboy crush' days to the second half of the seventies. In addition, there are comments about him from close associates. His Christian testimony is highlighted several times. There is also an inspiring and nostalgic live recording of Cliff's testimony delivered at the Billy Graham Crusade meeting, Earls Court, London, in 1966. TC EXSP 1601.

Start the Day (first series) Bible-reading cassettes: eighteen in the series, available separately. Each with an introduction by Cliff: 'Galatians', 'Exodus', 'Psalms', 'Proverbs', 'Acts', 'Isaiah', 'Matthew', 'Mark', 'Luke', 'John', 'Romans', 'Timothy', 'Job', 'James', 'Hebrews', 'Ephesians', 'Philippians', 'Colossians'. The second series

has six cassettes covering the books of 'Job', 'Hebrews', 'Colossians', 'Philippians', 'James' and 'Ephesians'. Each contains twenty three-minute programmes made up of a reading by Cliff, a question, a prayer and general thoughts for the day. Cassettes are available from Scripture Union bookshops or Scripture Union, P.O. Box 38, Bristol BS99 7NA, or from The Record Scene, 3 Church Parade, Ashford, Middlesex.

All My Love: Sway/I Only Came to Say Goodbye/Take Special Care/Magic in the Moonlight/House Without Windows/Razzle Dazzle/All My Love/I Don't Wanna Love You/You Belong to My Heart/Again/Perfidia/Reelin' 'n' Rockin'. Music For Pleasure MFP 1420. Late 1970.

Everybody Needs Somebody (originally *Love Is Forever*): Everyone Needs Someone to Love/Fly Me to the Moon/Have I Told You Lately That I Love You/Long Ago (and Far Away)/(All of a Sudden) My Heart Sings/Theme From a Summer Place/I Found a Rose/My Foolish Heart/My Colouring Book/Look Homeward Angel/Paradise Lost/Through the Eye of a Needle/I'll Walk Alone/Somebody. Sounds Superb SPR 90070.

How Wonderful to Know: same tracking as *21 Today* (see album list) minus 'Happy

205

Birthday'. World Records STP 643.

Cliff Richard: I'll String Along With You/The Touch of Your Lips/Temptation/We Kiss in a Shadow/Long Ago (and Far Away)/I'll Walk Alone/Come Closer to Me/Maria/ All I Do is Dream of You/ I'll See You in My Dreams/When I Grow Too Old to Dream/Dream. World Records ST 1051.

Cliff Richard (Reader's Digest offer): as above.

Cliff Live: Music For Pleasure MFP 50307. October 1976.

Rock On With Cliff: Move It/High Class Baby/My Feet Hit the Ground/Mean Streak/Living Doll/Apron Strings/Travellin' Light/Dynamite/Willie and the Hand Jive/A Voice in the Wilderness/Please Don't Tease/Gee Whizz It's You/Theme for a Dream/It'll Be Me/We Say Yeah/Do You Want to Dance. Music For Pleasure MFP 50467. February 1980.

Listen to Cliff (double): same tracking as *Listen to Cliff* and *32 Minutes and 17 Seconds With Cliff Richard.* Music For Pleasure MFP 1011. July 1980.

Cliff: a limited edition sampler specially manufactured for the trade to commemorate the reissue of twelve Cliff singles from the period 1959–1979. It contains single excerpts and a back sleeve showing the sleeve covers of the reissued records. EMI PSLP 350. February 1982.

Cliff. B.B.C. Transcription Service. Six tracks of London Hammersmith recordings made for overseas market (not commercially available) in conjunction with T.V. series.

Summer Holiday: limited edition, eighty copies. Elstree extra large recordings. Three sides plus one blank. Double-record set. Film dialogue, original song recordings.

Wonderful Life: limited edition, 150 copies. Four sides. Dialogue and songs.

Robert W. Morgan Special of the Week promotional record. Cliff interview, bits of album tracks. Issued by Capitol, U.S.A.

Interview with Cliff by music writer and poet Steve Turner at Greenbelt, August 1979. Christian Audio Vision Services Ltd, 171 Chase Side, Enfield, Middlesex, England. Cassette, GBO 083.

Demo for trade purposes: 'Don't Forget to Catch Me' from *Established 1958.* Columbia PSR 316.

Sampler album for *Every Face Tells a Story.* PSRS 410.

Sampler E.P. for 40 Golden Greats. Bits of each cut segued. PSR 414/415.

Test recordings: 'Breathless', 'Lawdy Miss Clawdy'.

Not issued: Recorded 7.3.1962 at Kingston ABC. Planned A side of Cliff, B of Shadows. Cliff songs: 'Do You Wanna Dance', 'Dim Dim the Lights', 'My Blue Heaven', 'Razzle Dazzle', 'Roving Gambler', 'Save My Soul', 'When the Girl in Your

Heart Is the Girl in Your
Arms', 'I Gotta Woman',
'Lessons in Love', 'Got a Funny
Feeling', 'The Young Ones',
'We Say Yeah'. (Tapes
believed to be in existence.)

K-TEL COMPILATIONS

The Summit: Cliff track: 'Devil
Woman'. NE 1067.
The Love Album: Cliff track:
'When Two Worlds Drift
Apart'. NE 1092.
Chart Explosion: Cliff track: 'We
Don't Talk Anymore'. NE
1103.
Love Is: Cliff track: 'Miss You
Nights'. NE 1129.

OTHER ARTISTS OR COMPILATION ALBUMS FEATURING CLIFF

Oh Boy: seven Cliff tracks: 'At the
Hop', 'Rockin' Robin', 'High
School Confidential', 'King
Creole', 'I'll Try', 'Early in the
Morning', 'Somebody Touched
Me'. Recorded 19 October
1958. Reissued in E.M.I.'s Nut
Gold series, 1978. Parlophone
PMC 7072.
Thunderbirds Are Go! The
Shadows, featuring one Cliff
song, 'Shooting Star'.
December 1966. SEG 8510.
Spree 73: Gospel/religious
convention album featuring
one track from Cliff: 'Jesus Is
My Kind of People'. Key KL
021.
Greenbelt: album of the religious
pop festival, held in 1979, with

one track by Cliff, 'Yes He
Lives'. Pilgrim MRT 1001.
Xanadu: film soundtrack album. Jet
JETLX 526. Cliff sings
'Suddenly' with Olivia
Newton-John, which was also
released as a single (Jet 7002).
Dick Saunders 10th Annual Rally:
album recorded live at Wembley
Stadium. One Cliff track, 'Love
Never Gives Up'. September
1975. Now only a cassette. Echo
ECR 008.
Alan Freeman's History of Pop: one
Cliff plus Shadows track, 'Living
Doll'. Arcade.
Best Shows of the Week: one song
from Cliff, 'The Day I Met
Marie'. B.B.C. Records BELP
002.
The Eddy Go Round Show: Cliff
sings 'It's Only Me', 'You're Left
Behind', 'Give Me Back That
Old Familiar Feeling'. European
release, EMI 5C062 25252X.
Stars Sing a Rainbow: Save the
Children Fund compilation
album, 1970. Cliff's song is
'Dancing Shoes'. Philips 6830
034.
Supersonic: T.V. show compilation,
1975. Cliff sings 'Take Me High'.
SSM 001.
Twenty With a Bullet: hits from the
E.M.I. roster. Cliff's track:
'Daddy's Home'. February
1982. EMTV 32.

BACK-UPS

Alexander John: 'Days Go By'.
Myrrh MYR 1010.
Dave Pope: 'Sail Away'. Also
produced by Cliff. MYR 1068.

Bryn Haworth: 'Keep the Ball Rolling'. A&M AMLH 68507.

Pat Carroll: 'To the Sun'. Pye 7N 25592.

Alan Shiers: 'Good on the Sally Army'. EMI 2423.

Garth Hewitt: 'I'm Grateful'. MYR 1078.

Joan Palethorpe, Faye Fisher, Audrey Bayley: 'This Was My Special Day'. Back-ups from *Aladdin* album. DB 7435.

Marietta (Parfitt): 'You're Only Lonely'. Polydor POSP 305.

Brian Bennett: 'The Girls Back Home'. Mercury 6016 048 (Sweden).

SONGS PRODUCED BY CLIFF FOR OTHER ARTISTS

Garth Hewitt: 'Did He Jump Or Was He Pushed'. Patch WOOF 001 (Cliff's Gospel label). 'I Can Hear Love'. Pye 7P 172.

Network Three (formerly Nutshell, RPM) single: 'Last Train Home', EMI 5120; 'Dangerous Game', EMI 5205.

Richard Loring (South Africa): 'Loving You'. EMIJ 1118. Wonderful Summer/Are You Sincere. EMIJ 11129.

Dave Pope: 'Sail Away' (also has backing vocals by Cliff). Myrrh MYR 1068.

SONGS WRITTEN BY CLIFF FOR OTHER ARTISTS

Cherry Wainer: 'Happy Like a Bell'. Columbia 45DB 4528.

Patti Brook: 'I Love You, I Need You'. Pye 7N 15422.

Brian James: 'It Just Happened That Way'. Written with Ian Samwell and Jet Harris. Olga OLE 005.

The Shadows: 'Some Are Lonely' (on the album *Out of the Shadows*). 33SX 1458. SCX 3449. 'With a Hmm Hmm Hmm on My Knee' (on the album *Jigsaw*). SX 6148. SCX 6148.

CLIFF SONGS BY OTHER ARTISTS

Lionel Bart: 'Living Doll'. Bronze BRO 3.

Andy Fairweather-Low: 'Travellin' Light'. A&M AMS 7248.

The Shadows: 'It'll Be Me Babe'. EMI 2461.

Don Lang: 'They Call Him Cliff' (a medley of Cliff hits). HMV POP 714.

Billie Joe: 'Power to All Our Friends' (European release). Sire SAA 707.

The Clee-Shays: 'Dynamite', instrumental (European release). Triumph TR 65.

Peter Noone: 'Goodbye Sam, Hello Samantha'. Bus Stop BUS 1057.

The Secret: 'The Young Ones'. Arista 142.

Bernd Cluver: 'Hey Mr Disc Jockey', retitled version of 'Hey Mr Dream Maker' (European release). Ariola AT 17711.

Dave Loggins: 'Please Remember Me' (on the album *One Way Ticket*). Epic PE 34713.

Mary Roos: 'We Don't Talk Anymore' (German cover version). Hansa 101 031.

Flamin' Groovies: 'Move It' (on the album *Now*). SRK 6067.

Ian Sinclair: 'I Can't Ask You for Anymore'. Creole CR 131.

Alvin Stardust: 'Move It' (on the album *Rock With Alvin*). Magnet MAG 39.

Mud: 'Living Doll' (on the album *Mud 2*). SRAK 513.

Lockjaw: 'The Young Ones'. Raw RAW 8.

New Seekers: 'Brand New Song' (on the album *Now*). Polydor. 'Give Me Love Your Way'. CBS 5235.

Larry Norman: 'Why Should the Devil'. MGM 2315 135.

Murray Head: 'Never Even Thought' (on the album *Say It Isn't So*). Island ILP 9347.

Dave Pope: 'Lord I Love You' (on the album *Sail Away*). Myrrh MYR 1068.

Ramones: 'Do You Want to Dance'. Sire 607 8618.

Flying Saucers: 'Apron Strings'. Charly CRL 5002.

Sidney Devine: 'Travellin' Light' (on the album *Almost Persuaded*). Philips 6308 29.

Richard Torrance: 'I Can't Ask for Anymore Than you'. Capitol CL 15985.

Shakin' Stevens: 'Apron Strings'. Epic EPC 9090.

Viv Stanshall: 'The Young Ones'. Harvest HAR 5114.

Quartet: 'Joseph'. Decca F13072.

Kevin Johnson: 'Rock and Roll'. UK UKR 84.

Deep Feeling: 'Do You Want to Dance'. DJM DJS 231.

Don Duke: 'Theme for a Dream'. Embassy WB 439.

Olivia Newton-John: 'Hey Mr Dream Maker' (on the album *Don't Stop Believin'*). EMI EMC 3126. 'Every Face Tells a Story' (on the same album). Also as a single: EMI 2574.

The Shadows: 'What'd I Say' (on the album *Shades of Rock*). Columbia SCX 6420.

Clout: 'Hot Shot'/'Under Fire' (on the album *Clout.*) Epic 36350.

The Shadows: 'The Day I Met Marie' (on the album *Hank, Bruce, Brian and John*). Columbia SX 6199. SCX 6199.

The Shadows: 'We Don't Talk Anymore' (on the album *Hits Right Up Your Street*). Polydor POLD 5046.

Plastique: 'A Heart Will Break Tonight'. Hansa 102333 100.

Hofmann and Hofmann: 'Warten' ('Dreamin''). Global 0033 239.

Holland and Bolland: 'Way Back to the Sixties' (tribute to Cliff). EMI 1A006 26561.

Shampoo: 'We Don't Talk Anymore'. Creole CRX 4.

Starshow: 'Devil Woman'. Creole CRX 4.

Diamond Orchestra: 'A Little in Love'. Arcade ADEH 303.

Barbara Dickson: 'Hold On'. Epic EPC 84551.

Barron Knights: 'Wired for Sound'. EPC 85319.

The Gorillas: 'Move It'. Chiswick CHIS 151.

The Sixties: 'Power to All Our

Friends'. (Cliff hit song medley). Telefunken CLIFF 1.

Stray: 'Move It'. Transatlantic. BIG 516.

The Californians: 'Congratulations'. Decca F12758.

The Rockin' Berries: 'Rock-a-Bye Nursery Rhyme' (includes 'Move It'). Pye 7N 45394.

B. A. Robertson: 'Language of Love'/'Hot Shot'. Asylum K12449. 'Sci Fi'. Asylum K12396. 'Fallin' in Love' (on the album *Initial Success*). Asylum K52216.

Angelic Upstarts: 'The Young Ones'. Warner K17426.

Glen Campbell: 'Give Me Back That Old Familiar Feeling'. Capitol 3735.

Kristine: 'Devil Woman'. Power Exchange PX 229.

Roger Whittaker: 'Miss You Nights'. Columbia SCX 6601.

Nolan Sisters: 'Miss You Nights'. Epic 83892.

Demis Roussos: 'Miss You Nights'. Mercury 6302 018.

David Pomeranz: 'If You Walked Away'. Arista ARTY 129.

Tito Burns: 'Salute to Cliff' (on the album *Bubbles*). Columbia SCX 6618.

Helen McBennett: 'Mr Dream Maker'. Emerald GES 1182.

J. J. Michaels: 'Tribute to Cliff'. Chevron CHVL 185.

Nearly all the songs on the Cliff album *Small Corners* (EMC 3219) have been recorded by other artists, including:

2nd Chapter of Acts: 'Goin' Home'. Myrrh MYR 1011. 'Hey Watcha Say'. Myrrh MYR 1026.

Larry Norman: 'I Wish We'd All Been Ready'. MGM 2315 135.

Malcolm and Alwyn: 'I Love'. Key KL 020.

Kris Kristofferson: 'Why Me Lord'. MNT 1482.

Randy Stonehill: 'I've Got News for You'. Rocky 2.

Non-U.K. Releases (selective listing)

Countless countries more or less follow the U.K. release schedules. However, licensing arrangements with E.M.I. U.K. allow foreign territories to issue their own album tracking and repackage existing material into whatever type of album content is desired. Also, deleted U.K. material may be reissued abroad.

Australia

ALBUMS

His Land (still available). SCX 06443.

Cliff Richard. WRCS 5019.

Me and My Shadows. SOEX 9716.

Portrait of Cliff Richard. SOEX 10061.

The Greatest. SCXO 7735.
The Greatest Volume 2. SCXO 7801.
The Greatest Volume 3 (as U.K. *Best of, Volume 2*). SCXO 6519.
Cliff Entertains. AXIS 6108.
Live. AXIS 6293.
20 Golden Greats. SCA 018.

Belgium

ALBUMS

When in France (recorded in French). 4C062 06234.
Cliff Sings. 335X 1192.
Me and My Shadows. SCX 3330.
When in Rome. 33 SX1762.
When in Germany Volume 1. 1A 062 07203.
When in Germany Volume 2. 1A 062 07204.
Golden Record. C066 05960.
V.I.P. C052 04569.
With the Shadows. 4M026 06996.
Expresso Bongo. K0522 07329.
When in Spain. 4C058 06728.
Cliff Alive plus *All My Love* plus *Love Is Forever*: three-album boxed set. MFP 4M128 54042 43 44.
Serious Charge (12-inch pressing). EMI K062 Z07528. Original enlarged picture cover. This is Cliff's first E.P. 'No Turning Back' and 'Mad About' are especially wanted by collectors. Both also on *Rock On With Cliff Volume 2* (EMI MD22 – see under New Zealand).
Carolsingers. Five traditional carols: 'God Rest Ye Merry, Gentlemen', 'In the Bleak Midwinter', 'Unto Us a Boy is Born', While Shepherds Watched' and 'O Little Town of Bethlehem'. Much wanted release. A0622 07571.
Dream (E.P.). 1A 0622 076154.
Holiday Carnival. 1A 0622 07616.

Brazil

ALBUMS

Rock Turbulo. Odeon MOFB 84.
Rock and Ballads. Odeon MOFB 123.
Listen to Cliff. 6 28 407 052.
Latino! Odeon MOFB 318.
Rock 'n' Roll Juvenile. EM 064 07112.

Bulgaria

ALBUM

I'm Nearly Famous. Balkanton EMI BTA 2117.

Canada

ALBUMS

Wonderful to Be Young. Dot DLP 34714.
Listen to Cliff. ABC Paramount, mono ABC 391, stereo ABCS 391.
Cliff's Hit Album. Capitol T6043.
Blue Turns to Grey. T6184.
In a Mod Mood. ST 6224.
All My Love. ST 6263.
Souvenir Album. DAO 6106.
Rock 'n' Roll Juvenile. Capitol Harvest ST 6461.

Far East

ALBUMS

Tom Jones and Cliff Richard. KP 7004.

211

The Young Ones. M6 1040.
Cliff Richard No. 7 (no record number, possibly bootleg).
24 Unforgettable Hits. TEP 514 740.
Cliff Richard. Universal K – Apple 7117.
Hits Volume 2. SCX 1513.
The Best of Cliff. URLP 311 76.

Finland

ALBUM

18 Greatest Hits. 9C 062 07320.

France

ALBUMS

Do You Want to Dance. FPX 254.
The Young Ones. CTX 40 284.
Cliff Richard. SCTX 340722.
Pathé Marconi. 2C068 06939.
Cliff Richard. C 150 06571/2.

French-Language Singles

Ah Quelle Histoire/Girl You'll Be a Woman Soon. CF 155.
La Ballade de Baltimore/L'Amandier Sauvage. 2C006 04841.
Il Faut Chanter la Vie/Come Back Billy Joe 2C006 05324.

Germany

SINGLES

Bin Verliebt (Fall in Love With You)/Die Stimme Der Liebe (Voice in the Wilderness). Recorded in German. C21703.
Schön Wie Ein Traum (Theme for a Dream)/Vreneli. Recorded in German. C21843.

Rote Lippen Soll Man Küssen (Lucky Lips)/Let's Make a Memory. Recorded in German. C22563.
Zuviel Allein (I'm the Lonely One)/Sag No Zu Ihm (Don't Talk to Him). Recorded in German. C22707.
Das Ist Die Frage Aller Fragen (Spanish Harlem)/Nur Mit Dir (On the Beach). Recorded in German. C22811.
Es War Keine So Wunderbar Wie Du (I Could Easily Fall in Love With You)/Es Könnte Schon Morgen Sein (The Minute You're Gone). Recorded in German. C22962.
Nur Bei Dir Bin Ich Zu Haus (Wind Me Up)/Glaub Nur Mir (On My Word). Recorded in German. C23103.
Du Bist Mein Erster Gedanke (Quiereme Mucho)/Was Ist Dabei (Time in Between). Recorded in German. C23211.
Das Glück Ist Rosarot/Was Kann Ich Tun (What Would I Do). Recorded in German. CS23371.
Ein Girl Wie Du/Bilder Von Dir (Visions). Recorded in German. C23510.
Es Ist Nicht Gut Allein Zu Sein/Ein Sonntag Mit Marie (The Day I Met Marie). Recorded in German. C23611.
Man Gratuliert Mir (Congratulations)/Ich Kann Treu Sein (I'll Come Running). Recorded in German. C23776.
London Ist Nicht Weit (London's Not Too Far)/ Mrs Emily

Jones. Recorded in German. C23777.

Zärtliche Sekunden (Don't Forget to Catch Me)/Wonderful World. Recorded in German. 1C006 28032.

Goodbye Sam Das Ist Die Liebe (Goodbye Sam Hello Samantha)/Kein Zug Nach Gretna Green. Recorded in German. 1C006 04523.

Ich Träume Deine Träume/Das Girl Von Nebenan. Recorded in German. 1C006 04706.

Wenn Du Lachst, Lacht Das Glück (Sally Sunshine)/Kleine Taube (You're My Pigeon). Recorded in German. 1C006 04903.

Gut, Dass Es Freunde Gibt (Power to All Our Friends)/Ein Spiel Ohne Grenzen. Recorded in German. 1C006 05315.

Es Gehören Zwei Zum Glücklichsein (Hanging On)/Liebeslied. Recorded in German. 1C006 05609.

Carrie (12-inch single). 052 07188.

ALBUMS

Hier Ist Cliff (recorded in German). Hör Zu SHZE 261.

Ich Träume Deine Träume (recorded in German). 1C062 04639, or 1C244 04639(s). Also German book club offer, 27301 1.

Congratulations (recorded in German). SMC 74430.

Supergold (previously known as *Edition 2000*). Has four German cuts, one in French, the remaining twelve in English. C188053 16/17.

When in Germany Volume 1(1A062 07203) and *Volume 2* (1A062 07204) have songs in German from Cliff.

When in Spain. C83518.

Cliff International. C83576.

Cliff and the Shadows Forever. A desirable album because it has the Shadows and a live South African track. C83767.

Cliff International Again. SMC 74223.

Good News SMC 74326.

Established. SMC 7448.

Cliff's Greatest. C062 04121.

Help It Along. C062 05581.

The Best of Cliff Richard. C062 04087.

Sincerely. C062 04136.

Tracks 'n' Grooves. C062 04617.

The Best of Cliff Volume 2. C062 05152.

Power to All Our Friends. C062 05355.

Take Me High. C062 05496.

The 31st of February Street. C062 05691.

I'm No Hero. 064 07342.

20 Rock 'n' Roll Hits. 064 07145.

Edition 2000 (reissued later as *Supergold*). C188053 16/17.

Cliff Richard and the Shadows. 134 05 316.

40 Golden Greats. 188 52 668/9.

Seine Grossen Erfolge. C054 05358 and M048 05358.

Me and My Shadows. SMVP 6150.

Cliff Richard. C048 04 318.

Spanish Harlem. M048 05 546.

In Concert. C056 05 553.

20 Grössten Hits. ADEG 17.

Move It. ADEG 85.

We Don't Talk Anymore. 052 07076.

Dreamin'. 052 07346.

Cliff's Songs – His Greatest Love Hits. K-Tel. No number available at time of printing. Material is different from U.K. *Love Songs* release.

Greece

ALBUM

20 Golden Greats Volume 1 (half of *40 Golden Greats*). 14C 062 06508.

Holland

ALBUMS

When in France (Recorded in French). 4C 062 06234.
Time to Rock (10-inch). 33 HP 165.
Cliff and the Shadows. SG HX 5001.
Portrait. 5C 056 04840.
Cliff Story Volume 1. 5C 052 05071.
Cliff Story Volume 2. 5C 052 05072.
Cliff Story Volume 3. 5C 052 05073.
Cliff Story Volume 4. 5C 052 05074.
Cliff Story Volume 5. 5C 052 05075.
When in Spain. 1A 052 06728.
When in Rome. 052 07147.
The Best of Cliff. 5C 054 04301.
The Best of Cliff Volume 2. 5C 054 05152.
Chanté en Français. 1A 062 06234.
Thank You Very Much. 062 06939.
Hits Grooste, Hitmaster (compilation of old and new titles). A062 07320.
Life. 1A 028 06226.
Rock on Cliff Richard. 1A 222 58054.
40 Golden Greats. 5C 154 06508/9.
'Live' at The Talk of the Town. C048 50738.
The Young Ones (previously deleted, reissued by E.M.I. Holland, March 1979). 5C 052 06963.
Summer Holiday (previously deleted, reissued by E.M.I. Holland, March 1979). 5C 052 06965.
Wonderful Life (previously deleted, reissued by E.M.I. Holland, March 1979). 5C 052 06961.
Aladdin and His Wonderful Lamp (previously deleted, reissued by E.M.I. Holland, March 1979). 5C 052 06962.
Finders Keepers (previously deleted, reissued by E.M.I. Holland, March 1979). 5C 052 06966.
Cinderella (previously deleted, reissued by E.M.I. Holland, March 1979). 5C 052 06967.
Two a Penny (previously deleted, reissued by E.M.I. Holland, March 1979). 5C 052 06964.
His Land (previously deleted, reissued by E.M.I. Holland, March 1979). 5C 052 04633.
Take Me High (previously deleted, reissued by E.M.I. Holland, March 1979). 5C 052 05496.

Italy

SINGLES

Immagina Un Giorno/Oh, No, No. Recorded in Italian. SCMQ 7075.
Congratulations/Girl You'll Be a Woman Soon. Recorded in Italian. SCMQ 7099.
Non Dimenticare Chi Ti Ama/Chi Lo Sa. Recorded in Italian. 3C0006 04056.

Constantly/I Only Know You.
Recorded in Italian. SCMQ
1751.

ALBUM
To My Italian Friends. 33 QPX
8024.

Japan

Generally, Japanese discs are of
better quality than in any other
country, with amazingly lush
packaging. *Live in Japan 72* (EOP
930773) contains, for many Cliff
collectors, the ultimate in live
recordings, with Farrar, Marvin,
Bennett, Pat Carrol and Olivia
Newton-John on backing vocals.

ALBUMS

Deluxe in Cliff Richard. OKB 021.
Cliff's Hit Volume. OR 7046.
Angel. OP 7371.
Dynamite. OP 7198.
Visions. OP 8080.
Finders Keepers. OP 8109.
Cinderella. 08 8128.
Greatest Hits! EOR 8166.
Deluxe. OP 8312.
Shout. OP 8197.
Two a Penny (different from the
U.K. version). OP 8534.
Latin à la Cliff. OP 8864.
Sings European Hits. OP 8885.
Cliff's Extra Special for You. OP
8925.
This is Cliff. OP 936813.
Brand New Cliff. OP 9537.
Cliff in Japan. OP 9701.
Cliff Richard. OP 9718.
Hit Album. OP 80315.
Best 20. OP 99004.
Best 20 Volume 2. OP 99022.

More Best. EMS 80491.
I'm Nearly Famous. EMS 80492.
Cliff's Love Sounds. EOP 80613.
Brand New Song. EOP 80860.
Cliff Live in Japan 72. EOP 93077.
*Live in Japan 72 + Marvin and
Farrar Live 72*. EOP 93077B.
Japan Tour 1974. Numerous songs
unique to this album: 'You've
Lost That Lovin' Feeling', 'The
Sun Ain't Gonna Shine
Anymore', 'Make It Easy on
Yourself', 'Get Back', 'Don't
Meet the Band', 'His Latest
Flame', 'Chantilly Lace',
'Crocodile Rock'. Available
Toshiba-E.M.I. import, EMS
67037/8.
Gold Disc Series (boxed set. EOP
95027B.
Cliff. The Best Artist Series. EOP
97003.
Cliff Richard 1958-1974. EMS
90001.
*Cliff Live with Olivia
Newton-John*. EMS 80538.
Every Face Tells a Story.
Toshiba-E.M.I. 80392.
Green Light. EMS 8115X.
Thank You Very Much. EMS
81204.
Rock 'n' Roll Juvenile. EMS 81258.
I'm No Hero. EMS 81369.
Rock 'n' Roll Best 20. EMS 90056.
Best 20 Volume 2. EMS 90067.
The Young Ones (10-inch). CW
1001.
Love Songs. EMS 90104.
Wired for Sound. EMS 17169.

Korea

ALBUM

Cliff Live in Korea. Includes eight

songs from *Cliff in Japan* album. Universal 7117.

Malaysia, Singapore

ALBUMS

All My Love. SMFP 1420.
Cliff Richard's Greatest Hits Volume 1. A number of unexpected tracks are included: 'Got a Funny Feeling' (flip side of 'When the Girl in Your Arms'), 'Thinking of Our Love' (B side of 'Nine Times Out of Ten'); and from the album *Listen to Cliff,* 'True Love Will Come to You'. Also included is the early single 'Livin' Lovin' Doll'. SREG 9713.
Cliff Richard's Greatest Hits Volume 2. This has four tracks from *21 Today*: 'My Blue Heaven', 'Y'Arriva', 'Poor Boy', and 'Outsider'; from *Cliff Sings*: 'Twenty Flight Rock', 'I'm Walking', and 'Little Things Mean A Lot'; and from *Listen to Cliff*: 'Blue Moon', 'It'll Be Me', 'Do You Want to Dance', 'The Young Ones', 'I'm Looking Out the Window'. SREG 9714.
Me and My Shadows. Issued in slightly different form from the U.K. version, without the original 1960 cover pictures, and in stereo only. SREG 1120.
It'll Be Me. SRS 5011.
Listen to Cliff. ABC 391.
Cliff Goes East. Double album. Cliff on three sides, Shadows on one side. Includes several tracks not found elsewhere: 'Can't Let You Go', 'Have a Little Talk With Myself', 'My Way'. LEAC 1041/2.

New Zealand

ALBUMS

His Greatest Hits. HITS 11.
20 Greatest Hits Volume 2. HITS 30.
Rock On With Cliff. Some differences from the U.K. M.F.P. (50467) version. Some of the less well known material includes 'Mumblin' Mosie' (B side of 'Theme For a Dream'), 'Ready Teddy', 'Livin' Lovin' Doll', 'Tough Enough', and 'Forty Days' from the album *21 Today*. MID 11.
Cliff Richard 1958-1981. HMV NZ6.
Rock On With Cliff Volume 2. An important release considering some of the titles included: Just Another Guy/Mad About You/ Your Eyes Tell on You/Thinking of Our Love/Now's the Time to Fall in Love/Boom Boom (that's how my heart beats)/A Forever Kind of Love/Never Knew What Love Could Do/True True Lovin'/No Turning Back/Somebody Loses/Lies and Kisses/I'm Afraid to Go Home/Pigeon/Watch What You Do With My Baby/What Would I Do for the Love of a Girl. EMI MD 22.

Scandinavia

ALBUMS

Four Sides of Cliff. E178 0524/5.
Cliff Richard and the Shadows. ST 3376.

South Africa

ALBUMS

Greatest Hits. JSX 33.
Something Old, Something New. JSX 118.
Goodbye Sam Hello Samantha. JSX 180.
25 Magnificent Memories of Cliff Richard. EMGJ 6009.
Forty Days. Long-deleted U.K. release titled *21 Today* minus 'Happy Birthday' and twenty-first birthday picture. SRS J6016.
The Best of Cliff Richard and the Shadows. MFB SR ST 6076.
Mr Dream Maker. SR ST 8059.
Souvenirs. CEY (M) 213.

Soviet Union

SINGLE

'If You Walked Away From Me Today' (flexi disc with Soviet artist on B side). Melodia T 62 07331 2.

ALBUMS

I'm Nearly Famous. Melodia C60 088 7516.
Best of Cliff Volume 1 Melodia C60 08875/6.

Spain

SINGLES

Que Buena Auarte!/High 'n'
Dry, La Voz De Su Amo. Recorded in Spanish. PL 63198.
Todo El Poder A Los Amigos/Come Back Billy Joe. Recorded in Spanish. 1J006 05340.

ALBUMS

Dias Maravillosos. LCLR 238.
Congratulations. LCLP 1454.
Gigantes De La Cancion Volume 26. Odeon J054 04621.

Sweden

ALBUM

Cliff Richard: 20 Rock 'n' Roll Hits. Includes a rare cut of 'Dynamite', different from the single. EMI Rock 11.

Turkey

ALBUMS

Blam. Compilation with sub-title *We Don't Talk Anymore,* but this is the only Cliff track on the album.
Green Light. RCA 1099 (wanted for the RCA logo).

U.S.A. (complete list)

SINGLES

Move It/High Class Baby. Capitol F4086.
Livin' Lovin' Doll/Steady With You. Capitol F4154.
Living Doll/Apron Strings. ABC Paramount 45 10042.
Travellin' Light/Dynamite. ABC

Paramount 45 10066.

A Voice in the Wilderness/Don't Be Mad at Me. ABC Paramount 45 10083.

Fall in Love With You/Choppin' 'n' Changin'. ABC Paramount 45 10109.

Please Don't Tease/Where Is Your Heart. ABC Paramount 45 10136.

'D' in Love/Catch Me I'm Fallin'. ABC Paramount 45 10175.

Theme For a Dream/Mumblin' Mosie. ABC Paramount 45 10195.

The Young Ones/We Say Yeah. Big Top 45 3101.

It's Wonderful to Be Young/Got a Funny Feeling. Big Top 45 16399.

Lucky Lips/The Next Time. Epic 5 9597.

It's All in the Game/I'm Looking Out the Window. Epic S 9633.

I'm the Lonely One/I Only Have Eyes for You. Epic 5 9670.

Bachelor Boy/True True Lovin'. Epic 5 9691.

I Don't Wanna Love You/Look Into My Eyes Maria. Epic 5 9737.

The Minute You're Gone/Again. Epic 5 9757.

I Could Easily Fall (in Love With You)/On My Word. Epic 5 9810.

The Twelfth of Never/Paradise. Epic 5 9839.

Wind Me Up (Let Me Go)/The Eye of a Needle. Epic 5 9867.

Blue Turns to Grey/I'll Walk Alone. Epic 5 10018.

Visions/Quando, Quando, Quando. Epic 5 10070.

Time Drags By/La La La Song. Epic 5 10101.

Heartbeat/It's All Over. Epic 5 10178.

All My Love/Our Story Book. UNI Records 55061.

Congratulations/High 'n' Dry. UNI Records 55069.

The Day I Met Marie/Sweet Little Jesus Boy. UNI Records 55145.

Throw Down the Line/Reflections. Seven Arts Records 7344.

Goodbye Sam Hello Samantha/You Can Never Tell. Monument MN 12211.

I Ain't Got Time Anymore/Monday Comes Too Soon. Monument MN 1229.

Living In Harmony/Jesus. Sire SAA 703.

Power to All Our Friends/Come Back Billie Joe. Sire SAA 707.

Miss You Nights/Love Enough. Rocket PIG 40531.

Devil Woman/Love On. Rocket PIG 40574.

I Can't Ask for Anything More/Junior Cowboy. Rocket PIG 40652.

Don't Turn the Light Out/Nothing Left for Me to Say. Rocket PIG 40724.

Try a Smile/You've Got Me Wondering. Rocket PIG 40771.

Green Light/Needing a Friend. Rocket YB 11463.

We Don't Talk Anymore/Count Me Out. EMI America 8025.

We Don't Talk Anymore/We Don't Talk Anymore. 12-inch, 33⅓ r.p.m., 7-minute version. EMI America SPRO 9252.

Carrie/Language of Love. EMI

218

America 8035.

Dreamin'/Dynamite. EMI
America 8057.

Little in Love/Everyman. EMI
America 8068.

Give a Little Bit More/Keep On
Looking. EMI America 8076.

All singles listed after 'Living in
Harmony' above had a
promotional copy released for
radio stations. Many of these had
only the A side.

Two a Penny/I'll Love You
Forever Today. Special
promotional single. Light L
601.

It's Wonderful to Be Young/The
Young Ones. Special
promotional single. Dot DGT
029X.

Wired for Sound/Hold On. EMI
America 8095.

Daddy's Home/Summer Rain.
EMI America 8103.

E.P.s

Two a Penny/Red Rubber
Ball/And Me (I'm on the
Outside Now)/Questions. UNI
EP 001. Reissued on Light
LSEP 101.

His Land/Over in Bethlehem/The
New 23rd. Light LSEP 102.

ALBUMS

The two prefixes to albums issued
by Rocket reflect a change of
distributor. Mono pressing ceased
with the album *Swinger's Paradise*.

Cliff Sings. The mono and stereo
have different track orders.
ABC Paramount, mono ABC
321, stereo ABCS 321.

Listen to Cliff. ABC Paramount,
mono ABC 391, stereo ABCS
391.

It's Wonderful to Be Young. Dot,
mono DLP 3474, stereo DLP
25474.

*Hits from the Soundtrack of
Summer Holiday*. Epic, mono
LN 24063, stereo BN 26063.

*Cliff Richard in Spain with the
Shadows and Norrie Paramor's
Strings*. Epic, mono LN 24115,
stereo BN 26115.

Swinger's Paradise. Epic, mono
LN 24145, stereo BN 26145.

Two a Penny. Light LS 5530 LP.
UNI Records also issued this
album. It was sold at cinemas.
There was no catalogue
number.

His Land. Light LS 5532 LP.

Good News. Word WST 8507 LP.

I'm Nearly Famous. Two different
covers adorned this album.
Rocket PIG 2210. Also BXL 1
3044. Reissued at budget price,
EMI SN 16221.

Every Face Tells a Story. Rocket
PIG 2268. Also BXL 1 3045

Green Light. Rocket BXL 1 2958.
Reissued at budget price, EMI
SN 16220.

We Don't Talk Anymore. EMI
America SW 17018.

I'm No Hero. EMI America SW
17039.

It's All in the Game. 7-inch jukebox
33⅓ r.p.m. version with I Only
Know I Love You/Secret Love
/Since I Lost You/I'm in the
Mood for Love/Fly Me to the

Moon/Magic Is the Moonlight. Epic, mono LN 24089, stereo BN 26089.

Wired for Sound. As U.K. release but without the track 'Say You Don't Mind'. EMI America SW 17059.

K-TEL COMPILATIONS

22 Fantastic Hits. Cliff track: 'Power to All Our Friends'. TV 233.

Stars. Cliff track: 'Devil Woman'. TV 2530.

Power Play. Cliff track: 'We Don't Talk Anymore'. TV 2630.

OTHER COMPILATIONS

Sound Express. Cliff track: 'We Don't Talk Anymore'. Ronco 3210.

History of British Rock. Cliff track: 'Blue Turns to Grey'. Sire SAS 3702.

Roots of British Rock. Cliff tracks: 'Move It', 'Living Doll'. Sire SASH 37112.

FILMS

Various Cliff films are available in the U.K. in part or in whole as Super 8 Home Movies. They can be obtained from Derann Film Services Ltd, 99 High Street, Dudley, West Midlands DY1 1QP, England.

Serious Charge. Stars: Anthony Quayle, Sarah Churchill, Andrew Ray. Cliff played the part of Curley Thompson. Thompson was the brother of the leader of a gang of youngsters who were into speed and lived for the next joy ride.

Songs sung by Cliff were 'Mad', 'No Turning Back', 'Living Doll'. He was backed by the Drifters but they did not appear on screen.

Director: Terrence Young. Producer: Michael Delamar.

Expresso Bongo. Stars: Laurence Harvey, Yolande Donlan, Sylvia Syms. Cliff was Bert Rudge, a young beat singer who became world famous as Bongo Herbert. Laurence Harvey played his rather unscrupulous manager.

Songs sung by Cliff were 'Love', 'Shrine on the Second Floor', 'A Voice in the Wilderness'.

Director and producer: Val Guest. Story: Wolf Mankowitz.

The Young Ones. Stars: Robert Morley, Carole Gray, Shadows. Cliff plays Nicky, the leader of a youth club. Their headquarters is a rundown hut in an equally deteriorating London district. A rich property owner wishes to buy the land on which the club stands. A many-variation fight follows between developer and youth group.

Songs sung by Cliff are on the album *The Young Ones* (SCX 3397). Singles from the film: When the Girl in Your Arms/Got a Funny

Feeling (DB 4716); The Young Ones/We Say Yeah (DB 4761); The Savage/Peace Pipe (The Shadows) (DB 4726).

Director: Sidney J. Furie. Producer: Kenneth Harper. Choreographer: Herbert Ross. Original screenplay and story: Peter Myers and Ronald Cass. Background score, orchestrations and musical direction: Stanley Black.

Summer Holiday. Stars: Ron Moody, Melvyn Hayes, Lauri Peters, Shadows, David Kossoff, Jeremy Bulloch Teddy Green, Pamela Hart, Jacqueline Daryl, Una Stubbs. Cliff is one of four London Transport mechanics who form a band named Don. They take an old bus and travel through five countries. The film depicts their adventures.

Songs sung by Cliff are on the album *Summer Holiday* (SCX 3462). Singles from the film: Summer Holiday/Dancing Shoes (DB 4977); The Next Time/Bachelor Boy (DB 4950): Foot Tapper/The Breeze and I (The Shadows – only the A side was in the film) (DB 4984). Two more Shadows songs were in the film and these, together with 'Foot Tapper', are included on the E.P. *Foot Tapping With The Shadows* (SEG 8286). Cliff co-wrote two songs: 'Big News' with Mike Conlin; 'Bachelor Boy' with Bruce Welch.

Director: Peter Yates. Producer: Kenneth Harper. Choreographer: Herbert Ross. Original screenplay and story: Peter Myers and Ronald Cass. Release: through Warner-Pathé.

Wonderful Life. Stars: Susan Hampshire, Shadows, Walter Slezak, Una Stubbs, Richard O'Sullivan, Gerald Harper, Derek Bond. Cliff plays Johnnie. He and friends entertain passengers on a luxury Mediterranean cruise but lose their jobs. They find themselves put to sea on a raft by an irritated ship's Captain. They reach land, which just happens to be the Canary Islands, and there they find themselves causing more than a minor disturbance in the filming of *Daughter of a Sheikh*.

Songs sung by Cliff are on the album *Wonderful Life* (SCX 3515). Single from the film: On the Beach/Matter of Moments (DB 7305). 'Theme for Young Lovers' by the Shadows is on the album *More Hits* (SCX 3578).

Director: Sidney J. Furie. Producer: Kenneth Harper. Associate producer: Andrew Mitchell. Choreographer: Gillian Lynne. Original screenplay and story: Peter Myers and Ronald Cass. Background score, orchestrations, musical direction: Stanley Black. Elstree Distributors.

Finders Keepers. Stars: Robert Morley, Graham Stark, Viviane Ventura, Peggy Mount, Shadows. Cliff and the Shadows play a group who have been booked into a hotel for the season but find the management cannot pay them. They become friendly with local people and hear how the traditional fiesta which surrounds the blessing of fishing boats is threatened by possible repercussions from a clutch of bombs which has been dropped in error by an American aircraft. Cliff plays himself.

Songs sung by Cliff are on the album *Finders Keepers* (SCX 6079). Singles from the film: Time Drags By/La La La Song (DB 8017). 'Finders Keepers' was issued as the B side of 'In the Country' (DB 8094). Tracks from the Shadows, other than 'Spanish Music', are on *The Shadows on Stage and Screen* (SEG 8528).

Director: Sidney Hayers. Producer: George H. Brown. Choreographer: Malcolm Clare. Original story: George H. Brown. Screenplay: Michael Pertwee. Music and lyrics: The Shadows. Inter-State Films Production for United Artists.

Two a Penny. Stars: Dora Bryan, Avril Angers, Ann Holloway, Nigel Goodwin and, as himself, Dr Billy Graham. Cliff plays Jamie Hopkins, a young drug peddler who encounters Christian faith thanks to his girlfriend Carol.

Songs sung by Cliff are on the album *Two a Penny* (SCX 6262). Cliff wrote three songs for the film: 'Two a Penny', 'Questions', and 'I'll Love You Forever Today', the latter two with J. F. Collier. Single from the film: I'll Love You Forever Today/Girl You'll Be a Woman Soon (only the A side was in the film) (DB 8437).

Director: James F. Collier. Executive producer: Frank R. Jacobson. Screenplay and original story: Stella Linden. Music composed and conducted by Mike Leander, and also Cliff Richard. A Worldwide film.

His Land. A documentary film which Cliff made in Israel. It was an hour long and was shown in youth clubs and church halls. A soundtrack album, *His Land* (SCX 6443), contained: 'His Land', 'Jerusalem Jerusalem', 'The New 23rd', 'Over in Bethlehem', 'Keep Me Where Love Is', and 'He's Everything to Me'. The songs were written by American Ralph Carmichael.

Take Me High. Stars: Debbie Watling, Moyra Fraser, George Cole, Hugh Griffith, Anthony Andrews. Cliff plays Tim Matthews, a rich, somewhat ruthless and ambitious young city gent. He works for a London merchant bank and expects an assignment to New York. Instead, he finds himself sent to Birmingham. Later he finds himself involved with a French restaurant owner, Sarah. They open a brumburger establishment, brumburger being a new form of hamburger! The film was Cliff's first major screen work for seven years.

Songs sung by Cliff are on the album *Take Me High* (EMC 3016). 'Hover' is an instrumental, as is 'Driving', though there is a vocal version of this song. 'Brumburger' is a duet between Cliff and Debbie

Watling. A poster with the album showed a portrait of Cliff on one side, and on the other, scenes from the film.

Director: David Askey. Producer: Kenneth Harper. Screenplay: Charles Penfold. Music: Tony Cole. Distribution: through Anglo-E.M.I.

Why Should the Devil Have All the Good Music. This was a 16mm Eastman colour film with a running time of 50 minutes. It was produced by Colin Rank of Abba Productions. Direction was by James Swackhammer. Cliff starred along with a number of well-known Jesus Music artists, including Larry Norman, Judy McKenzie and Dave Cooke, Malcolm and Alwyn, Graham Kendrick, the Arts Centre Group director and actor Nigel Goodwin, and pop singer Dana. It was a documentary of the 1972 London Festival for Jesus, basically a celebration of Christian beliefs.

A World of Difference. This was a 16mm colour documentary for Tear Fund centring on the Fund's director George Hoffman. Cliff contributed to the film.

Loved into Life and *Love Never Gives Up.* Two Tear Fund filmstrips about Cliff's visit to Bangladesh.

Cliff: Flipside. This was filmed at Cliff's Tear Fund concert at the Royal Albert Hall, 1979, and also at his home. He talks about his faith. The director and scriptwriter was Mike Pritchard. Intamedia produced the film for International Films, 235 Shaftesbury Avenue, London WC2H 8EN. It runs for 30 minutes and is a 16mm colour presentation.

A Day With Cliff. As the title indicates, the film follows Cliff through a day. It was made by Dutch television in the early seventies and is available via International Films.

Come Together. A film of the popular religious musical by American Jimmy Owens. Cliff is interviewed by Pat Boone. The film is 16mm colour, from International Films.

Let's Join Together. Cliff plus Johnny Cash and Choralerna. The music and message of the Spree festival, London 1973. International Films.

Life with Johnny series. Three films: *Johnny Up the Creek (The Good Samaritan); Johnny Faces Facts (The Mote and the Beam);* and *Johnny Come Home (The Prodigal Son).* These were made in 1969 when Cliff was invited by the religious department of Tyne Tees Television to present a series of contemporary religious programmes. Now available via Worldwide films, International Films. Each film places a New Testament parable in a musical modern setting.

Greenbelt Live! Some of the highlights of the major British religious festival held in 1979 where music is an important ingredient. Cliff gives a brief interview, is glimpsed from time to time, and has one stage song, 'Yes, He Lives'. Also in the film, among many, are Garth Hewitt, After the Fire, Randy Stonehill, and Larry Norman. A Tony

Tew film for Grenville Film Productions in association with Marshalls Publishing.

Judge for Yourself. This Scripture Union filmstrip deals with basic religious questions like: Does it make sense? Does it work? Does it fit in with what I know? Can it be applied to God's message?

London Crusade. Documentary in which Cliff makes an appearance. 1966. Worldwide films.

I'm Going to Ask You to Get Out of Your Seats. Richard Causton's documentary on Billy Graham for B.B.C. T.V. Cliff makes an appearance.

Rhythm 'n' Greens. The Shadows starred in this 1964 32-minute film. There are those who swear the part of King Canute was play by Cliff! It was.

VIDEO

The first U.K. Cliff video was issued in March 1981. This was of *The Young Ones* (EVH 20242) with a U.K. price of £28.30.

The Kenny Everett Show (EVH 36207). Cliff makes an appearance.

Thank You Very Much (TVE 9003292). Video cassette of T.V. show. VHS or Betamax.

STAGE APPEARANCES

December 1959: Cliff and the Shadows appear at Stockton Globe in *Babes in the Wood.*

June-December 1960: *Stars in Your Eyes* at the London Palladium. This starred Joan Regan, Russ Conway, Edmund Hockeridge, David Kossoff, the Shadows and Cliff.

28 August and for six weeks, 1961: Blackpool Opera House.

June-September 1963: *Holiday Carnival* at the A.B.C. Theatre, Blackpool. This starred Carole Gray, Dailey and Wayne, Arthur Worsley, Norman Collier, Ugo Garrido, and Cliff.

December 1964-April 1965. *Aladdin and His Wonderful Lamp* at the London Palladium. This starred Arthur Askey, Una Stubbs, Charlie Cairoli and Company and Cliff. The music and lyrics were by the Shadows. An album of the show was issued December 1964 (SCX 3522).

11 May 1970: *Five Finger Exercise* by Peter Schaeffer, Bromley New Theatre. Three-week run. Producer Patrick Tucker. Cliff plays Clive, a twenty-year-old university student.

10 May 1971: *The Potting Shed* at Bromley New Theatre. Cast included Patrick Barr, Margo Jenkins, Margot Thomas, Kathleen Harrison. Performance cancelled owing to fire.

17 May 1971: *The Potting Shed* opens at Sadlers Wells Theatre, London.

Same cast as above. Cliff plays James Calliger, a thirty-year-old who is denied family love and attempts to find out why. The original production was twenty years previously when Sir John Gielgud played James Calliger. Press reviews for the play and for Cliff were good. Numerous friends of Cliff attended the first night.

3 July 1974. *A Midsummer Night's Dream* performed by the Riversmead School Dramatic Society. Cliff played Bottom. Actors were past and present pupils of his old school. Cliff took six weeks off normal show and business engagements to rehearse. The play ran until 12 July with a break on 9 and 10 July. It was performed at Riversmead School, College Road, Cheshunt. Mrs Jay Norris produced. The same day that Cliff opened at the school Olivia Newton-John opened a season at Las Vegas!

TELEVISION AND RADIO

Cliff has taken part in so many television and radio programmes throughout the world that it is impossible to trace them all. This section gives some of his most important television and radio broadcasts, with most of the information relating to the U.K. His many appearances year by year on the long-running high-audience B.B.C. T.V. show *Top of the Pops* are not listed save for early bookings. The same goes for other long-running television and radio shows.

13 September 1958: A.B.C. T.V., *Oh Boy*. Cliff makes his programme debut and becomes a resident. The *New Musical Express*, describing his regular appearances on the show, writes, 'the most crude exhibitionism ever seen on T.V.' and adds, 'If we are expected to believe that Cliff Richard was acting naturally then consideration for medical treatment before it's too late may be advisable.'

25 October 1958: Cliff makes his debut on the popular B.B.C. Light Programme *Saturday Club*.

21 January 1960: *Pat Boone Show* (U.S. T.V.). Cliff sings 'Forty Days', 'Dynamite', 'Voice in the Wilderness', 'Living Doll', and 'A Whole Lot of Shakin'.

8 April 1961: Cliff appears on the panel of the B.B.C. T.V. *Juke Box Jury* show where four panel members give their opinions on latest single releases. Chairman is David Jacobs.

26 April 1961: *Parade of the Pops*, B.B.C. Light Programme.

20 May 1961: *Thank Your Lucky Stars*, I.T.V.

2 August 1961: records for *Easy Beat*, B.B.C. Light Programme.

10 October 1961: records special material for Radio Luxembourg.

17 December 1961: records for I.T.V.'s *Thank Your Lucky Stars* Christmas Hit Parade for 1961.

17 January 1962: on *Parade of the Pops* Cliff sings 'The Young Ones' and 'Who Are We to Say'.

11 April 1962: interviewed for Radio Free Europe.

28 August 1962: sings 'It'll Be Me' for the B.B.C.1 *Billy Cotton Show*.

14 December 1962: for *Saturday Club* Cliff records 'Do You Want to Dance', 'Bachelor Boy', 'The Next Time' and 'It'll Be Me'.

18 December 1962: takes part in *Pop Inn* (B.B.C. Light Programme).

21 January 1963: for the first time in the history of Radio Luxembourg's programme *ABC of the stars* it devotes the whole show to one person – Cliff.

22 April 1963: B.B.C. T.V. Cliff records his own special.

3 November 1963: Cliff and the Shadows on A.T.V.'s *Sunday Night at the London Palladium*.

12 May 1964: Cliff in German T.V. show in Munich.

1 July 1964: A.T.V. gives Cliff and the Shadows a one-hour special.

June 1965: Cliff and the Shadows record three one-hour specials for A.T.V.

10 August 1965: tenth anniversary edition of *Thank Your Lucky Stars*. Cliff receives a gold disc for 'Bachelor Boy' coupled with 'The Next Time'.

22 September 1965: Cliff records for U.S. T.V. *Ed Sullivan Show*.

6 March 1966: Cliff stars in B.B.C.2's *Show of the Week*. It's his first B.B.C. T.V. for three years.

9 October 1966: comperes and takes top billing for the A.T.V. show *Sunday Night at the London Palladium*.

7 December 1966: Granada T.V. show *Cinema*. Cliff talks about his films.

14 October 1967: in Tokyo for Japanese T.V. special.

19 December 1967: announcement made that Cliff will take a straight acting role in the play *A Matter of Diamonds*. Transmitted on I.T.V. April 1968.

23 February 1968: Cliff is on *Dee Time* (B.B.C. T.V.).

27 February 1968: *The Golden Shot*, German T.V. Cliff sings 'Don't Forget to Catch Me' in German.

5 March 1968: B.B.C.1. Cliff sings the six short-listed titles for the Eurovision Song Contest.

31 March 1968: *Morecambe and Wise Show*, B.B.C. T.V.

April 1968: *A Matter of Diamonds* is transmitted on I.T.V. It is a thriller in which Cliff has a straight acting role. He plays a young man who has decided he will steal a girl's diamond necklace but when he meets her he falls in love with her.

6 April 1968: *Eurovision Song Contest*, B.B.C. T.V. Cliff comes second with 'Congratulations'.

17 May 1968: *Cliff's T.V. Show* (B.B.C.). He sings 'My Babe', 'Congratulations' (backed by the Breakaways), 'It's All in the Game', 'Feeling Groovy' (with Hank Marvin), 'Perhaps I Had a Wicked Childhood', 'There Must Have Been a Moment of Truth', 'The Minute You're Gone', 'The Day I Met Marie', 'Take a Bird Who Can Sing' (with help from Una Stubbs, Sheila White and Hank Marvin), 'Oh No John No' (Cliff and others), 'Passing Strangers' (with Cilla Black), 'Big Ship', and 'Visions'.

22 May 1968: B.B.C. Light Programme. Cliff is a member of the panel for *Any Questions*.

23 June 1968: I.T.V. *Big Show*. Cliff sings 'The Day I Met Marie', 'All My Love', and 'Shout'.

28 June 1968: *Talk of the Town*, relayed on I.T.V. He sings 'Shout', 'All My Love', 'Nothing But a House-Party', 'If Ever I Should Leave You', 'Girl', 'London's Not Too Far', 'The Dreams That I Dream', 'The Day I Met Marie', 'A Taste of Honey', 'The Lady Came from Baltimore', 'When I'm Sixty-Four', 'The Young Ones', 'Lucky Lips', 'Living Doll', 'In the Country', 'Congratulations', and a brief snatch of 'Visions'. Vocal back-ups from the Breakaways.

17 July 1968: takes part in David Jacobs' B.B.C. T.V. show *Juke Box Jury*.

2 October 1968: interviewed by Keith Skues for B.B.C. Light Programme *Saturday Club*.

5 November 1968: records for B.B.C. Light Programme *Off the Record*. Chooses eight favourite discs and talks about them.

4 December 1968: interviewed by Adrian Love for B.B.C. World Service.

17 December 1968: records 'Congratulations' for B.B.C. T.V. *Top of the Pops* Christmas show.

18 and 19 December 1968: records for Scottish T.V.

19 February 1969: on the *Cilla Black Show* (B.B.C. T.V.), sings 'Good Times' and 'Don't Forget'.

22 February 1969: B.B.C. Radio, *Pete Murray Show*.

7 and 8 March 1969: records for *Rolf Harris Show*, B.B.C. T.V.

17 March 1969: takes part in *Sooty*, B.B.C. T.V. show. Transmitted 12 May.

25 March 1969: *Dave Cash Show*, B.B.C. Radio One.

7 June 1969: *Dee Time*, B.B.C. T.V. recording.

4 September 1969: interview on B.B.C. Radio One *Scene and Heard*.

29 September 1969: B.B.C. Radio, *Open House* with Pete Murray.

28 November 1969: French T.V., Paris. Sings 'Throw Down a Line' and 'Eyes of a Child'.

24 December 1969: B.B.C.1 *Cilla Black Show*.

3 January 1970: Cliff's own B.B.C. T.V. show. The series showcased prospective British entries for the Eurovision Song Contest.

20 February 1970: *Dave Cash Show*, B.B.C. Radio One.

7 March 1970: *Children's Favourites*, B.B.C. Radio One.

13 April 1970: B.B.C. Radios One and Three, *The Cliff Richard Story* with Robin Boyle.

19 May 1970: records contribution for Disney show, B.B.C. T.V.

31 August 1970: Cliff special, B.B.C. T.V. Aretha Franklin is the star guest, with others taking part, including Hank Marvin and Una Stubbs. The show lasts fifty minutes.

4 October 1970: *Sing a New Song*, B.B.C. T.V. First of three shows, with the Settlers, for the religious department. (The Settlers are also resident for six weeks from 20 September in the A.T.V. Sunday programme *Beyond Belief*.)

2 January 1971: new B.B.C. T.V. series *It's Cliff Richard* with Hank Marvin and Una Stubbs resident. Thirteen weeks.

24 January 1971: 'Lollipop Tree', B.B.C.2. Cliff provides the commentary for this section of *The World About Us*. The segment tells of a home for 800 children located at the foot of the Himalayas where for a time Cliff's aunt was a teacher.

27 March 1971: final screening of Cliff's T.V. series which began 2 January.

30 August 1971: B.B.C.1 *Getaway With Cliff* holiday special. Cliff joined by Olivia Newton-John, Hank Marvin, Bruce Welch and John Farrar. The show, which lasts fifty minutes, is filmed in various parts of Britain.

24 December 1971: B.B.C. T.V., Cliff's own Christmas Eve special.

1972: *It's Cliff Richard*. A thirteen-week B.B.C. T.V. series beginning January. Resident guests were Olivia Newton-John and the Flirtations. The Breakaways provided the vocal backing and the Pamela Davis Dancers provided the dancing. Hank Marvin declined a residency for this series. Another familiar face, that of Una Stubbs, was prevented from appearing in the early programmes because she was expecting a baby. Dandy Nichols provided the early replacement. Also guesting in the series were the New Seekers. They sang the songs which were short-listed for Britain's entry to the 1972 Eurovision Song Contest. Among other series guests were Elton John and Labi Siffre. The series gained over two million viewers more than the one in 1971. It was scripted by Eric Donaldson and produced by Michael Hurll.

27 February 1972: last programme of the series in which Cliff presents *Music for Sunday* for B.B.C. Radios One and Two. In this series he played records by other Christian artists and some of his own. Programme devised and produced by Jack Hywel Davies.

19 August 1972: Cliff makes a guest appearance on the *Lulu* show. He sings 'Reason to believe' and his new single 'Living in Harmony'.

2 September 1972: *The Case* is screened in the U.K. This film was specially made for the B.B.C. and Swedish, Norwegian and Finnish broadcasting companies. It starred Cliff, Tim Brooke-Taylor, Olivia

Newton-John and two Scandinavians, Mathi Rannin and Pekka Laitho. The plot was scripted by Eric Donaldson. It was described as a musical comedy thriller. Some reviewers likened Tim Brooke-Taylor and Cliff to Bob Hope and Bing Crosby! The programme producer was Michael Hurll. It took ten days of filming.

2 January 1973: B.R.T. T.V., Belgium, shows Cliff in Scotland with the songs 'Hail Caledonia', 'Skye Boat Song', 'Courting in the Kitchen', 'Let's Have a Ceilidh', 'Bonnie Mary of Argyll', and, among others, 'Scotland the Brave'.

10 January 1973: Cliff appears on the *Cilla Black Show* and sings the six entries for the Eurovision Song Contest (he had been chosen for the second time to represent Britain at this event). The six songs are 'Come Back Billie Joe', 'Ashes to Ashes', 'Tomorrow's Rising', 'The Days of Love', 'Power to All Our Friends', and 'Help It Along'. The song selected was 'Power to All Our Friends'.

13 January 1973: British Forces Broadcasting Service interview with Brian Cullingford.

19 January 1973: B.B.C.2 *They Sold a Million*.

2 April 1973: B.B.C. Radio One *Top 12*. Cliff chooses his top twelve records. Compere Brian Matthew, producer Paul Williams.

7 April 1973: Cliff appears at the Eurovision Song Festival and sings the British entry 'Power to All Our Friends', which comes third. The song was written by Guy Fletcher and Doug Flett. An estimated 300 million in thirty-two countries saw the show. Cliff was very disappointed at not winning and told reporters he was getting too old. However, 'Power to All Our Friends' became a worldwide pop hit.

4 May 1974: B.B.C. T.V. *Mike Yarwood Show*. When Cliff appears it is to find Mike impersonating Hughie Green, a well-known British T.V. presenter of new acts. Cliff sings his latest single '(You Keep Me) Hanging On.'

9 May 1974: *The Nana Mouskouri Show*. B.B.C. T.V. Cliff sings 'Give Me Back That Old Familiar Feeling'. Later he sings 'Constantly', sporting a yellow jacket and multi-coloured tie, and with his fringe parted in the middle. With Nana he sings 'I Believe in Music'.

24 August 1974: the first of the 1974 *It's Cliff Richard* series is transmitted.

9 April 1975: *Shangalang*, Bay City Rollers' Granada T.V. show. Interview.

19 April 1975: Cliff is a special guest on London Weekend Television's *Saturday Scene*, compere Sally James. The original version of 'Travellin' Light' is played. Cliff remarks on another and better version which is on his new album *31st of February Street*. He says he has recently been in Vienna 'Plugging my new record "It's Only Me You've Left Behind" '.

9 July 1975: *Jim'll Fix It*. Cliff fan Helen Moon of Cromer writes in to the

B.B.C. asking if she could meet her pop hero. The wish is granted. With the Shadows Cliff sings 'Run Billy Run'. After the show spot Helen Moon receives from Cliff an autographed copy of *31st of February Street*.

6 September 1975: first of a new series on B.B.C. T.V., *It's Cliff and Friends*. Major guests are Su Shiffron, David Copperfield and Alan Shiers. Musical director, Ronnie Hazelhurst; sound, Adrian Bishop-Laggett; lighting, Robbie Robinson; design, Chris Pemsel; producer, Phil Bishop. Cliff sings 'All You Need Is Love', 'Good on the Sally Army', 'With Su', 'All I Wanna Do', 'I've Got Time', 'Love Train'.

20 September 1975: *Supersonic*, I.T.V. programme produced by Mike Mansfield. Cliff wears a blue denim suit. He sings 'Honky Tonk Angel', 'Let's Have a Party', and does a brief take-off of Elvis.

3 October 1975: *Pop Quest*, I.T.V. A clip of Cliff is shown.

14 October 1975: Noel Edmonds on his Radio One show at 07.40 welcomes 1940-born Cliff into the world and plays 'Please Don't Tease'.

November 1975: Cliff appears on Capital, the London radio station, for a nostalgia show which recalls February 1959, with compere Roger Scott. 'High Class Baby' is played.

4 January 1976: B.B.C. Radios One and Two. New *Gospel Road* series. Cindy Kent, ex-Settlers, reviews new records while Cliff, as before, contributes material of his own and introduces songs by other people.

14 February 1976: I.T.V. *Supersonic*. Wearing a white jacket and trousers with a green shirt Cliff sings 'Miss You Nights'.

26 April 1976: records T.V. special, Holland. *Eddy Go Round* show. Broadcast 15 June 1976.

3 May 1976: Radio Luxembourg. Cliff previews his new album *I'm Nearly Famous*.

17 May 1976: Begins recording *Insight* with Tim Blackmore, Radio One.

19 and 26 June 1976: *Supersonic*, I.T.V. On the 19th Cliff sings 'Honky Tonk Angel'; on the 26th 'Let's Have a Party'.

6 September 1976: interviewed on B.B.C. T.V. *Nationwide* and on Thames T.V.

30 December 1976: Belgian T.V., *Adamo Special*. Cliff sings 'Living Doll' (with Adamo), 'Power to All Our Friends', and 'Honky Tonk Angel'.

28 September 1977: *DLT Show*, Radio One. D.J. Dave Lee Travis talks with Cliff from 6 p.m. to 7 p.m. Producer Dave Atkey.

1 October 1977: *Michael Parkinson Show*, B.B.C. T.V. Cliff is a guest along with Robert Morley, who was with Cliff in his films *The Young Ones* and *Finders Keepers*.

November 1977: *TisWas*, A.T.V. Cliff talks with compere Sally James

and undergoes the usual rituals for programme participants –
something squashy stuffed in the face and cold water to soothe a high
temperature.

15 February 1978: B.B.C. T.V., *Pebble Mill*. On this lunchtime show Cliff
speaks about his new album *Small Corners* and sings two songs from it.

21 September 1978: *Star Parade*, German T.V. Cliff sings 'Please
Remember Me' and 'Lucky Lips'.

1 October 1978: B.B.C. Radio One. *20 Golden Years*. First in a series
which tells the Cliff show business story.

30 October 1978: Australian T.V. *Australian Music to the World*. Cliff
sings 'Devil Woman', an interview is shown which had been filmed at
his English home and in which he talks of John Farrar and Olivia
Newton-John.

1 January 1979: Korea. K.B.S. T.V. shows *The Young Ones* in a New
Year programme.

12 June 1979: Dutch T.V. *AVRO Gala Special*. Cliff records on 31 May
and 1 June items for inclusion in this show, in aid of the fiftieth
anniversary of the Dutch Youth Hostel organization, N.J.H.C. Cliff
sings 'Miss You Nights', 'When Two Worlds Drift Apart'.

27 August 1979: B.B.C. Radio One broadcast a special programme on the
Greenbelt Jesus Music Festival in which Cliff is interviewed and heard
on stage.

5 September 1979: Capital Radio, London. Cliff takes part in the
top-rated *Roger Scott Show*. The two chat and a number of Cliff record
tracks are played.

19 September 1979: Manchester's Radio Piccadilly. Cliff is the guest of
well known D.J. Roger Day between 3 and 4 p.m. Several Cliff tracks
are played and Cliff also talks about his new record label Patch and his
first signing, Garth Hewitt.

23 December 1979: B.B.C. Radio One. *Star Special*. Cliff becomes a D.J.
for two hours and plays his favourite records. He names 'Rock 'n' Roll
Juvenile' as the recording of his own that he most likes.

26 December 1979: *Two Sides of Cliff*. B.B.C. Radio Two. Cliff plays his
own and Shadows' records.

7 January 1980: *Mike Douglas Show*, U.S.A. T.V. Cliff is interviewed by
the well-known chat-show personality. Douglas talks to Cliff about his
O.B.E. He tells how a great chunk of his career could be labelled
'European' and that he doesn't need America for finance.

8 January 1980: *The Dinah Shore Show*, U.S.A. T.V. Dinah tells of Cliff's
current U.S. hit 'We Don't Talk Anymore'. Cliff explains what an
O.B.E. is and shows the audience his Union Jack coloured socks. He
talks of his childhood memories, explains why he is not married, and
discusses the pros and cons of American girls.

March 1980. *Pop Gospel* I.T.V. series begins. Cliff appears in two shows.

22 June 1980: B.B.C. T.V., *Greenbelt*. An edited version of the film which has Cliff in film shots, in interview and in concert, but for Cliff fans the live footage is meagre.

23 July 1980: B.B.C. Radio One. Cliff on his O.B.E. day takes part in a telephone link-up with friend and Radio One D.J. Mike Read on his breakfast show.

23 September 1980: B.B.C. Radio Two, *The John Dunn Show*. A general chat and interview, one of many which Cliff has had over the years with this popular B.B.C. presenter. Cliff defines himself on this programme as 'basically a pop-rock singer'.

27 September 1980: B.B.C. *Swapshop*. Cliff appears on this high-audience younger listener programme and talks about himself and his music.

13 December 1980: B.B.C.1, *Michael Parkinson Show*. He sings 'Heartbreak Hotel'. In a finale with other programme guests Cliff joins in singing 'All the Way'. This programme was repeated 28 March 1981.

4 January 1981: U.S. T.V. *The John Kelly Show*, Los Angeles.

5 January 1981: U.S. T.V. *The John Davison Show*, Los Angeles.

6 January 1981: U.S. T.V. *Dionne Warwick's Solid Gold Show*, Los Angeles.

7 January 1981: U.S. T.V. *Merv Griffin Show*, Los Angeles.

20 March 1981: *Cliff in London*, B.B.C.1. Excerpts from Cliff's autumn concerts at the Apollo. The first part of the programme has Cliff accompanying himself on acoustic guitar.

7 September 1981: new British commercial radio station Centre Radio (Leeds) opens for transmission. Its first record is Cliff's 'Wired for Sound'.

30 September 1981: Cliff is in the United States on a promotional visit which includes filming four T.V. shows in Hollywood.

23 November 1981: B.B.C.2 transmits the first of four programmes on Cliff's career in show business. The focal point of each is a recent concert given by Cliff. The programmes also include other items with some overlapping of the people interviewed. The series title is *Cliff*. It was made by the B.B.C. in co-operation with Lella Productions, produced and directed by Norman Stone. This first programme shows the Rock 'n' Roll Special concert which was recorded and filmed at the Hammersmith Odeon on 1 May 1981. There are also film extracts from *Expresso Bongo* (Pendennis Pictures), *The Young Ones* (E.M.I. Elstree), *Oh Boy* (E.M.I./Pathé)' Pathé newsreels and B.B.C. T.V. newsreels.

Music: 'Rock 'n' Roll Juvenile', 'Stood Up', 'Move It', 'Shakin' All Over', 'Gee Whizz It's You', 'Whole Lotta Shakin' Goin' On', 'Blue Suede Shoes', 'Great Balls of Fire', 'Lucille', 'When Will I Be Loved', 'Teddy Bear', 'Long Tall Sally', 'Rip It Up'.

Interviewees: Adam Faith, John Foster, Jack Good, Marty Wilde, Hank Marvin, Bruce Welch, Tito Burns, Carl Perkins, Neil Spencer, Phil Everly.

27 November 1981: *A.T.V. Today.* Cliff with the authors of this book, Tony Jasper and Patrick Doncaster.

30 November 1981: B.B.C.2 series on Cliff, second programme. It focuses on a Gospel concert which was recorded at the Apollo, Manchester, on 6 February 1981.

Music: 'Why Should the Devil Have All the Good Music', 'Better Than I know Myself', 'Son of Thunder', 'You Can't Get to Heaven by Singing', 'Like Hell', 'Fool's Wisdom', 'Take Me Where I Wanna Go', 'Under the Influence', 'I Wish We'd All Been Ready', 'Lost in a Lonely World', 'The Rock that Doesn't Roll'.

Interviewees: Mike Read, Olivia Newton-John, Kenny Everett, Dave Lee Travis, Bill Latham, David Winter, Larry Norman, Pat Boone, Andrae Crouch, Network Three.

7 December 1981: B.B.C.2 series on Cliff, third programme. It centres on Cliff's American tour and a concert at the Savoy Theatre, New York, 2 April 1981.

Music: 'Travellin' Light', 'Move It', 'Devil Woman', 'Give a Little Bit More', 'Green Light', 'Monday Thru Friday', 'I'm Nearly Famous, 'We Don't Talk Anymore', 'Miss You Nights', 'Thank You Very Much'.

Interviewees: Buzz Brindle, Dave Lee Travis, Una Stubbs, Adam Faith, Don Grierson, David Bryce, Tim Messer, Olivia Newton-John, Steve Mann.

14 December 1981: B.B.C.2 series on Cliff, fourth programme. Cliff's birthday concert at London's Apollo, Victoria.

27 December 1981: *Everyman,* B.B.C.1. Cliff discusses his personal faith and beliefs.

Radio Specials

Cliff talking about *Every Face Tells a Story* with Roger Scott of London's Capital Radio.

Radio One *Insight* programme where Cliff chats about the album *I'm Nearly Famous.*

1976 Royal Albert Hall concert broadcast on Capital Radio, London.

1977 Croydon concert broadcast on Radio Two.

Cliff's Christmas 1977 programme broadcast on Radio Two.

Cliff singles file 1958-69 broadcast on London's Capital Radio, and his singles file continued, 1970-78.

Radio One *20 Golden Years* programme, part 1 to 5 with Tim Rice.

Gospel Concert, Royal Albert Hall, 10 October 1978, broadcast on
    Hilversum Radio.
D.J. Roger Scott introducing *Green Light* and also Cliff's Top 10 records
    broadcast on London's Capital Radio.

BOOKS ON OR BY CLIFF

Cliff Around the Clock (Daily Mirror Publications).
The Cliff Richard Story by George Tremlett (Futura).
D.I., Issues 1-63 (International Cliff Richard Movement).
From Cliff to You by Janet Johnson (International Cliff Richard
    Movement – for members only).
Happy Xmas from Cliff by Cliff Richard (Hodder and Stoughton).
It's Great to Be Young by Cliff Richard (Souvenir).
Me and My Shadows by Cliff Richard (Daily Mirror Publications).
New Singer, New Song by David Winter (Hodder and Stoughton).
Questions, Cliff answering reader and fan queries (Hodder and
    Stoughton).
The Wonderful World of Cliff Richard by Bob Ferrier (Peter Davies).
Two a Penny, film story by David Winter and Stella Linden (Hodder
    and Stoughton).
Visions (Cliff Richard Fan Club of London).
The Way I See It by Cliff Richard (Hodder and Stoughton).
Which One's Cliff? by Cliff Richard and Bill Latham (Hodder and
    Stoughton).
Cliff In His Own Words edited by Kevin St John (Omnibus).

FAN CLUBS

There is no official Cliff fan club, but the long-standing and efficiently run
International Cliff Richard Movement (I.C.R.M.) has gained the
co-operation of the Cliff Richard management.

The I.C.R.M. publishes a bi-monthly club paper *D.I. (Dynamite
International)*. Its headquarters is I.C.R.M., Postbox 4164, 1009AD,
Amsterdam, Netherlands. The editor of *Dynamite* is Harry De Louw.
Secretary is Anton Husmann Jr. The I.C.R.M. supplies a wide range of
information and material for members. There is a yearly subscription.
Listed below are the worldwide locations of the I.C.R.M. as of April
1982.

U.K. I.C.R.M. Groups

Avon and Somerset: Mrs M. Merritt, 14 Newlyn Way, Yate, Bristol BS17 5AX.

Birmingham: Tricia and Cath Smith, 24 Larkspur Croft, Bromford Bridge, Birmingham B36 8QE.

Buckinghamshire and Middlesex: Desmond D'sa, 15 Hardwicke Avenue, Heston, Middlesex.

Derbyshire and Nottinghamshire: Pamela Huggins, 25 South Avenue, Littlecover, Derby.

Devon and Cornwall: Jan Cowan, 2 Crescent Road, Bugle, St Austell PL26 8PQ.

Dorset: Freda Hector/Maureen Wakefield, 22 Benmoor Road, Creekmoor, Poole, Dorset BH17 7DS.

Essex: Cliff Marshall, 25 Cricketfield Grove, Leigh-on-Sea, Essex.

Glasgow: Elizabeth Daly, 15 Ryedale Place, Drumchapel, Glasgow G15 7HP.

Gloucester and Oxford: William Hooper, 17 Podsmead Road, Tuffley, Gloucester GL1 5PB.

Hampshire: Mrs Marion Cunningham, 67 Park Road, Freemantle, Southampton SO1 3DD.

Hereford and Worcester: Mrs Annette Bufton, 17 Seward Road, Badsey, Evesham, Worcs.

Isle of Wight: Mrs Dawn Nott, 5 Charnwood Cottages, West Street, Brading, Isle of Wight PO36 0DN.

Kent: Jacquey Hartree, Walsingham Cottage, Manor Park, Chislehurst, Kent.

Lancashire: Linda Gilmour, 18 Park Farm Road, Feniscowles, Blackburn, Lancs.

Leicestershire and Nottinghamshire: Angela Barcock, 28 The Morwoods, Oadby, Leics. LE2 5ED.

Lincolnshire: Dianne Holmes, Ings House, Fendyke Road, Firsby, Lincs.

London: Janet Johnson, 142 Weston Park, Hornsey, London N8 9PN.

South London and Surrey: Eileen Edwards, 1 Links View Road, Spring Park, Shirley, Surrey CR0 8NB.

Manchester: Alan Elliott, 144 Overdale Road, Stockport, Manchester SK6 3EN.

Merseyside and Cheshire: Susan Langley, 14 Wheatfield Close, Old Roan, Bootle 10, Merseyside L30 8RH.

Northern Ireland: Mrs Ann Thompson, 409 Ballysillan Road, Belfast BT14 6RE.

North-East England: Mrs Lynne Martin, 6 Grantham Road, Norton, Stockton, Cleveland TS20 1PP.

Staffordshire and Salop: Brenda Davies, 36 Waterbrook Close, Penkridge, Stafford.

Suffolk, Norfolk and Cambridgeshire: Miss A. R. Baker, 86 Levington Lane, Bucklesham, nr Ipswich, Suffolk IP10 9DZ.

Sussex: Mrs Carole Davis, 8 Lansdowne Court, Lansdowne Road, West Worthing, Sussex

BN11 5HD.

Wales: Peter Roberts, 11 Glos Gorsfawr, Grovesend, Swansea, South Wales SA4 2GZ.

Warwickshire: Mrs Joy M. Dyer, 'Stowupland', 22 Monument Way, Stratford-on-Avon, Warwicks. CV37 6YA.

Wiltshire and Berkshire: Mrs Christine Rowling, 17 Baydon Close, Moredon, Swindon, Wilts. SN2 3DP.

Yorkshire: Mrs Jennifer Chatten, 26 Wentworth Drive, Harrogate HG2 7LA.

Non-U.K. I.C.R.M. Groups

Australia: Glenys Grundy/Sheila Lewis, 106 Richards Drive, Morphett Vale, South Australia 5162.

Belgium: Miss Suykerbuyk Marleen, Julius de Geyterstraat 258, B-2610, Wilrijk, Belgium.

Canada: Denise Magi, 368 Eglinton Avenue East, Apt. 1111, Toronto, Ontario M4P 1L9.

West Germany: Christine Thon, Wedauer Strasse 42, D-4030 Raingen 4.

South Africa: Robert Witchell, P.O. Box 3505, Pretoria 0001.

U.S.A.: Dixie Gonzalez, 724 West Bard Road, Oxnard, California 93033.

The Shadows Circle of Friends is located at 69 Station Road, Portslade, East Sussex BN4 1DF. It is not an official fan club. John Friesen, 3 Church Parade, Ashford, Middlesex, is appointed official distributor of Shadows material.

An Olivia Newton-John fan club is run from Holland, P.O. Box 5050, 3502, JB Utrecht, Netherlands.

MEETING HOUSES

These enjoy the support of the I.C.R.M. They provide a place for members of the I.C.R.M. and affiliated clubs to meet each other, talk about Cliff, play his records, examine scrapbooks, arrange Cliff show visits, and so on. There is no additional membership fee, but the expenses for the activities of the meeting houses are shared by the fans taking part. The meeting houses listed below are affiliated to the I.C.R.M.:

U.K. Meeting Houses

Basingstoke: Sandra Boulter, 86 Warwick Road, Winkelbury, Basingstoke, Hampshire.

Blaydon: Rose Nesbit, 15 Cowan Close, Stella Park, Blaydon, Tyne and Wear.

Coventry: S. McAvoy, 14 Mount Nod Way, Broad Lane, Coventry. West Midlands CV5 7GX.

Exeter: Margaret Gouch, 7 Rosebud, Sandy-Acre Park, Clyst St Mary, Exeter EX5 1BB.

Fareham and Gosport: Sheila Cheeseman, 143 Turner Avenue, Rowner, Gosport, Hants. PO13 0BT.

Glasgow: Gertrude Hill, 20 Fairholm Street, Shettleston, Glasgow G32 7QB.

Leeds: June Cartwright, 104 Carden Avenue, Sutton Estate, Leeds LS15 0EQ.

London South-East: Joanne Wood, 27 Lynton Rd, Bermondsey, London SE1 5QU.

Newbury: Maureen Thirkill, 43 Dene Way, Newbury, Berks. RG13 2JL.

Nuneaton: Kath Rouse, 44 Portland Drive, Whittleford, Nuneaton, Warwicks.

Oxford: Pat Giles, 6 John Snow Place, Headington, Oxford OX3 8BB.

Plymouth: Susan Woodward, 205 Hamerdon Heights, Chaddlewood, Plympton, Plymouth, Devon.

Sheffield: Tina Bellamy, 3 Birley Rise Crescent, Birley Carr, Sheffield 6.

Stockton: Freda Boynton, 8 Barrhead Close, Stockton-on-Tees, Cleveland.

Stourport-on-Severn: Joy Reading, Lower Poolands Farm, Titton, Stourport-on-Severn, Worcs.

Stratton St Margaret: Wendy-Janice Martin, 57 Hathaway Road, Upper Stratton, Swindon.

Sutton: Elaine Davis, 6 Effingham Close, Sutton, Surrey.

Tamworth: Beryl Groves, 120 Broadsmeath, Kettlebrook, Ramsworth, Staffs. B77 1DQ.

Twickenham and Teddington: Karen Wright, 72 Twining Avenue, Twickenham, Middlesex TW2 5LP.

Waterlooville: Ruth Wylie, 14 Beresford Close, Waterlooville, Portsmouth, Hampshire.

West Bromwich: Maureen Powell, 14 St. Paul's Crescent, Golds Hill, West Bromwich, West Midlands.

Woking: Joyce Dunford, 115 Walton Road, Woking, Surrey GU21 5DW.

The fan clubs for Birmingham, Devon and Cornwall, Dorset, London, Wiltshire and Berkshire also run Meeting Houses.

Non-U.K. Meeting Houses

Australia: Alva Garton, 131 Huntriss Road, Doubelview, Perth, Western Australia 6018. Sue Cardon, 10 Dunsford Street, Whyalla 'Stuart', Whyalla, South Australia 5608.

Belgium: Viviane Mees, Kruisbeekstraat 18, 2060 Merkshem, Antwerp.

Finland: Merja Reponen,
   Taivaapankontie 33 C22,
   70200, Kuopio 20.
Japan: Taeko Takahashi, 3-27-31
   Nakakasai, Edogawa-ku,
   Tokyo 132.
South Africa: T-M & S-M
   Whitehead, P.O. Box 10653,
Marine Parade, Durban, Natal
   4056.
Sweden: Regina Rexberg, Nilsson
   Berg 36, 411 43 Göteborg.
   Eva Söderman, Terapivägen
   4E 2tr, 141 55 Huddinge,
   Stockholm.

THE CHRISTIAN FRIENDS OF CLIFF RICHARD

Originally there were two groups, one based in Denmark, the other in
France. In 1981 the Danish group was the only one functioning, with a
magazine titled after their organization. They say the object of this group
is to let those interested know about Cliff's Christian life and work, and to
support him through prayers and Christian love. They see Cliff as the
singer who is 'loving every second of his work, and looking forward to
Jesus coming back', and 'the one who cannot separate his job from God,
and he, like everyone else, needs the support of prayers, and love from
others'. They see their magazine not as a fan magazine but as a fantastic
chance to reach people who like Cliff with a 'Christian word, and that's
what we really want – to do a mission through it, and we have already seen
it work – people tell us about it in letters'. The Danish group say they
prayed a great deal before taking their decision and consulted with Bill
Latham, who is Cliff's Christian brother and responsible for arranging
Cliff's Christian activities. The address of this movement is The Christian
Friends of Cliff Richard, Christiansgade 6, 7800 Skive, Denmark.

GRAPEVINE

Grapevine came into being in September 1978 and claims a worldwide
membership of 1,950. It initially began under the name of The Cliff
Richard Meeting House Society. It was started by a group of
Colchester-based fans for the purpose of linking together all the clubs in
the U.K., providing information about Cliff's concert tour dates and
supporting his charitable activities. The concept of Grapevine is described
by the organizers as 'developing from the need to give a better and faster
information service than had been available elsewhere, particularly
regarding ticket applications'. Grapevine publishes a sixteen-page
magazine-format illustrated newsletter every three months, and holds its
own annual convention.

Grapevine says that all profit realized from the sale of Grapevine
T-shirts, photographs, and so on, is donated to charity. In two-and-a-half

years it has given over £1,250 to the Cliff Richard Charitable Trust Fund. Grapevine also sponsors a little girl called Suparti in Indonesia through the Tear Fund child care programme.

Several of those responsible for running Grapevine are committed Christians and this is reflected in the content of the magazine, which encourages members to think about the Christian message associated with Cliff's Gospel songs and his faith.

U.K. membership costs £1.50 per year plus five stamped addressed envelopes (9″ x 6″), four for magazines and one for urgent information.

Membership for those in Eire is £2.50 and for those overseas £3.50 (both inclusive of envelopes and stamps). Irish cheques, postal orders or Irish pound notes cannot be accepted. Payment must be made in sterling or by International Money Order made out in sterling. British postal rates frequently change – usually upwards – and the authors of this book therefore suggest that readers should consult Grapevine further about costs if they decide to contact the organization regarding membership etc. The Grapevine address is P.O. Box 55, Colchester, Essex, CO4 3XJ.

The Chairman of Grapevine is Diana Duffett. Vice-Chairman, Gordon Donaldson. Treasurer, Veronica Owen. Secretary, Jennie Harding. Social Secretary, Sylvia Austin. Photographer, Peter Noad. Clerical Assistant, Jocelyn Leyland.

THE CLIFF RICHARD CHARITABLE TRUST

Clubs and meeting houses of the I.C.R.M. and those of the Grapevine movement make donations to Cliff's fund. The fund is a small one but was established so that Cliff had a convenient channel for his support of the many charities with which he sympathizes, but for which he is unable, owing to pressures on his time, to present special fund-raising concerts. The trust makes a series of donations each quarter – a maximum of £200 to any organization. All recipients have to be registered charities and appeals from individuals cannot be considered. Obviously, the trust makes no public appeal for funds and is essentially a channel for Cliff's own personal donations. If fans from time to time make a donation then this is included in the funds to be distributed at the next quarter.

INTERNATIONAL CLIFF WEEK

This is held during the week of Cliff's birthday, 14 October. During this special week every single member of the I.C.R.M. writes to their local radio station telling them of the week and asking for Cliff records to be played.

OBTAINING NON-CURRENT RECORDS

The following sources are recommended by the I.C.R.M. (a stamped addressed envelope or International Reply Coupon should always be sent with requests.:

John Friesen, Record Scene,
   3 Church Parade, Ashford,
   Middlesex.
Dieter Boek,
   Kölner Landstrasse 179,
   4000 Düsseldorf, W. Germany.

Arie de Kwaadsteniet,
   Kroonkruid 31,
   2914 BS Nieuwerkerk,
   a/d Ijssel, Holland.

CLIFF AND THE SHADOWS ON TOUR

Cliff's tours have always been and still are organized by Eddie Jarrett.

24 January 1959: Rialto Theatre, York. Among his numbers Cliff sang: 'Move It', 'High Class Baby', 'Make Believe', 'King Creole', 'Whole Lot of Shaking' Goin' On', 'Schoolboy Crush'. Also on the bill: Wee Willie Harris, Tony Crombie and His Rockets.

17 August 1961: Tivoli Gardens, Stockholm. The Shadows: 'Apache', 'Frightened City', 'F.B.I.'. Cliff backed by the Shadows: 'Move It', 'Please Don't Tease', 'Living Doll', 'My Blue Heaven', 'A Girl Like You', 'What'd I say'.

2 April 1964: ABC, Kingston. The Shadows: 'Chattanooga Choo Choo', 'Dance On', 'In the Mood', 'That's the Way It Goes', 'Theme for Young Lovers', 'Little Bitty Tear', 'Big B', 'Foot Tapper', 'F.B.I.'. Cliff backed by the Shadows, Bob Miller and his Millermen: 'I Wanna Know', 'Don't Talk to Him', '24 Hours From Tulsa', 'Da Doo Ron Ron', 'Moon River', 'It's All in the Game', 'Maria', 'I'm the Lonely One', 'Constantly', 'Whole Lot of Shaking' Goin' On', 'What'd I Say', 'Bachelor Boy'.

7 and 9 September 1964: ABC, Great Yarmouth. The Shadows (Hank, Bruce, Brian and John): 'In the Mood', 'Dance On', 'Nivram', 'The Rise and Fall of Flingel Bunt', 'Theme for Young Lovers', '500 Miles', 'Little Bitty Tear', 'Tonight', 'Big B', 'F.B.I.'.

16 February 1965: Pantomime Season, London Palladium, *Aladdin and His Wonderful Lamp*. The Shadows: 'Me Oh My', 'Genie With the Light Brown Lamp'. Cliff backed by the Shadows and the Palladium Orchestra: 'I Could Easily Fall', 'This Was My Special Day', 'I'm in Love With You', 'There's Gotta Be a Way', 'Friends', 'Make Every Day a Carnival Day', 'I've Said Too Many Things', 'Evening Comes', 'Havin' Fun'.

8-14 June 1965: Hippodrome Theatre, Birmingham. The Shadows (Hank, Bruce, Brian and John): 'Brazil', 'In the Mood', 'Apache', 'Stingray', 'Mary Anne', 'Let It Be', 'Big B', 'The Rise and Fall of Flingel Bunt', 'Tonight', 'F.B.I.'.

3 October 1965: Gaumont, Derby. The Shadows (Hank, Bruce, Brian, and John): 'Brazil', 'Foot Tapper', 'Apache', 'Don't Make My Baby Blue', 'Let It Be Me', 'Stingray', 'Tonight', 'Big B', 'F.B.I.'. Cliff backed by the Shadows: 'Do You Want to Dance', 'Angel', 'Don't Talk to Him', 'On the Beach', 'The Minute You're Gone', 'The Time in Between', 'The Twelfth of Never', 'Long Tall Sally', 'It's All in the Game', 'Da Doo Ron Ron', 'I Could Easily Fall', 'The Young Ones', 'Living Doll', 'Lucky Lips', 'Bachelor Boy', 'Razzle Dazzle', 'What'd I say'.

21 February 1966: Cabaret Season, Talk of the Town, London. The Shadows (Hank, Bruce, Brian and John): 'Brazil', 'Dance On', 'Nivram', '500 Miles', 'A Little Bitty Tear', 'Tonight', 'Little B', 'F.B.I.'. Cliff backed by the Shadows: 'I Could Easily Fall', 'The Minute You're Gone', 'Do You Want to Dance', 'Wind Me Up', 'My One and Only Love', '24 Hours From Tulsa', 'On the Beach', 'Girl from Ipanema', 'My Colouring Book', 'What'd I Say', 'The Young Ones', 'Living Doll', 'Bachelor Boy'.

3 April 1966: Empire Pool, Wembley, Record Star Show in aid of spastics. The Shadows (Hank, Bruce, Brian, and John): 'The Rise and Fall of Flingel Bunt', 'Somewhere', 'Dance On'. Cliff backed by the Shadows: 'I Could Easily Fall', 'Wind Me Up', 'Blue Turns to Grey', 'The Young Ones', 'Living Doll', 'Lucky Lips', 'Bachelor Boy'.

3 July 1966: ABC, Great Yarmouth. The Shadows (Hank, Bruce, Brian, and John): 'In the Mood', 'Dance On', 'Don't Make My Baby Blue', 'Nivram', 'Sloop John B', 'Let It Be', 'Will You Be There', 'Somewhere', 'Little B', 'The Rise and Fall of Flingel Bunt'.

10 March 1967: Pantomime Season, London Palladium, *Cinderella*. The Shadows (Hank, Bruce, Brian, and John): 'The Flyder and the Spy', 'Autumn'. Cliff backed by the Shadows and the Palladium Orchestra: 'Why Wasn't I Born Rich', 'Peace and Quiet', 'In the Country', 'Come Sunday', 'If Our Dreams Come True' (with Pippa Steel), 'Poverty', 'Peace and Quiet' (reprise), 'The King's Palace', 'She Needs Him More Than Me', 'Hey Doctor Man.

27 August 1967: Winter Gardens, Bournemouth. The Shadows (Hank, Bruce, Brian, and John): 'In the Mood', 'Dance On', 'Don't Make My Baby Blue', 'Let It Be Me', 'Apache', 'Nivram', 'Bombay Duck', 'Foot Tapper','Little Bitty Tear', 'Death of a Clown', 'San Francisco', 'The Rise and Fall of Flingel Bunt', 'Somewhere', 'Little B', 'F.B.I.'.

15 and 18 January 1968: Cabaret Season, Talk of the Town, London. The Shadows: 'Sleepwalk', 'In the Mood', 'Dance On', 'Don't Make My Baby Blue', 'Let It Be Me', 'Wonderful Land', 'Nivram', 'Apache', 'Foot Tapper', 'Cool Water', 'Little Bitty Tear', 'The Rise and Fall of Flingel Bunt', 'Somewhere', 'Little B', 'F.B.I.' On the 15th Hank, Bruce, Brian and Liquorice played. On the 18th, Hank, Bruce, John

and Tony. 'Little B' was not played on the 18th. At the start of the season John Rostill was unwell and was replaced by Brian 'Liquorice' Locking. Later in the season Brian Bennett was taken to hospital with appendicitis and was replaced by Tony Meehan, by which time John Rostill had recovered sufficiently to rejoin the group.

23 May 1968: The Tom Jones Season, London Palladium. The Shadows (Hank, Bruce, John, and Brian): 'Dance On', 'Lara's Theme', 'Dear Old Mrs Bell', 'Niram', 'Putting on the Style', 'Somewhere', 'Little B', 'F.B.I.'.

11 October 1968: season at the London Palladium. The Shadows (Hank, Bruce, Brian, and John): 'In the Mood', 'Lara's Theme', 'Foot Tapper', 'For Emily', 'Putting on the Style', 'Somewhere', 'F.B.I.'. Cliff backed by the Breakaways and the Palladium Orchestra: 'Shout', 'Marianne', 'Bachelor Boy', 'Somewhere in My Youth or Childhood', 'If Ever I should Leave You', 'The Day I Met Marie', 'La La La La La', 'The Young Ones', 'Lucky Lips', 'Living Doll', 'In the Country', 'Don't Forget to Catch Me', 'When I'm 64', 'Congratulations', 'Visions'.

7 October 1969: The Alaska, Tokyo. The Shadows appeared in the first half as part of the orchestra that accompanied Cliff. Cliff had the support of three Japanese girl singers. 'Shout', 'Move It', 'It's All in the Game', 'Something Good', 'If Ever I Should Leave You', 'Nothing But a House-Party', 'Throw Down a Line', 'The Day I Met Marie', 'La La La La La', 'Taste of Honey', 'The Lady Came From Baltimore', 'Big Ship', Medley: 'The Young Ones', 'Living Doll', 'In the Country', 'Bachelor Boy', 'Early in the Morning', 'When I'm 64', 'Congratulations', 'Visions'.

7 November 1969: Astoria, Finsbury Park, London. The Shadows (Alan, Brian, and John): 'Nivram', 'Exodus', 'Little B'. Cliff backed by the Brian Bennett Orchestra (including John Rostill, A. Hawkshaw, Marcie and the Cookies): 'Shout', 'Move It', 'It's All in the Game', 'Good Times', 'Somewhere in My Youth or Childhood', 'If Ever I Should Leave You', 'Throw Down a Line', 'The Day I Met Marie', 'La La La La La', 'A Taste of Honey' (instrumental with Cliff on guitar), 'The Lady Came From Baltimore', Big Ship', 'The Young Ones', 'Living Doll', 'In the Country', 'Bachelor Boy', 'With the Eyes of a Child', 'When I'm 64', 'Congratulations', 'Visions'.

21 November 1970: Odeon, Golders Green, London. Hank Marvin, Bruce Welch, and John Farrar: 'Hide Your Love Away', 'My Home Town', 'You're Burning Bridges', 'Silvery Rain', 'Throw Down a Line', 'Faithful', 'Keep the Customer Satisfied'. Cliff backed by the Cookies and the Brian Bennett Orchestra: 'La La La La La', 'Goodbye Sam Hello Samantha', 'Words', 'The Young Ones', 'Living Doll', 'Move It', 'Travellin' Light', 'Bachelor Boy', 'Congratulations',

'The Day I Met Marie', 'Soul Deep', 'I Ain't Got Time Anymore', 'I Who Have Nothing', 'Proud Mary', 'Walk on By', 'The Look of Love', 'The Girl Can't Help It', 'Great Balls of Fire', 'Lucille', 'Jailhouse Rock', 'Good Old Rock 'n' Roll', 'Rock 'n' Roll Music', 'Do You Want to Dance', 'I Saw the Light'.

13 June 1971: A Night With the Stars, tribute to Dickie Valentine, London Palladium. Hank Marvin, Bruce Welch, and John Farrar: 'Down on the Corner', 'Lady of the Morning', 'My Home Town', 'Faithful', 'Apache', 'Keep the Customer Satisfied.' Cliff backed by the Cookies and the Jack Parnell Orchestra conducted by Norrie Paramor: 'Get Ready', 'Sunny Honey Girl', 'The Day I Met Marie', 'Fire and Rain', 'Today, Tomorrow, Forever', 'Congratulations,' 'Silvery Rain', 'I Saw the Light', 'I Want to Hold Your Hand' (with Petula Clark).

25 October 1971: season at the London Palladium. Hank Marvin, Bruce Welch, and John Farrar: 'Lady of the Morning', 'My Home Town', 'Faithful', 'Black Eyes', 'Keep the Customer Satisfied'. Cliff backed by the Flirtations and the Palladium Orchestra, leader Brian Bennett: 'We Can Work It Out', 'Flying Machine', 'Fire and Rain', 'Yesterday, Today, Forever', 'Congratulations', 'Silvery Rain', 'The Day I Met Marie', 'Walk on By' and 'The Look of Love' (with Olivia Newton-John), 'The Girl Can't Help It', 'Great Balls of Fire', 'Lucille', 'Jailhouse Rock', 'Good Old Rock 'n' Roll', 'Rock 'n' Roll Music', 'Do You Want to Dance', 'Sing a Song of Freedom' (with Olivia Newton-John, Marvin, Welch, and Farrar).

17 November 1972: Fairfield Hall, Croydon. Cliff backed by Bones and the Brian Bennett Band: 'I Can't Let You Go', 'Gonna Have a Little Talk With Myself', 'The Day I Met Marie', 'Make It Easy on Yourself', 'The Sun Ain't Gonna Shine Anymore', 'Jesus', 'Mr Business Man', 'What the World Needs Now', 'I've Got God', 'My Way', 'Reflections', 'Living in Harmony', 'Brand New Song', 'It's a Saturday Night at the World', 'Don't Move Away' and 'Love' (both with Olivia Newton-John), 'Congratulations', 'Whole Lot of Shakin' Goin' On', 'Keep a Knockin', 'Tutti Frutti', 'Rave On', 'Long Tall Sally', 'Rip It Up', 'Dancing Shoes', 'Sing a Song of Freedom'.

17 September 1973: in aid of John Grooms Association for the disabled, Royal Festival Hall. Cliff backed by Barry Guard and the Orchestra: 'The Day I Met Marie', 'The Next Time', 'Jesus', 'Jesus Loves You', 'Jesus Is My Kind of People', 'Silvery Rain', 'Guitar Man', 'His Latest Flame', 'Chantilly Lace', 'Bony Moronie', 'Do You Want to Dance', 'Crocodile Rock', 'I Could Easily Fall', 'Higher Ground', 'Visions', 'Power to All Our Friends', 'Living in Harmony', 'Come Back Billy Joe', 'The Minute You're Gone', 'Goodbye Sam Hello Samantha', 'You Will Never Know', 'Guitar Tango' (instrumental, Cliff on guitar), 'Fireside Song', 'Travellin' Light', 'Throw Down a Line', 'It's

a Saturday Night at the World', 'Give All Your Love to the Lord', 'Got to Get You Into My Life', 'Congratulations', 'In the Country', 'Dancing Shoes', 'Sunny Honey Girl', 'On the Beach', 'Sing a Song of Freedom'.

31 March 1974: Lakeside Country Club in Surrey. Hank Marvin and John Farrar backed by Cliff Hall (keyboards), Dave Ackley (bass), Andrew Steel (drums), Jean Hawker (vocals): 'Keep the Customer Satisfied', 'Lonesome Mole', 'Wonderful Land', 'Music Makes My Day', 'Marmaduke', 'Turn Around and Touch Me', 'The Rise and Fall of Flingel Bunt', 'Lara's Theme', 'Tiny Robin', 'Time Drags By', 'Take Me Home, Country Roads', 'The Banks of the Ohio', 'In the Country', 'The Day I Met Marie', 'Apache', 'F.B.I.', 'Lucille', 'Rip It Up', 'Blue Suede Shoes'.

17 April 1974: The Cliff Richard Show, London Palladium. Cliff backed by Barry Guard and the Orchestra: 'Dance the Night Away', 'Can't Help Myself', 'Do You Want to Dance', 'Constantly', 'Take Me High', 'You Got What It Takes' (with Pat Carroll), 'Summer Holiday', 'The Next Time', 'Amazing Grace', 'Jesus Is My Kind of People', 'I've Just Realized', 'Living in Harmony', 'Give Me Back That Old Fashioned Feeling', 'Congratulations', 'In the Country', 'Dancing Shoes', 'The Day I Met Marie', 'On the Beach', 'Visions', 'Power to All Our Friends'.

27 October 1974: The Colin Charman Benefit Gala, London Palladium. Cliff backed by the Shadows (Hank, Bruce, Brian, John, and Alan): 'Willie and the Hand Jive', 'Don't Talk to Him', 'Bachelor Boy', 'A Matter of Moments', 'Power to All Our Friends'.

9 March 1975: The Shadows in Concert, Fairfield Hall, Croydon. Hank Marvin, Bruce Welch, Brian Bennett, John Farrar, Alan Tarney with John Piddy (keyboards): 'The Rise and Fall of Flingel Bunt', 'Man of Mystery', 'Lady of the Morning', 'Lonesome Music', 'Black Eyes', 'Turn Around and Touch Me', 'Guitar Tango', 'Faithful', 'Tiny Robin', 'Marmaduke', 'Foot Tapper', 'Apache', 'Dance On', 'Let Me Be the One', 'Nivram', 'Wonderful Land', 'Music Makes My Day', 'Silvery Rain', 'My Home Town', 'Frightened City', 'Honourable Puff Puff', 'Somewhere', 'Lucille', 'Rip It Up', 'Blue Suede Shoes', 'Sleepwalk', 'F.B.I.'.

12 May 1977: The Shadows in Concert, 20 Golden Dates, Royal Albert Hall. Hank Marvin, Bruce Welch, and Brian Bennett with Alan Jones (bass guitar) and Francis Monkman (keyboards): 'Shazam', 'Man of Mystery', 'Kon-Tiki', 'Marmaduke', 'Atlantis', 'Don't Throw It All Away', 'Shadoogie', 'Guitar Tango', 'Please Don't Tease', 'Summer Holiday', 'The Day I Met Marie', 'Bachelor Boy', 'I Could Easily Fall in Love With You', 'In the Country', 'Shindig', 'Apache', 'Foot Tapper', 'The Rise and Fall of Flingel Bunt', 'Dance On', 'Nivram',

'Walk Don't Run', 'Don't Make My Baby Blue', 'Theme for Young Lovers', 'Frightened City', 'Peace Pipe', 'The Savage', 'Little B', 'Sleepwalk', 'Let Me Be The One', 'Wonderful Land', 'F.B.I.'.

8 March 1978: two-week season at the London Palladium. The Shadows comprised Hank Marvin, Bruce Welch, Brian Bennett, Cliff Hall, Alan Jones. The band credits read Terry Britten (lead guitar), Stu Calver (guitar), Clem Cattini (drums, percussion), Dave Christopher (guitar), Mo Foster (guitar), Graham Jarvis (drums, percussion), Graham Murray, John Perry and Tony Rivers (vocals), Graham Todd (keyboard). Cliff and the Shadows: 'The Young Ones', 'Do You Want to Dance', 'The Day I Met Marie'. The Shadows: 'Shadoogie', 'Atlantis', 'Apache', 'Nivram', 'Walk Don't Run', 'Little B', 'Let Me Be the One', 'Wonderful Land', 'F.B.I.'. Cliff and the band: 'Please Don't Tease', 'Yes He Lives', 'Every Face Tells a Story', 'Up in the World', 'Miss You Nights', 'Up in Canada', 'Melting Into One'. Cliff and the Shadows: 'Move It', 'Willie and the Hand Jive', 'The Minute You're Gone', 'Bachelor Boy'. Cliff, Hank and Bruce: 'All Shook Up'. Cliff and the band: 'Devil Woman', 'Why Should the Devil Have All the Good Music'. Cliff, the Shadows and the band: 'We All Have Our Dreams'.

29 January 1979: Tear Fund Concert, Chichester Festival Theatre. Local group of boys and girls: 'Sons and Daughters'. Cliff: 'Rock 'n' Roll Juvenile', 'Night Time Girl', 'Up in Canada', 'Can't Take the Hurt Anymore', 'Why Should the Devil Have All the Good Music', 'Moving In', 'Why Me Lord', 'Reflections'.

1979: European Tour. Cliff plus Skyband. Skyband consisted of Terry Britten (lead guitar), George Ford (bass guitar), Mart Jenner (guitar), Graham Todd and Adrian Lee (keyboards), Graham Jarvis (drums), Stu Calver, John Perry and Tony Rivers (back-up vocals). The three vocalists joined Cliff up front for 'Theme for a Dream' and 'Spanish Harlem'. Cliff: 'Move It', 'Doing Fine', 'The Young Ones', 'Rock 'n' Roll Juvenile', 'If You Walked Away', 'Hot Shot', 'Visions' (with Graham Todd and Adrian Lee), 'Theme for a Dream', 'Spanish Harlem', 'Lucky Lips', 'Give Me Love Your Way', 'Did He Jump or Was He Pushed', 'Why Should the Devil Have All the Good Music', 'Sci Fi', 'Carrie', 'Never Even Thought', 'My Luck Won't Change', 'Green Light', 'Miss You Nights', 'Do You Want to Dance', 'Monday Thru Friday', 'Devil Woman', 'We Don't Talk Anymore', 'Thank You Very Much'.

1-3 November 1979: Oxford. Cliff with Skyband and back-ups as on European tour: 'Move It', 'Doing Fine', 'The Young Ones', 'Rock 'n' Roll Juvenile', 'If You Walked Away', 'Hot Shot', 'Theme for a Dream', 'Spanish Harlem', 'The Shape I'm In Tonight','Under Lock and Key' (later titled 'I'm Nearly Famous'), 'Did He Jump or Was He

Pushed', 'Why Should the Devil Have All the Good Music', 'Sci Fi', 'Carrie', 'Never Even Thought', 'My Luck Won't Change', 'Green Light', 'Miss You Nights', 'Do You Want to Dance', 'Monday Thru Friday', 'Devil Woman', 'We Don't Talk Anymore', 'Living Doll', 'Summer Holiday'.

1980: Cliff in Germany. Cliff and band – Mike Moran (keyboards), Martin Jenner, Mark Griffiths (guitars), Graham Jarvis (drums), Dave McRea (synthesizers), Tony Rivers, John Perry and Stu Calver (back-up vocals). 'Living Doll', 'Lucky Lips', 'The Minute You're Gone', 'I'm Nearly Famous', 'Take Another Look', 'The Twelfth of Never', 'Hey Mr Dream Maker', 'Green Light', 'Learnin' to Rock 'n' Roll', 'Heartbreak Hotel', 'Move It', 'In the Night', 'Carrie', 'When Two Worlds Drift Apart', 'I'm No Hero', 'Dynamite', 'Give a Little Bit More', 'Devil Woman', 'Sci Fi', 'Miss You Nights', 'Everyman', 'The Rock That Doesn't Roll', 'A Heart Will Break', 'Dreamin', 'We Don't Talk Anymore'.

1980: The Best of British Gospel Rock, South Africa. Gospel concerts with Nutshell (later known as RPM, then Network Three), Garth Hewitt. The concerts were before mixed audiences. Cliff: 'Sweet Little Jesus Boy', 'O Little Town of Bethlehem', 'Silent Night', 'In the Bleak Midwinter', 'Away in a Manger', 'We're All One' (with Garth Hewitt and Nutshell). Garth Hewitt: 'Jesus Is a Friend of Mine', 'Under the Influence', 'Did He Jump or Was He Pushed' (with Cliff, vocal back-up and guitar). Nutshell: 'You Can't Get to Heaven By Living Like Hell' (with Cliff), 'Lifeline', 'I Am Nothing Without You', 'Jesus Is the Answer' and 'Get Up and Dance' (both with Garth and Cliff). Cliff: 'Dreamin' '. Garth Hewitt: 'Riding On the King's Highway', 'Come Out Fighting' (Cliff backing), 'May You Live to Dance on Your Grave'. Nutshell: 'Don't Let me Fall', 'Like a Thief in the Night'. Cliff: 'Everyman', 'Song for Sarah', 'The Rock That Doesn't Roll', 'How Great Thou Art'.

14 October 1980: Cliff's birthday night. Five nights at the Apollo Theatre, London. The first night began with the audience singing 'Happy Birthday', and Cliff singing some lines of 'I'm 21 Today'. Cliff and band: 'Living Doll', 'The Young Ones', 'The Minute You're Gone', 'I'm Nearly Famous', 'Take Another Look', 'Twelfth of Never', 'Hey Mr Dream Maker', 'Suddenly' (Olivia Newton-John's voice on backing track, face on a screen), 'Green Light', 'Learning to Rock 'n' Roll', 'Heartbreak Hotel', 'Move It', 'In the Night' segueing into 'Carrie', 'When Two Worlds Drift Apart', 'I'm No Hero', 'A Little in Love', 'Give a Little Bit More', 'Devil Woman', 'Sci Fi', 'Miss You Nights', 'Everyman', 'The Rock That Doesn't Roll', 'A Heart Will Break', 'Dreamin'', 'We Don't Talk Anymore'.

1981: Tear Fund tour. Lasted two and a half weeks and raised around

£50,000 for the Fund. Network Three provided the support act and included in their set 'Long Train Home', 'Lifeline', 'Thief in the Night', 'Solo' and 'Keep Your Eyes on Jesus'. Cliff: 'Son of Thunder', 'Loving Me Lord Forever', 'Under the Influence', 'Better Than I Know Myself', 'You Can't Get to Heaven' (joined by Mo and Annie of Network Three), 'Summer Rain', 'Moving In', 'You and Me and Jesus', 'Fool's Wisdom' (Cliff guitar duet with Paul Field of Network Three), 'Take Me Where I Wanna Go', 'Lost in a Lonely World', 'I Wish We'd All Been Ready', 'Everyman', 'The Rock That Doesn't Roll', 'How Great Thou Art'.

1981: U.S. tour. Cliff: 'Son of Thunder', 'Monday Thru Friday', 'Dreamin'', 'When Two Worlds Drift Apart', 'Green Light', 'Move It', 'Heartbreak Hotel', 'Why Should the Devil Have All the Good Music', 'Hey Mr Dream Maker', 'Carrie', 'Miss You Nights', 'A Little in Love', 'Everyman', 'Sci Fi', 'Summer Rain', 'Devil Woman', 'The Rock That Doesn't Roll'. Encore: 'Give a Little Bit More', 'A Heart Will Break', 'We Don't Talk Anymore', 'Thank You Very Much'. Other titles substituted: 'Take Another Look', 'Do You Want to Dance', and 'My Luck Won't Change'.

1981: British tour. 'Son Of Thunder', 'Better Than I Know Myself', 'Wired for Sound', 'Lost in a Lonely World', 'The Next Time', 'The Day I Met Marie', 'Don't Talk to Him', 'Miss You Nights', 'Dreamin'', 'We Don't Talk Anymore', 'Learning How to Rock and Roll', 'Move It', ' "D" in Love', 'Gee Whizz It's You', 'Dynamite', 'All I Have to Do Is Dream', 'When Will I Be Loved', 'Shakin' All Over', 'Teddy Bear', 'Stood Up', 'Daddy's Home', 'Blue Suede Shoes', 'Great Balls of Fire', 'Lucille', 'Long Tall Sally', 'Razzle Dazzle', 'Whole Lotta Shakin' Goin' On', 'It'll Be Me'. (In the original tour programme 'Miss You Nights' was not included but such was the reaction from the audience in Glasgow, where the tour began, that the number was added.

1-2 September 1981: special concerts at Wembley, London. Gospel-religious event with Garth Hewitt and Network Three. All three: 'Get Up and Dance' (1 September only), 'I'm Nearly Famous (2 September only), 'Travellin' Light' (2 September only), 'Up in Canada' (2 September only), 'Get Up and Dance', 'Sing a Song of Freedom'. Garth Hewitt: 'Somebody Calls Your Name', 'Under the Influence' (Cliff on back-ups). Cliff, Annie and Mo (of Network Three): 'You Can't Get to Heaven'. Network Three: 'Come Go with Me' (Cliff on harmony vocals), 'Dreamin'', 'Summer Rain', 'Shakin' All Over', 'We Don't Talk Anymore', 'Jesus Is the Answer', 'Lean on Me' (with Network Three), 'Son Of Thunder' (2 September only), 'Bye Bye Love', 'Fool's Wisdom', 'I Wish We'd All Been Ready', 'Lost in a Lonely World', 'Better Than I Know Myself', 'Wired for Sound', 'Daddy's Home', 'The Rock that Doesn't Roll', 'The One for All'.

1981: Gospel tour. 'Son Of Thunder', 'Loving Me Lord Forever', 'Such Is a

247

Mystery', 'Under The Influence', 'No One Loves Me Like I Know', 'You Can't Get to Heaven', 'Summer Rain', 'Moving In', 'Fool's Wisdom', 'Take Me Where I Wanna Go', 'You and Me and Jesus', 'Lost in a Lonely World', 'I Wish We'd All Been Ready', 'Everyman', 'The Rock That Doesn't Roll', 'How Great Thou Art'.

1-6 February 1982: Blazers Club, Windsor. 'Son of Thunder', 'Young Love', 'A Little in Love', 'Better Than I Know Myself', 'We Don't Talk Anymore', 'Move It', 'Broken Doll', 'Summer Rain', 'Dreamin'', 'Sci-Fi', 'Carrie', 'The Next Time', 'The Day I Met Marie', 'Miss You Nights', Devil Woman', 'Thief in the Night', 'Daddy's Home', 'Wired for Sound', Rock 'n' Roll medley: 'Blue Suede Shoes', 'Great Balls of Fire', 'Lucille', 'Long Tall Sally' and 'Rip It Up'. 'It'll Be Me'.

Band line-up: keyboards – Dave Cooke (first time with the band, has written song material for Cliff, including 'Better Than I Know Myself), and Alan Park; drums – Graham Jarvis; bass – Mark Griffith; guitar – Mart Jenner; guitar – Tony Clark; back-up vocals – Tony Rivers, John Perry, Stu Calver. At the beginning of the set Cliff said Blazers was the 'first week of our World Tour'!

Index